The Crowns of Apollo

SWINBURNE

JAMES MCNEILL WHISTLER

Dry-point, second state

Courtesy of the Smithsonian Institution, Freer Gallery of Art, Washington, D. C.

SWINBURNE'S

PRINCIPLES OF LITERATURE AND ART

The CROWNS of APOLLO

A STUDY IN
VICTORIAN CRITICISM AND AESTHETICS

ROBERT L. PETERS

University of California at Riverside

Detroit   Wayne State University Press   1965

This book is the winner of the Hilberry Publication Prize
awarded annually, and for the first time in 1964,
by the Board of Advisers to the Wayne State University Press
in cooperation with the Wayne State University Press.

FOR JEAN

The Muses can bear children and Apollo can give crowns to those only who are able to win the crown and beget the child; but in the school of theoretic sentiment it is apparently believed that this can be done by wishing.

SWINBURNE
"Matthew Arnold's New Poems"

❈❈❈❈❈❈❈❈❈❈

PREFACE

❈❈❈❈❈❈❈❈❈❈

This study is an attempt to rescue from near oblivion Algernon Charles Swinburne's contributions to the aesthetics of his time and to provide a more detailed arrangement and evaluation of his principles of literature and art than have yet appeared. His reputation as a poet has tended to overshadow his abilities as a critic; it is a long time since, as Edmund Gosse said, "the advent of the *Fortnightly Review* with a critical article by Swinburne in it was looked forward to as a great event." Swinburne's commitment to criticism was a deep one, springing from his love for literature, founded upon a wide knowledge, and supported by the liveliest temper and mind. What he means in the sentence from which the title of this book comes is this: Apollo, god of the imagination, awards his crowns only to the rare followers who are dedicated to the highest standards of genius and craftsmanship. Begetting the child, as Swinburne saw it, is no easy task; even the most gifted artist can waste his seed on the popular, the facile, and the cheap. There is no danger that Parnassus will ever be crowded.

Chapter I surveys some initial problems encountered in Swinburne's criticism and suggests its more obvious defects and merits. Chapter II sketches the critical framework and serves as background for the ensuing chapters, which present specific aspects of his theories. While a neat design may seem inharmonious with Swinburne's reputation as an impetuous, rambunctious critic, the principles are all his, and many of them he theorized about at length. Although his discussions of a topic may be separated by a passage of years, they very frequently seem to be parts of a single whole, and I have found it both convenient and necessary to treat them as such. The Code of Short Titles, Abbreviations and Dates will assist the reader to keep the chronology straight. Chapter III explores the problems of didacticism and the moral tone, and describes Swinburne's response to the widespread Victorian belief that didacticism is a main function of art. Chapter IV treats the use of detail and contains what I believe to be an original interpretation of Victorian aesthetic aims. Chapter V is an extension of the preceding chapter, since various fusions of the senses were in part attempts to define beauty in a complex world of natural phenomena. Chapter VI outlines one of Swinburne's more original contributions to Victorian critical theory, the drawing of distinctions between the varieties of *passion*. Chapter VII presents his theory of the progressive and dynamic aesthetic whole toward which all fine art moves.

I have been generous with illustrative plates, which are intended to complement the text at those points where the works are discussed. Swinburne himself followed this practice. In the first edition of *William Blake* (1867) he reproduced eight illustrations, six hand-colored and two in black and white, most of them from the prophetic books.* The best represented artists are Blake, Rossetti, Whistler, and Simeon Solomon, those painters who are most prominent in Swinburne's criticism. It is curious, I might note, that Swinburne had so little to say publicly about the work of his friend Edward Burne-Jones. The frontispiece requires a word or two of comment. Although this dry-point portrait was never completed by Whistler, it is one of the most powerful of all portraits of Swinburne, and is a fine antidote to the contemporary romanticized likenesses by Watts, Rossetti, Solomon, and Scott. The penetrating gaze, the fine modelling of the forehead and temples, and the swiftly rendered mouth and chin contrast boldly with the impetuous, heavy lines massed around and upon the figure. The work was probably begun during the early sixties when Whistler was doing the *Six Projects* for F. R. Leyland. In its first state the dry-point was thought to be a portrait of Leyland, which was changed in the second state to Swinburne. This may be the etching which Swinburne's publisher originally intended to prefix to the first edition of *Chastelard* in 1865 (*Letters*, I, 126). Whether Whistler's renowned and highly fastidious standards for his own work or the cooling off of his friendship with Swinburne explains his never having completed the portrait is at best a matter for surmise. A cropped version of the work appears in Vol. I of Georges Lafourcade's *La Jeunesse de Swinburne* (Paris, 1928).

Since the Bonchurch edition of Swinburne's works, edited by Edmund Gosse and T. J. Wise, remains the basic prose collection, it is from this work that any analysis of the criticism must chiefly derive. In addition I have drawn upon the letters, paying particular attention to those which Swinburne wrote to the newspapers and intended for a public hearing. I have also consulted the late essays in manuscript, "Changes of Aspect" and "Short Notes," both in the Henry E. Huntington Library collection and published with a perceptive introduction by Clyde Kenneth Hyder in *PMLA*, LVIII (1943), 227-244; since I have access to the manuscripts, however, I have quoted directly from them. An edition of the rare *Undergraduate Papers,* also in the Huntington Library, has proved useful. I have referred to certain passages in the manuscript, "Notes on Poems and Reviews," which were never published, and to passages in the first edition of the pamphlet *Notes on the Royal Academy Exhibition, 1868,* which were not included in the Bonchurch; and I have been fortunate in being able to use one of the most fascinating of all Swinburne's unpublished works, "The Chaotic School," an essay on Robert Browning which Cecil Y. Lang has industriously assembled. In deciding the issue of Swinburne's exact contributions to the *Spectator* I have accepted W. D. Paden's recent determinations; I should imagine that his essay, "Swinburne, the *Spectator* in 1862, and Walter Bagehot," in *Six Studies in Nineteenth-Century English Literature and Thought*, edited by Harold Orel and G. J. Worth, will remain the authoritative word on the subject.

Because the Bonchurch edition is not always easily available (the edition was limited, if we can believe Wise and Gosse, to 780 numbered sets, and by some avid librarians is thought rare enough to be kept under lock and key) I have quoted liberally. I apologize to those readers who may find the quotations surfeiting; I simply know of no better way to make clear the solidity of Swinburne's contribution. Fortunately we have his vigor, elegance, and wit to grace the page.

I have identified the sources of the quotations by the key tables. This should be more helpful to the reader than the simpler and usual method of noting the appropriate volume and page of the Bonchurch edition. The bibliography is confined to works cited in the text. In the Bonchurch edition there are no indexes; so, to assist those scholars and students who try unsuccessfully to trace references there, I am appending a fairly complete list of names and topics. Parts of my study have appeared in journals. I am grateful to the editors for permission to republish a section on literalism in *Victorian Studies* (June, 1962); some of the material on organic form in *Criticism* (Winter, 1963); and a version of Chapter III in *Victorian Poetry* (Summer, 1964).

I am indebted to Professors Jerome H. Buckley of Harvard University, Herbert M. Schueller of Wayne State University, and Robert F. Gleckner of the University of California at Riverside for their encouragement, for drawing my attention to some points I had overlooked in the Romantics and in the aestheticians, and for their painstaking reading of the entire manuscript. I am indebted to Cecil Y. Lang not only for his edition of the letters, a source of much initial inspiration, but for his aid in other matters. Mr. Dennis Farr, Assistant Keeper, the Tate Gallery, was of help in locating some elusive paintings which are reproduced as plates in the book. Mr. Lionel Lambourne, The William Morris Gallery, Walthamstow, England, shared his knowledge of Swinburne's early favorite, the elusive Simeon Solomon. Bertha M. Usilton, Librarian, Freer Gallery of Art, assisted by supplying crucial information on James McNeill Whistler, particularly on the puzzling dry-point of Swinburne and the *Six Projects* series. Dr. Harold Basilius, Director of the Wayne State Press, and Professor Alexander Brede, Chief Editor Emeritus of the Press, deserve thanks for their help and counsel, as do Professors Hazard Adams of the University of California at Irvine, Milton A. Voigt of the University of Utah, and Donald Howard of the University of California at Riverside. I also wish to thank Naomi Dicker, Felice Levine, and the library and clerical staffs of Wayne State University and the University of California at Riverside. The dedication to my wife Jean is an inadequate token of my admiration for her critical astuteness and her willingness to devote time to Swinburne's cause. I hesitate to think of the many tatters in this book's mortal dress which she detected and helped to mend.

My aim, once more, has been to correct the reputation of a great and neglected essayist, one who if he were still alive would be my severest critic and, I am sure, the most colorful and trenchant of the lot.

ROBERT L. PETERS

Riverside, California

June, 1964

* Here is the note Swinburne and his publisher supplied to introduce his "List of Illustrations" for *William Blake:*

In justice to the facsimilist who has so faithfully copied the following designs from Blake's works, the publisher would state they were made under somewhat difficult circumstances, the British Museum authorities not permitting tracing from the copies in their possession. In every case the exact peculiarities of the originals have been preserved. The colouring has been done by hand from the designs, tinted by the artist, and the three illustrations from "Jerusalem" have been reduced from the original in folio to octavo. The paper on which the facsimiles are given has been expressly made to resemble that used by Blake.

❇❇❇❇❇❇❇❇❇❇❇❇

CONTENTS

❇❇❇❇❇❇❇❇❇❇❇❇

ILLUSTRATIONS*

Illustrations 2 through 31 follow page 34

16

CODE OF SHORT TITLES, ABBREVIATIONS, AND DATES

CODE	TITLE	VOL. & PAGES OF BONCHURCH EDITION	DATE*
AL	"Aurora Leigh"	XVI, 3-8	1898
AV	"Auguste Vacquerie"	XII, 431-449	1875
B	"Byron"	XV, 120-139	1866
B&F	"Beaumont and Fletcher"	XII, 409-437	1910
BJ	"A Study of Ben Jonson"	XII, 3-124	1888
C	"Coleridge"	XV, 140-154	1869
CB	"Charles Baudelaire"	XIII, 417-427	1862
CD	"Charles Dickens"	XIV, 57-90	1913
CEP	"A Century of English Poetry"	XIV, 120-143	1880
CM	"Christopher Marlowe"	XI, 271-280	1883
COA	"Changes of Aspect," MS. in Huntington Library		[late 1890's]
Col	"Collins"	XIV, 149-154	1880
Con	"Congreve"	XIV, 144-148	1877
CS	"The Chaotic School," MS.		[1866]
CT	"Cyril Tourneur"	XI, 460-480	1887
D	"A Relic of Dryden"	XIV, 411-421	1880
DGR	"The Poems of Dante Gabriel Rossetti"	XV, 3-49	1870
EB	"Emily Brontë"	XIV, 45-54	1883
E&S	*Essays and Studies*		1875
GC	"George Chapman"	XII, 136-251	1876
GPL	"Greene, Peele, and Lodge"	XII, 127-135	1914
H	"Robert Herrick"	XV, 260-263	1891
J	"Recollections of Professor Jowett"	XV, 243-259	1893
JD	"John Day"	XII, 289-306	1897
JF	"John Ford"	XII, 371-408	1871
JM	"John Marston"	XI, 353-380	1888
JN	"John Nichol's 'Hannibal'"	XV, 461-466	1872
JW	"John Webster"	XI, 281-314	1886
JS	"James Shirley"	XII, 339-367	1890
K	"Keats"	XIV, 295-302	1882
KR	"King Richard II"	XI, 255-266	1903
L	"Landor"	XIV, 287-294	1882
L&W	"Lamb and Wither"	XIV, 245-286	1885
LC	*"Les Cenci"*	XV, 319-329	1883
Le	"King Lear"	XI, 232-241	1902
M	"Morris's 'Life and Death of Jason'"	XV, 50-61	1867
MA	"Matthew Arnold's New Poems"	XV, 62-119	1867
NCB	"A Note on Charlotte Brontë"	XIV, 3-42	1877
NEP	"Short Notes on English Poets"	XIV, 97-119	1880

*Unless otherwise noted the date given is for the earliest published version of the work, usually in periodical form.

CODE	TITLE	VOL. & PAGES OF BONCHURCH EDITION	DATE*
NP	"Notes on Some Pictures of 1868"	XV, 196-216	1868
NPR	"Notes on Poems and Reviews"	XVI, 353-373	1866
NRA	*Notes on the Royal Academy Exhibition, 1868*		1868
NTS	"Notes on the Text of Shelley"	XV, 348-397	1869
O	"Othello"	XI, 242-254	1904
OMF	"Notes on Designs of the Old Masters at Florence"	XV, 155-195	1868
P	"Pericles"	XI, 225-231	1905
PA	"Prudhomme on Art and Science"	XV, 401-408	1909**
PM	"Preface: *Miscellanies*"	XIV, 91-96	1886
PMa	"Philip Massinger"	XII, 252-288	1889
PVH	"Posthumous Works of Victor Hugo"	XIII, 263-389	1866, 1887, 1889
R	"Charles Reade"	XIV, 346-375	1884
RB	"Richard Brome"	XII, 326-338	1892
RD	"Robert Davenport"	XII, 307-320	1890
S	"Journal of Sir Walter Scott"	XV, 219-242	1891
Sh	"Percy Bysshe Shelley"	XV, 330-347	1903
SN	"Short Notes," MS. in Huntington Library		[c. 1900]
SS	"A Study of Shakespeare"	XI, 3-222	1875–1879
SSV	"Simeon Solomon's 'Vision of Love'"	XV, 443-458	1871
SV	"Social Verse"	XV, 264-288	1891
T	"Théophile"	XIII, 397-414	1915***
T&M	"Tennyson and Musset"	XIV, 303-341	1881
TD	"Thomas Dekker"	XI, 315-352	1887
TH	"Thomas Heywood"	XI, 419-459	1895
TM	"Thomas Middleton"	XI, 381-408	1886
TN	"Thomas Nabbes"	XII, 321-325	1914
ToD	"Tennyson or Darwin"	XIV, 342-345	1888
UM	"Under the Microscope"	XVI, 377-444	1872
UP	*Undergraduate Papers*		1858
VH	"Victor Marie Hugo"	XIII, 3-259	1877, 1883, 1885
W&B	"Wordsworth and Byron"	XIV, 155-244	1884
WB	"William Blake"	XVI, 51-350	1868****
WC	"Wilkie Collins"	XV, 289-306	1889
Wh	"Whitmania"	XV, 307-318	1887
WLA	"Whistler's Lecture on Art"	XVI, 21-32	1888
WR	"William Rowley"	XI, 409-418	1907

** The essay was written in the spring of 1862—See T. J. Wise, *A Bibliography of the Writings in Prose and Verse of Algernon Charles Swinburne, The Complete Works of A. C. Swinburne* (20 vols., London and New York, 1925–1927), XX, 317.

*** Gosse says that the work was "doubtless written in 1862"—*Works of A. C. Swinburne*, XX, 375.

**** The work was completed two years earlier.

XXXXXXXXXXXXXXXXXXXXXXX

The Crowns of Apollo

XXXXXXXXXXXXXXXXXXXXXXX

"What!" cries the reader, *"are we to* study *Poetry? To pore over it as we do over Fluxions?"* Reader, *it depends upon your object: if you want only* amusement, *choose your book, and you get along, without study, excellently well.* "But is not Shakespeare *plain, visible to the very bottom, without study?" cries he. Alas, no, gentle Reader; we cannot think so. . . ."*
—**Thomas Carlyle,** *"Goethe"*

It is empty to charge criticism with going hungrily into minute things and paltry questions of verbal or metrical quibbling. Upon these things depends the form of a poem; and upon the form depends the value of a man's work.
—**Swinburne,** *"The Chaotic School"*

Doubtless . . . the test of true and great poetry is just this: that it will endure, if need be, such a process of analysis or anatomy; that thus tried as in the fire and decomposed as in a crucible it comes out after all renewed and re-attested in perfection of all its parts, in solid and flawless unity, whole and indissoluble.
—**Swinburne,** *"Under the Microscope"*

⬡⬡⬡⬡⬡⬡⬡⬡⬡⬡⬡⬡⬡

CHAPTER I

⬡⬡⬡⬡⬡⬡⬡⬡⬡⬡⬡⬡⬡

MERITS AND DEFECTS: A SURVEY

My awareness of the wealth of Swinburne's criticism developed gradually. Conditioned at first by the outright and often flippant dismissal of his prose by various critics, my intention was to skim and proceed to the poems, which have always seemed to me more considerable in their art, more complex in ideas, and more modern in appeal than his general reputation has allowed. The going was difficult. Swinburne is not always an easy critic either to enjoy or to understand. The well-advertised crotchets of style and tone, the willful disregard for progressive argument, and the great passages of elaborate pastiche, all too often brought low by vituperation, excessive enthusiasms, and other lapses of taste, were formidable deterrents. At the start it was like trying to force one's way through briars. And the quantity of Swinburne's prose, excluding the novels *Lesbia Brandon* and *Love's Cross-Currents*, is considerable, and would constitute an achievement in sheer bulk even for a man who wrote nothing but criticism.

As I read I became increasingly impressed by certain judgments which were well in advance of their time. Surely any critic who made sensitive distinctions between the quartos of *Hamlet*, who placed Donne and Collins above Gray, *Paradise Regained* (for its organicism) above *Paradise Lost*, Emily Brontë above George Eliot, Jonson's *Discoveries* above Bacon's *Essays*, *Don Juan* above *Childe Harold*, and *Bleak House* above *The Old Curiosity Shop*, deserves our attention. In his treatment of widely disparate figures, not only from all periods of English literature but from various European literatures, Swinburne was sure and adept. Cecil Lang observes of Swinburne: he "leaves the impression that he had read *all* of English and French literature and most of Greek, Latin, and Italian."[1] Moreover, he was a pioneer in solving problems of Shakespearean authorship and in dating the plays; Chapman's currently high reputation has been traced to him; the analyses of Blake's elusive prophetic books remain fresh and undated;[2] more effectively than anyone in his generation, he introduced the English to contemporary French literature. His knowledge of painters and sculptors, though not as imposing as his knowledge of writers, was second only to Ruskin's. Finally, his style, with its vigorous blending of wit, sarcasm, and high seriousness, was striking almost in spite of itself; few critics have produced such lively work.

I discovered shortly that passages of theory seemed to group themselves into a system, the tenets of which were largely formed by 1858, the date of his *Undergraduate Papers*, and well before the appearance of the *Spectator* pieces (1862), *Atalanta in Calydon* (1865), *William Blake* (1866, though completed more than two years earlier), and *Poems and Ballads* (1866). His main formulas, outlined so early, and unvaried throughout his long career, preceded Walter Pater's *Renaissance* (1873) by seven years; Whistler's "Ten O'Clock" lecture (first delivered in 1885, though not published until 1888) by eighteen; Oscar Wilde's "Decay of Lying" (1889) by twenty-two; and William Butler Yeats's "Autumn of the Flesh" (1898; later printed under the slightly less flamboyant title, "Autumn of the Body") by thirty-one. These cardinal titles in the history of English aestheticism were all to some degree stimulated by Swinburne.

Despite some shifts in taste, the most notable being reappraisals of Whitman, Byron, and Arnold, Swinburne's literary judgments, like his critical principles, remained consistent. Reviewing his career from the distance of the late nineties,[3] he defended himself against interpreters who called him a fickle, restless, and ultimately dishonest critic. "I have written," he said in "Changes of Aspect," "much in praise of others, & a little now & then in dispraise. I have never found occasion to recall or to modify one syllable of satire or of blame. And when I have felt impelled to qualify tho' never to recant my praise, I have had no reason to regret the liberal & loyal excess of its original expression" (*COA*, 3-4).[4] Among his best known attacks are those upon Byron, Arnold, Tennyson, Andrew Lang, and Longfellow; in others he refers to the "Caledonian Coprophile" Thomas Carlyle, the "Archquack" Emerson, and the "bisexual" George Eliot. Edward Dowden wittily modified Sainte-Beuve's definition of the motto "Chattertonism," "Admire me, or I kill myself," to a "less distressing" motto for Swinburne: "Admire me, and all that I admire, or I select some odorous animal from the Natural History and name you after it."[5] Yet, as Swinburne himself declared, his views were often equivocal. Even though he regarded *Merope* as a dismal croak from "the hoarsest of the Oxonian frog-pond," he loved much of Arnold's poetry and saw the value of his best criticism; he adapted some of Arnold's ideas and at times imitated the flow of Arnold's graceful sinewy style.[6] He regarded Byron as a "greater" poet than Tennyson, though not a "better" one. He could appreciate Browning's "mind" while condemning his verbal pyrotechnics and lapses of taste. (In Browning's hands "the miserable English language, garotted, gouged, her jaw broken, and the teeth driven down her throat, howls helplessly for mercy . . . apparently to the ineffable and delicious excitement of Mr. Browning: whose supple energy of continuous verbiage it seems impossible to tire out"—*CS*,3).[7] He read Carlyle with pleasure and paid him too the compliment of imitating his style; Carlyle had a "perverse and sinister and splendid genius" and was Swift's "most distinguished imitator and most unabashed disciple"—*J*,245; *PM*,92. He had many discerning and positive things to say about George Eliot. His change towards Whitman was not so much a reappraisal as an expression of distaste for the imitators and adulators; the fact that he had seen weaknesses from the start did not diminish his admiration for "Out of the Cradle Endlessly Rocking," "Sleep," "Camp of Green," and "When Lilacs Last in the Dooryard Bloomed."[8] His attitude toward Ibsen, as expressed in the manuscript "Short Notes," was similar:

> The celebrity of Ibsen is the very reason why a loyal Shakespearean & Hugoist should & must feel bound—or shall we say free?—to protest, by no means against the recognition of his [Ibsen's] unquestioned capacity, but against the cult of his iconoclastic idolators who blaspheme & revile the name that is above every name

in order to exalt that of a writer who has rivalled or exceeded Wychereley in obscenity of subject. . . .

Of people like Marlowe, Shakespeare, Chapman, Blake, Shelley, Landor, Arnold, Dickens, Baudelaire, Flaubert, and Balzac, Swinburne held basically the same opinions at the close of his career that he had at the beginning.

We should not, however, underplay Swinburne's eccentricities. There is in his work an effusive element of dreamy withdrawal from the world of everyday which strikes us as dated and is largely antithetical to our more realistic approaches. There is a luxuriance of prolonged emotion, sustained to the point of exhaustion and too often ungraced by the brilliant irony he was capable of writing. His fondness for snarling at the lesser fry, a delight which equalled the one he took in barbing greater fish, makes us wonder if he did not overlook the value of journalistic criticism. There are abrupt changes of tone, at times as harsh as the sound of shattering glass. His interminable critical accolades often make us uncomfortable—he sometimes sounds as if he worked for an ambitious advertising agency dedicated to furthering the arts. Nor has his zeal for ranking nearly every poet and artist worn well. "Gods and Godlings" and "Giants and Titans" were two of his favorite comparisons. Hugo is an almost unquestioned god. T. E. Welby has said that though Swinburne's judgments "do not imply a critical philosophy as profound as Coleridge's" they "are less fallible, and might indeed be described as infallible if it were not that he insisted on the supreme worth of virtually everything written by Hugo."[9] There is also a faded complacency about such absolutes as beauty and truth and the usual Victorian confidence in progress. Neither has Swinburne's reputation as a proponent of art-for-art's sake encouraged a calm appraisal of his theories. Moreover, some of the monographs and essays scarcely rise above a competent journalism and others contain severe lapses of taste.

The problem we have with Swinburne is similar to the one René Wellek has faced with Pater, some of whose essays, says Wellek, "are only book reports or exercises in translation from the French which should never have been reprinted. . . ."[10] We might guess that Swinburne never intended to republish many of his essays, and we are obliged to isolate the weak from the meritorious ones. He himself apparently had some such selectivity in mind when he chose not to re-print in a collection an essay on John Nichol's drama *Hannibal*, a piece which Wise and Gosse, however, included in their edition of the works.

Much of Swinburne's crankiness came from a compelling desire to be exact. During the "Fleshly School" controversy he explained to Theodore Watts that in *Under the Microscope* he had sought to de-liver "the plain truth as against foes and friends alike . . ." (*Letters,* II, 209). His victims would, of course, interpret "plain truth" differ-ently. He had refused to gloss over Blake's faults: "Apology shall now and always remain as far from us as it was in life from Blake himself" (*WB*, 250); poets who deserve "gratitude at our hands" also deserve "candour" (*MA*, 104), and "to excuse and to explain" are, after all, "different offices." If criticism is more "than the ephemeral cackle of casual praisers and blamers; if it is to be thoughtful and truthful . . . handmaid of higher arts," it must show us "how and why this man excels that, what are the stronger and what the weaker sides of his attempted or achieved work when set fairly by the work of others" (*M*, 50).

We may note here, not so much in his defense as in his favor, that he was sensitive to the prolixity and oddnesses of his own style. In 1889 he referred to the "laborious length" of his analysis of Victor Hugo's *L'Année terrible*; he wrote to John Morley of the "luscious form of verbosity" he had to guard against so that his works would not lose their foothold and sweep "down a flood of effeminate and monotonous music, or [be] lost and split in a maze of . . . draggle-tailed melody"; "Nephelidia" parodies his ornate verse manner; and he abruptly shut off a section of elaborate praise of Keats and Arnold with humorous self-perspective: "sweeping aside all this accumulated panegyric," he said, and then proceeded to the French writer Gúerin's significant traits (*MA*, 110).[11]

And of course Swinburne was not always a pioneer. There are originality and freshness in his insights and in some of his precepts, and certainly in his judgments he was independent; but to say that he was a great creative thinker would be wrong. He reflected many of the limitations of the age, and he was as eclectic an English critic as there has ever been. His principles came from such diverse sources as Chapman and Carlyle, Pope and Hazlitt, Ben Jonson and Coleridge,

Sidney and Shelley, Dryden and Blake, Gautier, Ruskin, and Arnold. He used Pope's aesthetic ideals of "justice" and "tact," Hazlitt's remarks on genius and the sublime, Coleridge's theories of the organic whole, Jonson's prose style as well as his contempt for the insensitive reader, Shelley's transcendentalism, Sidney's belief in the poet's elevated role, Blake's vibrant art "gathering" its form, Dryden's ideals of aesthetic decorum, Carlyle's equations of art with an enlightened moral role, Chapman's exuberance of style and taste, and Ruskin's several theories of an art work shaped to meet the demands of a personal aesthetic.

Swinburne seemed to feel that his own function was to remind fellow critics of a number of standards they had begun to neglect: the merits of artistic tradition, particularly the neoclassical one; the necessity for a thorough grounding both in the literature of one's own country and in foreign literatures; the need for establishing accurate texts of earlier writers; the importance of complete candor and honesty in the exercise of the critical office; and the value of one's own response to the distinctive temperaments of artists and their works.

In his intention chiefly to influence other critics and dedicated readers whose tastes in art were similar to his own, he differed somewhat from Ruskin, Arnold, Bagehot, Dowden, Henley, Birrell, and Gosse, who on the whole addressed themselves to a broader public. Arnold's explorations of the functions of criticsm, for example, were intended mainly to alert middle-class readers to the neo-Hellenic virtues of beauty, serenity, and order; and although he ranked the critical activity below the creative he refused to absorb the refined prismatic hues of aestheticism. The artist clearly functions in society and his work depends for its quality upon a cultural tone. The "creative power" in literature, said Arnold, works with "the best ideas . . . current at the time." This we expect since "creative literary genius does not principally show itself in discovering new ideas. . . ." Its work is "synthesis and exposition, not . . . analysis and discovery; its gift lies in the faculty of being happily inspired by a certain intellectual and spiritual atmosphere. . . ." There must "concur, the power of the man and the power of the moment, and the man is not enough without the moment; the creative power has, for its happy exercise, appointed elements, and those elements are not in its own control.[12]

For Swinburne, art was on the whole more autonomous than this, timeless and above place or caste:

> For art is very life itself, and knows nothing of death; she is abso-lute truth, and takes no care of fact; she sees that Achilles and Ulysses are even now more actual by far than Wellington and Talleyrand; not merely more noble and more interesting as types and figures, but more positive and real . . . she need not climb mountains or cross seas to bestow on all nations at once the light of her countenance; she is omnipresent and eternal, and forsakes neither Athens nor Jerusalem, Camelot nor Troy, Argonaut nor Crusader . . . (*VH,* 248, 249).

It is unfortunate for Swinburne's reputation as a critic that he failed to arrange a logical presentation of his ideas; but he was not a formal aesthetician. Beneath his flamboyancies we find principles balanced between freedom and control, wisdom and emotion, the ideals for an art created by dedicated men transmuting the resistant materials of an imperfect, various, and sullied world. It is typical of his honesty and perspicacity that he refused to regard criticism as a fine art. He believed that criticism is important and he tried to do litera-ture a service with his own; but he would not rank it with poetry. His critical ends were practical, often journalistic, and feverishly of the moment; in depth of perception and accuracy of judgment, and in a faithful application of his principles, he makes his mark. H. W. Garrod has said, ". . . there is more truth in two pages of Swinburne than in twenty of Taine."[13] Since he moved between a fervent romanticism stimulated by the Elizabethans, by Lamb, Blake, Hazlitt, Shelley, Gautier, and Hugo, and the constants of a classicism derived from Greek literature and from Jonson, Dryden, and Arnold, it has been easy for his readers to miss the fact that his insights were struck from a set of basic critical and aesthetic standards, and that many of his preoccupations were those which continue to aggravate the serious artist well into the twentieth century. To realize the accuracy of this statement, we need only to review Yeats's troubled concern over the fragmentation of life and his quest for "unity of being," his awareness of the divided nature of the arts, of the phases of the creative mind and its enigmatic waverings between the broad spectrum of the subjective and the objective inspirations, and his resolution of the issues between artist and public achieved with no little pain through the assembling of a private mythology. All of these concerns were Swinburne's too. The aim of art, he believed, was to enable both artist and perceiver to transcend the immediate fragmented world and achieve repose, "the supreme pause of soul and sense," as he wrote of Rossetti, "where we feel and accept the quiet sovereignties of a happy harmony and loyal form, whose service for the artist is perfect freedom."

CHAPTER II

CRITICISM: THE PRINCIPLES

Among the "certainties" Swinburne announced for his ideal critic were the perception of true works of art and the accurate discovery of "how and in what way" they succeed (*M*, 50). The critic is both advocate and judge; he pleads the cause of genius and awards the crowns of Apollo to the deserving. These are more ambitious aims than Hazlitt's "to feel what is good" and then "to find reasons," and differ insofar as to discover differs from to feel. They vary also from Walter Pater's practice of delaying judgments for the sake of sensitive discriminations and for capturing the *virtue* or flavor of single artists and works. Swinburne's aim is less a quest for reasons to support a gifted private taste than it is a search for rapport between true creative and critical talent, with final judgment suspended until discovery is made and the rapport achieved. The ideal critic must be impressed before he can hope to produce a memorable criticism. There is severity in Swinburne's principle. His ideal critic is no fashioner of a comfortable journalese publishing his chats in libraries, his polite letters on literature, or his critical kit-kats; nor is he one who frames generalities and skims over surfaces. The proper critical task, Swinburne declared, is to sift and test genius "by proof of syllable and letter" and then to evaluate. The significant, published results of this effort are the conclusions. It was an "apocalyptic fact" that an artist can be understood only through an analysis of both his method and material (*SS*, 5).

In Swinburne's prose there are numerous strictures and warnings set forth as guide-lines, and records of various sorts of critical failures. Frequently he names critics in order to lambaste them. For the Furnivall Shakespeareans[1], with whom he had protracted quarrels, he supplied this jawbreaker: the "Polyseudocriticopantodapomorosophisticometrico-glosssematographicomaniacal Company for the Confusion of Shakespeare and Diffusion of Verbiage (Unlimited)" (*SS*, 221). Much of the time his remarks seem to belong to a continuing discussion; whether he wrote them in 1868 or in 1909 seldom seems to matter. I ask the reader to keep this in mind not only throughout this chapter but throughout the ones to follow.

One of the easiest critical evasions was "to dilate at length" on genius—a besetting weakness, we might add, of much Victorian criticism, not excluding Swinburne's own. Like Arnold's poet, the slack critic too often preferred the wide rather than the deep gaze; he generalized or recorded first impressions. Swinburne felt that Arnold himself was subject to censure, especially when he employed broad theological terms to equate poets.

> "A criticism of life" becomes such another term or form of speech as "prevenient grace," or "the real presence," or "the double procession of the Holy Ghost": if, Hamlet-like, we consider too curiously what it may mean, the reverent reader may haply find himself on the high road to distraction, the irreverent will too probably find himself on the verge of laughter. (*W&B*, 158)

Swinburne complained, and with some justification—though at the same time he did not in this instance sufficiently appreciate Arnold's attempt to relate art to society—that Arnold was too fond of definitions, that his "passion" for them deprived his criticism of depth. When he let his mind range too freely "upon all subjects," he was apt to become willful and superficial. An example is the early essay on the Celtic spirit in English literature, certainly not one of Arnold's best. Said Swinburne,

> The Celt we have always with us, & never notice him; neither as poet nor as critic can a Macpherson, a Moore, a Mangan, &

a Maginn be taken into serious account by the countrymen of
Chaucer & Shakespeare, of Milton & Wordsworth, of Coleridge
& Landor. . . . the amateur or would-be Celt, brutal if not bloody
& Saxon if not sane, who pretends to discover a visible vein of
Celtic fancy, a visible thread of Celtic influence, in the master-
works of English inspiration, is almost too absurd a figure to pass
underided & unnoticed among the ranks in which he has enlisted.
. . . (*COA*, 11-12)

Criticism, Swinburne had observed much earlier, is "a something not
ourselves, making for paradox." Arnold's defect, a "smiling academic
irony," made him "something not himself—something, shall we say,
definable as a stream of tendency making for unrighteousness in
criticism and inconsistent with righteousness in poetry" (*PM*, 94). This
parody of Arnold, like Swinburne's other strictures on him, did not,
it must once more be said, preclude Swinburne's admiration for that
large part of Arnold's critical work which Swinburne thought good.
He called Arnold the "eye of English criticism" (*MA*, 101). But when
Arnold was vulnerable, Swinburne never hesitated to attack.

A minor but annoying critical evasion was the use of pseudo-
nyms by critics who feared retaliation. These were "animalcules and
infusoria," Swinburne declared in a jibe at Robert Buchanan, the
"Thomas Maitland" who had perpetrated "The Fleshly School of
Poetry" (1871), a neurotic attack upon Rossetti and Swinburne. These
also included the writers for the detested *Quarterly Review*. One coward in particular had greeted *Jane Eyre* with the comment that "its
author must be a woman who long since had deservedly forfeited the
society of her own sex" (*NCB*, 39). Swinburne's animus on behalf of
Charlotte Brontë was as intense as that he had felt for himself when
attacked by Buchanan. Charlotte Brontë's commentator, an "obscene
animal," for his offense "now nailed up by the ear," remains unidenti-
fied:

> its particular name being as undiscoverable as its generic designa-
> tion is unmistakable—to the undecaying gibbet of immemorial
> contempt. When a farmer used to nail a dead polecat on the out-
> side of his barndoor, it was surely less from any specific personal
> rancour of retaliatory animosity towards that particular creature
> than by way of judicial admonition to the tribe as yet untrapped,

the horde as yet unhanged, which might survive to lament, if not
to succeed, the malodorous malefactor. No mortal can now be
curious to verify the name . . . of the typical specimen which then
emitted . . . at once the snarl and the stench proper to its place
and kind. But we know that from the earlier days of Shelley
onwards to these later days of Tennyson, whatsoever things are
true, whatsoever things are honest, whatsoever things are just,
whatsoever things are pure, whatsoever things are lovely, whatsoever things are of good report, become untrue, dishonest, unjust,
impure, unlovely, and illfamed, when passed through the critical
crucible of the *Quarterly Review.* (*NCB,* 39-40)

Of the good critic, Swinburne expects the large view, the grand vision,
full-faced and clearly revealed.

It followed that Swinburne was contemptuous of critics who failed
to judge honestly and forcibly. He sneered at Leigh Hunt for having
a "dainty palate . . . nauseated by the . . . greasy flavour of the dramatic
viands . . . served up in such prodigality of profusion" by Ben Jonson
(*BJ,* 42), viands which Swinburne himself found quite palatable. Even
the great favorite Percy Shelley fell short. Although the "Defense of
Poetry" is "sensitive and candid," it is not "intelligent or acute"; the
style, "generally rather than particularly good," lacks "force and
point" (*S,* 339). Swinburne remarked of Shelley as a critic of Shakespeare: "As surely as there has seldom been a poet of greater or of
equal genius, so surely has there seldom been a critic of greater or
of equal imbecility' (*PM,* 93-94).[2] When poets failed as critics of
other poets, Swinburne was particularly distressed; for he believed that
creative genius requires a comparable critical genius, and, ideally at
least, who should be better equipped for this than a critic who was
himself a poet? (This is not the place to explore the soundness of his
idea.) Arnold and Shelley, at least upon occasion, failed; so did Poe,
in his fondness for the poetry of R. H. Horne and his admiration of
"bad" Byron. In its way a remarkable synthesis of ideas current in England and America, Poe's "The Poetic Principle" praises Byron's "Stanzas
to Augusta" as one of Byron's minor poems "which has never received
from critics the praise which it undoubtedly deserves."[3] Swinburne,
perhaps unfairly, selects the twenty-seventh line for comment; Poe

had reproduced the whole poem. This line, said Swinburne in a letter to Paul Hamilton Hayne,

> is not so much bad metre or harsh metre as no metre at all. I defy anybody to read or sing that line, as it stands, so as to make verse—even very bad verse—of it; and for this reason—that it is very bad prose; lumbering, limping, and dissonant. Poe himself *could* not have written such a line: nor, I am convinced, could you. Byron has written hundreds upon thousands as bad. And I hope he is almost the only man who ever did. (*Letters*, V, 72-73)

Equally at fault were those who perpetrated the biographical fallacy, or the "Johnny Keats stage of criticism" (*W&B*, 193). These critics, among whom Shelley himself was numbered, confused their sympathies for Keats and his reputed suffering at the hands of the *Quarterly* reviewer with the virtues of his poetry. It is typical of Swinburne that he was one of the first[4] to point out that Keats was "above the pitiful level of a creature whose soul" could be "snuffed out by an article" (*K*, 302). As late as the "Changes of Aspect," written in the nineties or even later,[5] he felt that confusion over Keats's true nature and his poetry still prevailed, and he contrasted Keats, in the matter of sensitivity, with the Victorian Tennyson. The "gentle courtier and moralist whom we all admire" was a notorious coward when faced with adverse criticism, and this dispite his many gifts and successes. Tennyson failed to pass the test of manhood. Dryden, though a lesser poet, "fought his enemies like a man." And

> those who quail & wail & wince & spit & sputter when attacked—who do not hit straight back, & whip their insulters openly out of the course—dishonour the standard with which they must be supposed to wish that their names should be associated. (*COA*, 7)

This passage becomes one of the most revealing of Swinburne's several energetic but frequently ambivalent dissertations on Tennyson.

> Tennyson could neither fight his enemies nor ignore them. He was a great poet at his best; a glorious figure among the almost incomparable glories of England; but he was also what Keats was not—an example of a poet who confirms, as far as it lies in him to confirm, the malignant and preposterous tradition that a poet must be something other and weaker if not meaner than a man. And,

great as was the charm of his genius, the intelligence which could "hail" a proposition or a definition of a principle common to all the arts whatever as "truest lord of hell"[6] was simply putid: stupid is no word for it. . . . And whenever Tennyson himself was not serving this lord of hell, the law which compels every artist to do his very best in his own line, & not allow the very noblest intention or instinct or emotion to deflect or distort or pervert his hand, he drivelled. . . (*COA*, 77-79)

It is to Swinburne's credit that he kept these matters, and others, in perspective, insisting upon a practiced, unsentimental glance at the relation between an artist's life and his work. If we recall the fusion of personal morality and aesthetics extolled in such ringing tones by Carlyle and Ruskin, both of whom denied ultimately that an "immoral" artist could create a great work,[7] we can better appreciate Swinburne's brisk sanity. Swinburne would never have said that the true artist, morally attuned, "conquers Heaven for us" (Carlyle), or that a noble picture without a noble painter is impossible (Ruskin). Swinburne did not reject the artist's life as meaningless to his art; but he felt rather, as do many of our best critics today, that history and personality matter after the work has been examined on its own terms.[8]

Swinburne inveighed too against the perennial critical practice of dismissing the present as a time of dissolution and hence failing to detect contemporary greatness. Dante, Shakespeare, and Milton, he said, were insufficiently appreciated in their time; in the nineteenth century Blake was overlooked and Shelley and Charlotte Brontë were undervalued. The forgotten point was that qualities of greatness remain constant; there is no sadder fact than the critical neglect of genius in its own day.

In every age there is some question raised as to its wants and powers, its strength and weakness, its great or small worth and work; and in every age that question is waste of time and speech . . . . There has never been an age that was not degenerate in the eyes of its own fools; the yelp of curtailed foxes in every generation is the same. To a small soul the age which has borne it can appear only as an age of small souls; the pigmy brain and emasculate spirit can perceive in its own time nothing but dwarfishness and emasculation. (*DGR*, 41-42)

BUBBLES

JOHN EVERETT MILLAIS

A woodcut after the painting of 1886.
Courtesy of A. & F. Pears, Ltd.

**THE CIRCLE OF THE
LUSTFUL: PAOLO AND
FRANCESCA**
1827

WILLIAM BLAKE

From *Illustrations to the Divine
Comedy of Dante by William Blake*,
printed for the National Art Collectors
Fund (London, 1922). Photo,
courtesy Special Collections Librarian,
University of California at Los Angeles.

**THE CIRCLE OF
THE THIEVES:
AGNOLO BRUNELLESCHI
ATTACKED BY A
SERPENT**
1827

WILLIAM BLAKE

From *Illustrations to the Divine
Comedy of Dante by William Blake*,
printed for the National Art Collectors
Fund (London, 1922). Photo,
courtesy Special Collections Librarian,
University of California at Los Angeles.

AUTUMN LEAVES signed 1856

JOHN EVERETT MILLAIS

An example of Millais at his best. There is a haunting introspective quality in the
faces of the girls, and the renderings of detail and broad landscape are equally
felicitous in their treatment of light and precise objects.

Courtesy of the City of Manchester Art Galleries

BEATRICE ADDRESSING DANTE FROM THE CAR c. 1827

WILLIAM BLAKE

THE SIMONIAC POPE c. 1825 WILLIAM BLAKE

Water-color illustration to
The Divine Comedy

This illustration and the preceding
one reveal Blake's highly individual
conception of the human form,
nature, and the visionary world—
a conception quite alien to
popular notions of the day on
such matters.

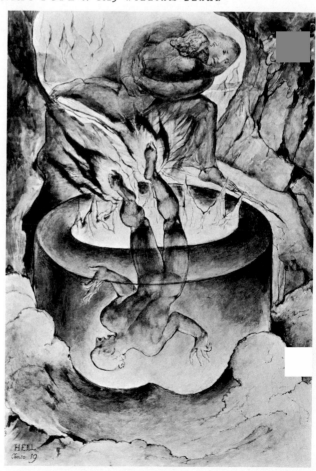

THE HIRELING SHEPHERD signed 1857

WILLIAM HOLMAN HUNT

An example of Hunt's subordination of skillfully rendered detail to a moral theme: the work illustrates
the dangers of ignoring one's obligations. The painting is crammed with still-life interest.

Courtesy of City of Manchester Art Galleries

A MEDLEY OF FLOWERS FROM TABLE MOUNTAIN, SOUTH AFRICA
1883

MARIANNE NORTH

Miss North's energy, fidelity to the facts of nature, and her contributions to scientific knowledge (some flower specimens which she discovered are named after her) would have delighted Ruskin. The description of this picture shows her passion for accuracy:

"On the right, the scarlet *Sutherlandia frutescens*, R. Br., followed by the white balls of the minute flowers of a *Brunia?* a blue and red *Lobostemon* (Boraginaceae); below the *Sutherlandia* are female cones of *Leucadendron platyspermum*, R. Br., and the yellow heads of the male inflorescence of the same shrub with a purple *Senecio* between them. Next comes a kind of "Everlasting" (*Helichrysum speciosissimum* Willd.) having white flower-heads with a yellow centre, and a blue *Lobelia*. Partly beneath the other flowers is the Ground-orchid, *Disa cornuta*, Sw. with dark blue and white hooded flowers and thick leaves mottled with red; and lastly the beautiful *Mimetes cucullata*, R. Br., a proteaceous shrub having whitish flowers supported by pink bracts."

Her best pictures, for their fine coloring, organization, and strong brush stroke are pleasing works of art. A Museum housing her works, her gift to the nation, is located in Kew Gardens.

[See her *Recollections of A Happy Life*, II, 228, for an account of her trip up Table Mountain.]

Courtesy of the Royal Botanic Gardens, Kew

THE BLIND GIRL
signed 1856

JOHN EVERETT MILLAIS

In addition to its fine detail, this picture has a unique symbolic force. The younger girl seems to communicate the spendid vision of the rainbow and the luminous town and field through the hand she clasps. The vision is so powerful that the seeing girl shields out some of the brilliance with the cape.

Courtesy of the City Museum and Art Gallery, Birmingham

PILGRIMS TO ST. PAUL'S 18(

JOHN EVERETT MILLA⟩

An engraving after the original, present whereabouts unknown. One can readily appreciate the attractic
this picture of the armless and the legless veterans at the tomb of their commander had for the middl
class viewer—an attraction other than the purely aesthetic.

[The Sisters, mentioned in the text, cannot be located
Courtesy of the Mansell Collecti⟨

THOMAS CARLYLE: ARRANGEMENT IN GREY AND BLACK NO. 2 1872

JAMES MCNEILL WHISTLER

Swinburne rightly detected character and intellect in this vigorous portrait. At the same time, however, in the silhouette of the seated figure Whistler created one of his most appealing purely visual designs.

Courtesy of Glasgow Museums and Art Galleries

MY SOUL AND I 1894

SIMEON SOLOMON

Reprinted from Julia Ellsworth Ford, *Simeon Solomon: An Appreciation* (New York, 1909)

THE BLESSED DAMOZEL 18

DANTE GABRIEL ROSSET

Rossetti's two paintings of the "Blessed Damozel" invite comparisons with one another and with the p
itself. While the painting of 1877 eliminates the heaven filled with cameo portraits of lovers and gains
concentration thereby, it lacks the complex, interwoven design and great sense of distance and scale of
earlier work. I present both plates for the reader who may want to consider them in the light of Swinbur
many comments on Rossetti's fusions of soul and sense and technique and spirit.

Courtesy of the Lady Lever Art Gallery, Port Sunlight, Ches

THE BLESSED DAMOZEL 1874

DANTE GABRIEL ROSSETTI

Courtesy of the Fogg Art Museum, Harvard University, Grenville Lindall Winthrop Collection

SIBYLLA PALMIFERA
1866-1870

DANTE GABRIEL ROSSETTI

Courtesy of the Lady Lever Art Gallery, Port Sunlight, Cheshire

WIFE OF PYGMALION 1868

G. F. WATTS

Swinburne said that this work recalls the Venus of Milos, that an ancient Greek painter must have painted women this way (*NP*, 197).

Courtesy of Lord Faringdon and the Courtauld Institute of Art, London

THE LITTLE WHITE GIRL: SYMPHONY IN WHITE, NO. 11
1865

JAMES MCNEILL WHISTLER

Courtesy of the Trustees of the Tate Gallery, London

AZALEAS 1868

ALBERT MOORE

Courtesy of the Municipal Gallery of Mod Art, Parnell Square, Dublin

THE SINGING OF LOVE
1870

SIMEON SOLOMON

Courtesy of the City Museum and Art Gallery, Birmingham

ACTAEA, NYMPH OF THE SHORE 1868

FREDERIC LEIGHTON

Swinburne felt that the charm of this work was limited to Leighton's draughtsman's skill, and that the Hellenic quality was artificial (*NP*, 199).

Courtesy of the National Gallery of Canada, Ottawa

VARIATIONS IN FLESH COLOUR AND GREEN: THE BALCONY
1868

JAMES MCNEILL WHISTLER

The first of the sketches Swinburne described resulted in this picture, one of the last of Whistler's paintings to pose figures against a broad background. The Japanese motifs of clothing, human pose, and the broken cluster of flowers and the rectangles formed by bamboo curtains are held to the foreground.

Courtesy of the Smithsonian Institution, Freer Gallery of Art, Washington, D. C.

SYMPHONY IN WHITE AND RED
c. 1868

JAMES MCNEILL WHISTLER

This is the third of the sketches Swinburne describes.

Courtesy of the Smithsonian Institution, Freer Gallery of Art, Washington, D. C.

LOVE BOUND AND WOUNDED
1870

SIMEON SOLOMON

Reprinted from Julia Ellsworth Ford, *Simeon Solomon: An Appreciation* (New York, 1909)

BEHEMOTH AND LEVIATHAN
c. 1820

WILLIAM BLAKE

Illustration for the Book of Job. A fine water-color illustration of Blake's "world of spirit" and strange natural forms, with difficult conceptions of space resolved by clouds, kneeling figures, and a Michelangelesque deity, his finger extended towards a globe containing the monsters of earth and sea.

Courtesy of the Pierpont Morgan Library, New York

TEMPTATION AND FALL OF EVE
1807

WILLIAM BLAKE

Illustration for *Paradise Lost.* Watercolor. This work displays well the "clarity of outline" Swinburne admired in Blake. The counterpoint of the central figures (Eve facing us, Adam seen from the rear) and the diagonal line position of the three heads are enhanced by the simplified landscape and the absence of all but the most essential details.

Courtesy of the Huntington Library and Art Gallery, San Marino, California

MEETING OF DANTE AND BEATRICE 1859-1863
SIMEON SOLOMON
Courtesy of the Tate Gallery, London

ILLUSTRATIONS TO
THORNTON'S *VIRGIL*
1821
WILLIAM BLAKE
Woodcut.
Courtesy of the British Museum,
London

HEAD OF A YOUNG BACCHUS
1867
SIMEON SOLOMON
Courtesy of the City Museum and Art
Gallery, Birmingham

TORSO OF APOLLO

*Courtesy of the Syndics of the Fitzwilliam
Museum, Cambridge*

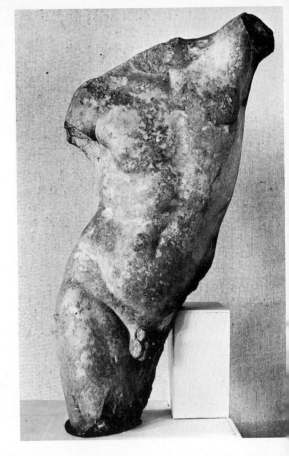

**THE BORGHÈSE
HERMAPHRODITE**

(*Hermaphrodite Endormi*)

RESTORED BY BERNINI

Courtesy of the Musée du Louvre, Paris

To detect greatness in any time requires a great critic;

> and if no man on earth be great in our day, who on earth can be
> great enough to know and let us know it on better authority than
> a pigmy's? Such champions as please may fight out on either side
> their battle of the sandbags and windbags . . . ; I am content to as-
> sume, and am not careful to dispute in defence of the assumption,
> that the qualities which make men great and the work of men
> famous are now what they were, and will be what they are: that
> there is no progress and no degeneracy traceable from Aeschylus
> to Shakespeare, from Athenian sculptors to Venetian painters;
> that the gifts of genius are diverse, but the quality is one; and—
> though this be a paradox—that this quality does not wait till a
> man be dead to descend on him and belong to him . . . and that
> the dawn of his faculty cannot reasonably be dated from the hour
> of its extinction. If this paradox be not utterly untenable, it follows
> that dead men of genius had genius even when yet alive, and did
> not begin to be great men by ceasing to be men at all; and that
> so far we have no cause to distrust the evidence of reason which
> proves us the greatness of men past when it proves to us by the
> same process of testimony the greatness of men present. (*DGR*,
> 43-44)

Swinburne had written his *William Blake* to prove this very thesis.
At Blake's death, the "world" obliged him by allowing him to be buried
"among his nearest kin" and to have the English burial service read
over him. There, however, obligations ceased. The world had called
him mad, kept him poor, and deprived him even of his grave.

> All which to him must matter little, but is yet worth a recollection
> more fruitful than regret. The dead only, and not the living,
> ought, while any trace of his doings remains, to forget what was
> the work and what were the wages of William Blake. (*WB*, 131)

Swinburne's feelings on these matters led him to stress, perhaps
to overstress, the value of praise as a critical function. In this he resembled one of his favorites, Walter Savage Landor, who had given
"much energy to praising merits" and little time to "assailing defects in
literature."[9] Swinburne's own "chief aim" as well as his "chief pleasure," announced in the preface to the third edition of *Essays and*

Studies, was "rather to acknowledge and applaud" what he again "found noble and precious than to scrutinize or to stigmatize . . . [the] worthless and base." His treatment of Blake, again, illustrates his method. Because Blake had been so ignored, Swinburne decided that outright adulation was necessary; for

> . . . when full honour has been done and full thanks rendered to those who have done great things, then and then only will it be no longer an untimely and unseemly labour to map out and mark down their shortcomings for the profit or the pleasure of their inferiors and our own; . . . however pleasant for common palates and feeble fingers it may be to nibble and pick holes, it is not only more profitable but should be more delightful for all who desire or who strive after any excellence of mind or of achievement to do homage wherever it may be due. . . . (*WB,* 345)

An example of the misguided critic is the anonymous reviewer of George Meredith's *Modern Love, and Poems of the English Roadside, with Poems and Ballads* (*Spectator,* June 7, 1862). Swinburne thought the critic unfair, partly because he had failed to acknowledge Meredith's previous work, and with notable restraint reminded him that

> Praise or blame should be thoughtful, serious, careful, when applied to a work of such subtle strength, such depth of delicate power, such passionate and various beauty, as the leading poem of Mr. Meredith's volume. . . .(*Letters,* I, 51)

This early statement, incidentally, was the only public expression Swinburne made regarding Meredith's work.

Yet another mistake was the false equation or comparison of writers. Swinburne thought it ridiculous to condemn one artist simply because he lacked the attributes of another; the critic's task is to make distinctions and adhere to them. With a typical flourish he complained of "eminent and exquisite critics" who are "surprised and indignant" not to "find grapes on a fig-tree or figs on a vine." Such men fail to see that while "art is one" its "service . . . is diverse" (*VH,* 245). Arnold, again, was guilty. His equation of Keats and Shelley set Swinburne's teeth on edge.

> What Shelley tries to do he does; and he does not try to do the same thing as Keats. The comparison is as empty and profitless

as one between the sonnets of Shakespeare and the sonnets of
Milton. Shelley never in his life wrote a poem of that exquisite
contraction and completeness, within that round and perfect
limit. This poem of the Euganean Hills is no piece of spiritual
sculpture of painting after the life of natural things. I do not pretend to assign it a higher or a lower place; I say simply that its
place is not the same. (*NTS,* 380)

Arnold was delinquent also when he bracketed Shelley and Byron[10] as
unsolid, fragmentary, and fleeting. Swinburne's own contrast of the
two poets demonstrates his talent for pointed characterization:

> With all . . . reverence for the noble genius and memory of Byron,
> I can no more accept him as a poet equal or even akin to Shelley
> on any side but one, than I could imagine Shelley endowed with the
> various, fearless, keen-eyed, and triumphant energy which makes
> the greatest of Byron's works so great. With all his glory of ardour
> and vigour and humour, Byron was a singer who could not sing;
> Shelley outsang all poets on record but some two or three through-
> out all time. . . . (*NTS,* 376)

Swinburne had some elaborate fun at the expense of the much-despised
New Shakspere Society, one of whose members made the unpardon-
able error of equating Shakespeare with Sophocles rather than Aeschylus. Swinburne's comments stand as a note to his parody-report of a
session at which the members settled the "disputed authorship" of
A Midsummer Night's Dream. The speaker holds for George Chapman, "on the ground of style," though he at first thought a "similarity
of subject" with *The Revenger's Tragedy* indicated Cyril Tourneur.
His concluding evidence is "that the character of Puck could hardly
have been the work of any English poet but the author of *Bussy
d'Ambois"* (*SS,* 198). Swinburne concludes his burlesque:

> Mindful of the good old apologue regarding "the squeak of the
> real pig," I think it here worth while to certify the reader of little
> faith, that the more incredibly impudent absurdities above cited
> are not so much or so often the freaks of parody or the fancies
> of burlesque as select excerpts and transcripts of printed and
> published utterances from the "pink soft litter" of a living brood—
> from the reports of an actual Society, issued in an abridged and

doubtless an emasculated form through the columns of a weekly newspaper. One final and unapproachable instance, one trans-cendant and pyramidal example of classical taste and of critical scholarship, I did not venture to impair by transference from those columns and transplantation into these pages among humbler specimens of minor monstrosity. Let it stand here once more on record as "a good jest forever"—or rather as the best and therefore as the worst, as the worst and therefore as the best, of all possible bad jests ever to be cracked between this and the crack of doom. Sophocles, said a learned member, was the proper parallel to Shakespeare among the ancient tragedians: Aeschylus—hear, O heaven, and give ear, O earth!—*Aeschylus was only a Marlowe.* (*SS*, 221-222)

Swinburne himself found the comparison of writers a useful tool. Comparison was, in fact, one of his favorite methods;[11] but he was usually careful to avoid the fault for which he had censured Arnold. (Arnold's rigidity and lack of humor also disturbed him.) When Swinburne compared writers he did not pretend, as he thought Arnold had, to be finally evaluative or to adjudge success and failure by the thematic or spiritual affinity of one writer with another; his com-parisons are linking points, useful as stimuli for more extensive analyses. They show Swinburne's talent for the swift, provocative judg-ment presented with style, pith, and wit. Here are some samples: Massinger, "if not buoyant and brilliant as Fletcher, or rich with the spiritual wealth and strong with the gigantic thews of Jonson, has his own place of honour in pure as well as mixed comedy" (*JF*, 385); Tourneur's "moral rhetoric" has an "earnest and fiery intensity" while that of "the less inspired and more inflated ventriloquist of *Childe Harold's Pilgrimage*" is "blatant and flatulent" (*CT*, 462); Middle-ton's command of dialogue and composition is "rather feminine than masculine," genuine and memorably poetic, while Marlowe's and Jonson's, Webster's and Beaumont's, Tourneur's and Ford's was "firmer if not . . . freer" and "graver if not . . . sweeter" (*TM*, 397); Shirley may remind the reader of "Jonson—with all the sap squeezed out of him, or of Fletcher—with all his grace evaporated" (*JS*, 340); Nash "is always readable, even when religious," Greene is not (*GPL*, 129); Collins somewhat resembles Tennyson, whose special mark was an "artistic tenderness of conscience and scrupulous self-mastery of hand" (*Col*, 152); in the ability to "pass beyond the idyllic details of land-scape, and put out from shore into the wide waste places of the sea," Hugo recalled Byron (*B*, 128). "Of all men of genius Ford was probably the worst jester and Byron the worst playwright that ever lived" (*JF*, 399). Dante made of the "moral image" a "living man," while Spenser made of the vital man a moral image (*NEP*, 103). Donne's rhymes were "rugged" while Jonson's were "stiff" (*BJ*, 68). Peacock's ripe and rich humor is "as superior to Praed's as dry champagne to sweet, or a Sultana grape to a green gooseberry" (*SV*, 280). George Eliot's talent (here Swinburne made what he called a "rough and sweeping" rather than "a loose or inaccurate division") was "a type of intelligence vivified and coloured by a vein of genius" while Charlotte Brontë's was dominantly a "genius directed and moulded by a touch of intelligence" (*NCB*, 10). Benjamin Jowett's estimate of Dryden and Pope was as "charitable (and therefore, in my humble opinion, as equitable and as reasonable) as Macaulay's was perversely one-sided and squint-eyed" (*J*, 244). Finally, the "author of *Roderick* is to the author of *Evangeline* as is the author of *Paradise Lost* to the author of *Roderick*. Southey is the moon of Milton as Longfellow is the moon of Southey" (*COA*, 19).

A letter to Norman MacColl not only anticipates one of Swinburne's better essays, "Tennyson and Musset," (1881), but presents a clear statement of his "comparing" principle. To examine Tennyson and Musset is "perfectly fair, natural, and profitable . . . for they are unquestionably poets of the same order, and may reasonably be set or weighed against each other—whereas to compare either with Shelley or Hugo for preference or postference, is purely absurd and profitless . . ." (*Letters*, III, 326). He quarreled with Taine's "plea" that Musset is greater than Tennyson. This is as preposterous as bracketing Tennyson with Shakespeare, or preferring Musset and Mérimée to Hugo. If comparisons are to work they must involve artists of similar achievement. He also compared separate works by the same author, and his comments at times reveal an almost frustrated search for the precise word or phrase. Jonson's *Alchemist* has a mastery of cumulative detail and a "triumphant simplicity of process and impeccable felicity of result." *Volpone*, however, reveals a greater "imagination," a "savour of something like romance, which gives a higher tone to the style and a deeper interest to the action" (*BJ*, 25).

Swinburne observed too the fondness of critics for basing judgments on the "selection and collocation of fragmentary passages," hardly "the best way," he said, "to attain a fair and serious estimate of either poet's worth or station." He was writing specifically of Alfred Austin, who in 1869 produced a series of magazine articles (issued the following year as *The Poetry of the Period*), recording his disgust with Tennyson's "feminine" art and his admiration for Byron's masculinity. Austin's method was to juxtapose weak passages from Tennyson, including lines written in his youth, against some powerful lines by Byron. For good measure, Austin took a swipe at Swinburne's "falsetto notes" and "emasculated poetic voice." For three pages in "Under the Microscope" Swinburne managed to keep calm:

> Byron may be or may not be as much greater than Tennyson as the critic shall please, but this is not a sufficient process of proof. Nor assuredly do I think it is; but the method chosen is none of mine; it is the method chosen by the critic whom for the moment I follow to examine his system of criticism. His choice of an instance is designedly injurious to the poet whom it shows at his weakest; but it seems to me, however undesignedly, not much less injurious to the poet whom it shows at his strongest. Such is frequently the effect of such tactics, the net result and upshot of such an advocate's good intentions. (*UM*, 396)[12]

On another occasion, Swinburne said that the reading of "glorious excerpts from Chapman's *Caesar and Pompey*" may give us "a nobler impression" than if we were to read the complete play, but only the consideration of a work's entire "merit as well as all its demerit" will produce an intelligent critical understanding (*GC*, 209). Of greater consequence was the selection of those details in a work of conjectural authorship which seemed best to resemble those of a master author. Critics were apt to be more concerned with establishing a favored attribution than with treating the evidence objectively. In a skillful study,[13] the "Note on the Historical Play of *King Edward III*" (1879), Swinburne demonstrated how easy it is to reach false conclusions if one weighs only details which give the "nobler impression." He observes of one scene that there is much pretty verbiage after the general manner of Elizabethan sonnetteers, touched here and there with something of a higher tone; but the whole scene drags, flags, halts onward at such a languid rate, that to pick out all the prettiest lines by way of sample would give a favourable impression but too likely to be reversed on further and fuller acquaintance. (*SS*, 176)

Moreover, the conscientious critic will acquaint himself with the entire body of an artist's work, the failures as well as the successes. We understand Thackeray better by knowing that *Pendennis*, "marvellous" in characterization, humor, and "living truth," is nonetheless inferior to *Henry Esmond* and *Vanity Fair*; a study of *Dombey and Son* enables us to appreciate *David Copperfield* (*CD*, 69). The defects of Marlowe's *The Jew of Malta* bring into higher relief the virtues of the other plays. *Edward II* is Marlowe's masterpiece "in dramatic power and positive impression of natural effect"; *Doctor Faustus* excels as "pure poetry." *Tamburlaine*, despite its "many and heavy faults," predicts Marlowe's greatness, and is, therefore, essential to the complete Marlowe (*CM*, 271, 274, 275). One revealing example of Swinburne's own application of his theory concerns itself with Blake's illustrations for the *Divine Comedy*, the last illustrations he was to make. Of the seven designs, Swinburne believed three equalled Blake's best work: the Paolo and Francesca, the Dante and Virgil observing "the grovelling and swine-like flocks of Malebolge," and the design for the circle of traitors. The other works Swinburne rejected, but not without first marking their expressionistic force [*See* Plates 3, 4, 6, 7]:

Into the other four designs we will not enter [he had spent over three pages on his favorites]; some indeed are too savagely reckless in their ugly and barren violation of form or law, to be redeemed by even an intenser apprehension of symbol and sense; and one at least, though with noble suggestions dropped about it, is but half sketched in. In that of the valley of serpents there is however a splendid excess of horror and prodigal agony; the ravenous delight of the closing and laughing mouths, the folded tension of every scale and ring, the horrible head caught and crushed with the last shriek between its teeth and the last strain upon its eyelids, in the serrated jaws of the erect serpent—all have the brand of Blake upon them. (*WB*, 124-125)

Swinburne's perceptive eye recognized the power in these impressive works. But he reminds us of Ruskin confronting the late Turner, and coming away nonplussed by what he had seen: the highly tonal canvasses in which barely discernible objects were immersed in shimmering atmospheres of gold, red, white, and orange tones seemed to Ruskin incomplete, reckless, and vaguely sketched in. The point I make here is not that Swinburne failed—as indeed he did—to observe an advance in Blake's technique but that he had carefully considered the whole before making a judgment.

Another obligation of the critic is to distinguish the qualities in an artist's work which he thinks are permanent from those which are "ephemeral." In particular he should note any voguish elements. Charles Dickens, for example, has a "literary and sentimental side" which makes him "a type of his generation and his class," the Victorian bourgeois. Little Nell is so overdrawn as to be incredible.[14] His enduring side, composed of his comic, pathetic, tragic, and creative elements, is far more consequential (*CD*, 60). Byron's flamboyancies in the Eastern tales and in *Childe Harold*, which at one time were so popular with readers, are far less enduring than his treatment of freedom or his "marvellous mastery of tragicomedy" in *Don Juan* (*COA*, 5).

The critic must be well acquainted with periods of literature and with movements in the arts. For example, if he is ill-apprised of the range, depth, and charm of Elizabethan lyrics he is apt to mistake poems "in the courtly or pastoral key of the season" for fine examples of the Renaissance lyric art, and in blinder moments may even equate fourth rate poets, with little more than a handful of skillful verses to their credit, with poems by Shakespeare, Spenser, Daniel, and Drayton. He will fail to see that the bulk of such poems is merely of "the idyllic or elegiac line of business," in Elizabethan days a business or a school "without a master or a head" (*SS*, 172). The informed critic will know that *fashionables* of any period are short-breathed runners and broken-winded athletes (*SS*, 170).

The supreme challenge for the English critic was, of course, Shakespeare, who more than any other writer required a comprehensive view. A fine critic should, for example, seek to "trace and verify . . . shades and gradations" of style in Shakespeare's "successive works," "the ebb and flow of alternate influences, the delicate and infinite subtleties of change and growth discernible" (*SS*, 7). He discerned such growth in the *Hamlet* quartos; his reading of the two versions is still important for economy, stylistic beauty, and depth of insight:

> In *Hamlet*, as it seems to me, we set foot as it were on the bridge between the middle and the final period of Shakespeare. That priceless waif of piratical salvage which we owe to the happy rapacity of a hungry publisher is of course more accurately definable as the first play of *Hamlet* than as the first edition of the play. And this first *Hamlet*, on the whole, belongs altogether to the middle period. The deeper complexities of the subject are merely indicated. Simple and trenchant outlines of character are yet to be supplanted by features of subtler suggestion and infinite interfusion. Hamlet himself is almost more of a satirist than a philosopher. . . . The Queen, whose finished figure is now something of a riddle, stands out simply enough in the first sketch as confidante of Horatio, if not as accomplice of Hamlet. There is not more difference between the sweet quiet flow of those plain verses which open the original play within the play and the stiff sonorous tramp of their substitutes, full-charged with heavy classic artillery of Phoebus and Neptune and Tellus and Hymen, than there is between the straightforward agents of their own destiny whom we meet in the first *Hamlet* and the obliquely moving patients who veer sideways to their doom in the second. (*SS*, 115-116)

Swinburne's conjectures about Shakespeare led him to an ambitious statement of theory, one in which a study of external qualities leads to a scrutiny of internal form, the somewhat elusive but real inner spirit characteristic of great art. This fusion constituted for Swinburne the proper "science" of criticism and is one of his most serious, if partially derivative, contributions to the critical thought of his age:

> Without study of his forms of metre or his scheme of colours we shall certainly fail to appreciate or even to apprehend the gist or the worth of a painter's or a poet's design; but to note down the number of special words and cast up the sum of superfluous syllables used once or twice or twenty times in the structure of a single poem will help us exactly as much as a naked catalogue of the colours employed in a particular picture. A tabulated statement

or summary of the precise number of blue or green, red or white draperies to be found in a precise number of paintings by the same hand will not of itself afford much enlightenment to any but the youngest of possible students; nor will a mere list of double or single, masculine or feminine terminations discoverable in a given amount of verse from the same quarter prove of much use or benefit to an adult reader of common intelligence. What such an one requires is the guidance which . . . may help him to discern at once the cause and the effect of every choice or change of metre and of colour; which may show him at one glance the reason and the result of every shade and of every tone which tends to compose and to complete the gradual scale of their final harmonies. This method of study . . . should also be recognized as the sole method by which the work of a great poet can be studied to any serious purpose. For the student it can be no less useful, for the expert it should be no less easy, to trace through its several stages of expansion and transfiguration the genius of Chaucer or of Shakespeare, of Milton or of Shelley, than the genius of Titian or of Raffaelle, of Turner or of Rossetti. (*SS*, 8-9)

A rock on which modern steersmen, "too enamoured of their own guesses and secret histories," frequently crashed was the dating of texts (*SS*, 9). Swinburne lamented that he himself was without the lifetime of authority needed to assign accurate dates to Shakespeare's works; the more he thought the more impossible it seemed that anyone, either through the analysis of "inner" or "outer" evidence, could determine a "lineal order" with any finality. But his aims were high. He decided that it would be helpful to separate the plays into classes, in order to study "the several stages or periods" of Shakespeare's "mind and art" (*SS*, 11-12). This was his new approach: he would study "by the ear alone" Shakespeare's "metrical progress" and discover a "corresponsive progress within" (*SS*, 19).

As for a related and similarly vexatious problem, that of double authorship, Swinburne maintained that collaboration was "naturally as impossible to refute as to establish by other than internal evidence" (*SS*, 14). In a tantalizing letter to the editor of the *Athenaeum*, March 10, 1883 (*Letters*, V, 3-5), evoked by the announcement of A. H. Bullen's discovery of *Sir John van Olden Barnavelt*, Swinburne wrote that the authorship of the play is "quite impossible to determine with anything like such positive certainty as is assumed by the editor and his correspondents; but on this matter I must make time to write again at greater length." So far as I know the time was never found. In a letter to Bullen himself two days later the matter was scarcely broached, and about a year later (*Letters*, V, 50), he tentatively agreed with Bullen that Massinger had helped with the play. But in the main, Swinburne's views on these textual problems were, to borrow Harold Nicolson's word, revolutionary. Nicolson singles out the essay on Shakespeare for the "useful light on the vexed question of collaboration" and dating; the essay is one of the impressive moments in nineteenth-century Shakespearean criticism.[15]

Related to his emphasis upon the complete canon and the dating of texts was the principle that editors must be scrupulous in their handling of textual matters. Few Victorians were as well qualified as Swinburne to make this point, and few made it with such vigor. Shakespearean "scholars" and "dunces" had perpetrated textual errors in Shakespeare's works, ignoring "the corrections, suppressions, alterations, and modifications—which distinguish the text of the quartos from the too frequently garbled and mangled, the sometimes transfigured and glorified text of the folio" (*BJ*, 82). In "Thomas Middleton," first printed in 1886, Swinburne lambasted defilers of texts, particularly of *Macbeth*.

> As for the supposed obligations of Shakespeare to Middleton or Middleton to Shakespeare, the imaginary relations of *The Witch* to *Macbeth* or *Macbeth* to *The Witch*, I can only say that the investigation of this subject seems to me as profitable as a research into the natural history of snakes in Iceland. That the editors to whom we owe the miserably defaced and villainously garbled text which is all that has reached us of *Macbeth*, not content with the mutilation of the greater poet, had recourse to the interpolation of a few superfluous and incongruous lines or fragments from the lyric portions of the lesser poet's work—that the players who mangled Shakespeare were the pilferers who plundered Middleton—must be obvious to all but those (if any such yet exist anywhere) who are capable of believing the unspeakably impudent assertion of those mendacious malefactors that they have left us a

pure and perfect edition of Shakespeare. These passages are all thoroughly in keeping with the general tone of the lesser work: it would be tautology to add that they are no less utterly out of keeping with the general tone of the other. But in their own way nothing can be finer: they have a tragic liveliness in ghastliness, a grotesque animation of horror, which no other poet has ever conceived or conveyed to us. The difference between Michel Angelo and Goya, Tintoretto and Gustave Doré, does not quite efface the right of the minor artists to existence and remembrance. (*TM*, 398)

English writers, including Swinburne's own contemporaries, were entitled to some of the attention editors and scholars ordinarily lavish on Catullus, Lucretius, and other ancients.

It is a shame that Englishmen should not be forthcoming who would think it worth while to expend as much labour, and would be competent to bring that labour to as good an end, in the service of their own immortal countrymen, as is expended and as is attained by classical scholars in the service of alien and not more adorable gods. (*BJ*, 83)

Swinburne's efforts to establish proper texts for Jonson and Shelley are well-known. His essay, "Notes on the Text of Shelley" (1869), though "slight and rapid," is a model of patience, close analysis, humor, and wisdom. His intention was to stimulate "a perfect and critical edition of the whole works" of Shelley. He was at first pleased to greet William Michael Rossetti's *The Poetical Works of Percy Bysshe Shelley: Including Various Additional Pieces from MS. and Other Sources* (2 vols., London, 1870) as he announced in a "Note," published in 1875:

He has lightened the darkness that perplexed us . . . ; he has delivered all students from the bondage of Medwin and Hogg . . . .[16] he has had the glory of giving to the world fresh verse of Shelley's. Whole poems and priceless fragments, fresh instalments of imperfect but imperishable work, we owe to the labour of his love. (*NTS*, 385)

Also, Rossetti supplied elaborate notes "to elucidate and to rectify much that was corrupt and obscure." Nevertheless, Swinburne detected shortcomings, and his complaints all derive from his thesis that a poet's text must remain inviolate:

> The punctilious if not pedantic precision which has reformed the whole scheme of punctuation, doubtless often loose enough in the original editions, compels us to remark that the last state of this text is worse than the first. This edition is beyond praise . . . as a book of reference; but no one, I should imagine, will ever read in it for pleasure, while he can procure instead the loosest and most incorrect of those previously printed. (*NTS*, 386)

In addition, Rossetti substituted "you" for "thou" and "thee" throughout *The Cenci*, "on some rigid system of regulation to which the editor himself does not pretend to suppose that his author ever proposed to conform." Six of these instances Rossetti acknowledged;

> but for the sentences broken up and recast, the interpolated periods which make two or three curt inharmonious sentences out of one most harmoniously prolonged through natural pauses to its natural end—for these and other vexatious pedantries or petty rigidities of rule, it does not seem that any defence or apology has been thought needful. (*NTS*, 387)

As Swinburne proceeds, he warms to his subject, accusing Rossetti of ignorance in perpetrating false readings which were inconsistent with his "high and rare intelligence in matters of art and imagination" (*NTS*, 392). Finally Shelley's unpublished "boyish absurdities and atrocities in the way of rhyme" should have been excluded; the exactitude which preserves what a poet himself would have suppressed is "pernicious" (*NTS*, 394). This mass of errors and misjudgments is particularly distressing since it distorts some of the fine qualities of England's finest lyric poet: it is

> certain that of all forms or kinds of poetry the two highest are the lyric and the dramatic, and that as clearly as the first place in the one rank is held among us by Shakespeare, the first place in the other is held and will never be resigned by Shelley. (*NTS*, 397)

Of William Gifford, who had edited a nine volume edition (1816) of Ben Jonson, Swinburne said a few complimentary things; but even Gifford "left not a little to be done," and the 1875 revision by F.

Cunningham was only slightly improved. Cunningham failed to revise or even to note Gifford's misreadings in the 1816 edition. The remarks he tossed into an appendix, his contribution, Swinburne found "somewhat provocative of strong language." A writer of Jonson's stature requires "nothing less than . . . a careful and complete edition of all his extant writings, with all the various readings of the various editions published during his lifetime" (*BJ*, 81-82). In a lengthy letter (July 1885) to A. H. Bullen, Swinburne returned to the problem. Bullen had just published the first half of his eight-volume *The Works of Thomas Middleton*, July 1885, which he dedicated to Swinburne. "It is really too absurd a pretence for . . . editors to play the Bowdler with Ben Jonson, of all men. But . . . the varying versions, cancels, and corrections of his plays ought to be given, that justice may be done to so great and conscientious an artist: and this would be a work worthier of your ability and energy than the re-editing of Shirley" (*Letters*, V, 119). Nor should editors and critics ever willfully censor texts to make them fit for "the hands of schoolgirls." When a work has been published it is "public property thenceforward and forever," and the pretence of a bowdlerizer is "inexpressibly preposterous" (*BJ*, 83-84). Similarly, in January 1885, he complained to Bullen, who had just published *The Works of Christopher Marlowe,* in three volumes, that Bullen might have assisted Marlowe's cause if he had chosen to reprint the whole of *Lust's Dominion* rather than R. H. Horne's inferior tragedy, *Death of Marlowe* (*Letters*, V, 94-95). *Lust's Dominion* contained internal evidence of Marlowe's hand and should have appeared in full; for "offensive and preposterous as are the cancelled articles, they help to show that the whole thing was either a bad joke or an impudent calumny." Particularly in an edition not intended for boys' schools, Swinburne jibed, all should be printed.

As we have seen, Swinburne's tenets for critics were various, and the illustrations he gave in support abundant. In his prose, he seldom forgot for long that he is a critic of serious intentions addressing minds as informed and as agile as his. He never talked down. In fact, nearly every book he wrote was criticized for its abstruseness and disregard for the reader who was not his match. When we realize how frequently in an age like our own, which prides itself on ambiguities and ironic tinctures, irony is either deflected or missed, we can afford some sympathy for Swinburne's critics. At the same time, on that level of art and mind requiring the fullest play of brain and imagination, his principles are well-executed and neatly framed; only, the gallery walls are sometimes jammed and frequently the pictures require straightening and realigning.

Newton Arvin has said of Swinburne's criticism: "His capacity for *feeling himself into* a piece of literature that enlists his devotion is almost incredible, and in reproducing the experience for another his voluble lyricism is for once no hindrance; his amazingly responsive vocabulary, his apparently illimitable expressiveness, are allies of the stoutest kind."[17] And this is quite true; Swinburne's uncanny ability to yield himself "to the object," and to reflect in his own writing the characteristics of the literature he was discussing, cannot fail to compel admiration. He himself wrote often of the strong critical talent required to transfix the inner vitality of a great work. "To analyse the style of the greatest among writers," he said, "would need the subtlety," and "to praise it would need the inspiration, of their own inaccessible genius" (*VH*, 201). He discussed the matter in writing of Hugo:

This style of Victor Hugo's is not easy to catch and reproduce effectively. To find fault with it, lay a finger on the flaws and knots of it, set a mark against this or that phrase—even to seize on some salient point and hold it up in the way of parody—these are the easy things to do. It has singular alternations of fluent power and sharp condensed angular thought; moves now softly and freely, now with a sort of abrupt military step, a tight-laced, short-breathed kind of march, as it were; a style broken and split up into bright, hard fragments of spar, that have a painful sparkle in them, and rough, jagged notches and angles; then, again, it shifts into quite another likeness, becomes flexible, soft, sinuous, as the over-growth of trees or grass; with a passionate eager beauty in it that dilates every word and sentence to the full; a feverish excess of blood, a tremulous intensity of life. It is hard at times to keep up with the pace of it; the very written words seem to have a conscience and a vitality in them, to heave and beat with the fever of excited thought, to quiver with actual sensuous passion. Moreover, the style expands and opens up into vast paragraphs, coherent, indeed, but only as water coheres; "tumbling, weltering spaces

49

of sea with no good anchorage for miles," that drift the reader
breathless out of reach of rope or spar. Evidently, however, this
matter, too, is best as it is; these are the forms into which the great
thought and purpose of the writer naturally cast themselves, they
fall and lap of their own accord into these folds and creases, and
so the meaning of the book gets clothed and set out as suits it best.
(*VH*, 169-170)

This passage strikes the reader with some of the creative force of
Hugo's work: Swinburne's style parallels Hugo's style, his mood
Hugo's mood.

A similar passage in *George Chapman* is notable both for its
imitation and its acute analysis of that Elizabethan's early manner.
Sympathetic readers, Swinburne said of Chapman's style, will at first
be shocked

> by the crabbed and bombastic verbiage, the tortuous and pedantic
> obscurity, the rigidity and the laxity of a style which moves as it
> were with a stiff shuffle, at once formal and shambling; which
> breaks bounds with a limping gait, and plays truant from all rule
> without any of the grace of freedom; wanders beyond law and
> straggles out of order at the halting pace of age and gravity, and
> in the garb of a schoolmaster plays the pranks of a schoolboy with a
> ponderous and lumbaginous license of movement, at once rheu-
> matic and erratic. (*GC*, 158)

Other instances of Swinburne's ability to mirror the style of his
subject are the essay on Keats, which is lucid, restrained, and "sculptured,"—to use a word Swinburne associated with Keats; a brilliant
defense of Browning's obscurity which employs touches of Browning's
angular colloquial diction as well as his mannered elisions; references
to Carlyle, garbed usually in a Carlylean idiom (he referred to
Thomas Cloacinus . . . and "his usual terse and unaffected elegance"—
Letters, V, 83); and an appreciation of Arnold's poems which is a clear
return to stylistic economy and restraint.[18]

The ambitious estimate of Wordsworth, which appeared in 1884,
was one of Swinburne's more notable efforts to transfix special qualities,
although it is Arnold's prose style that he chiefly echoes. It illustrates
well Swinburne's ability to produce a sustained analysis of a difficult

writer and is a masterly fusion of the aesthetic response and the practical suggestion. I shall here only present the contours of his argument,
passing over the many references to specific poems. He had earlier, in
the 1867 essay on Matthew Arnold, underscored the challenge Wordsworth presented to his critical powers: his "greatness" was his own
and "incommunicable" to any disciple (*MA*, 87). His prevailing note,
he observes in the 1884 essay, is philosophic rather than tragic; he is
not a poet of action. For the hostile critic who might object to this
delineation of a passive Wordsworth, Swinburne had this rejoinder:
Wordsworth never wished nor pretended to be an action poet. Even as
"a poet of introspection, of spiritual insight or ethical doctrine," Wordsworth "has been—if it may be said without irreverence—perhaps alike
overrated by others and by himself: but as the poet of suffering and
of sympathy with suffering, his station is unequalled in its kind"
(*W&B*, 219). He belongs with Milton and Pindar, though he lacks
the "constancy of impulse" and "steadfastness of inspiration" by which
they are "sustained through the whole course of their spiritual flight
from summit to summit of majestic imagination and moral ardour"
(*W&B*, 218). In his best poems he does, however—and there is nothing
more Pindaric in modern poetry—possess ardency and serenity, "the
flameless fire of imaginative thought." Some of the lines in "Tintern
Abbey," particularly, are for majesty surpassed only by Milton: "the
music of some few almost incomparable passages seems to widen and
deepen the capacity of the sense for reception and enjoyment and
understanding of the sublimest harmonies" (*W&B*, 221). The "peculiar
note" of this "great, though most unequal and uncertain, most lawless
and irregular poet," is "sublimity in tenderness" (*W&B*, 225).[19]

Swinburne's efforts to reflect and cite the individual characteristics
of the writer or painter under discussion were important in the stream
of nineteenth-century criticism. He belongs to the second class of "impressionist" critics, as distinguished by Herbert M. Schueller in a study
of the theories of John Addington Symonds. A member of the first
class, the kind Swinburne was suspicious of, recounts his "adventures
among masterpieces," presenting as pure a transcript of his emotions
as he can. He is "the sybarite of artistic experience . . . the Des Esseintes
of criticism." Members of the second class, like Lamb, De Quincey,
Hazlitt, and Pater, are aware that the logical end of a refined impressionism is solopsism, and in addition to recording their reactions

they describe aesthetic features and make judgments.[20] The principle of identifying and transmitting the "temperament" of a writer appears as a central issue in Pater, Wilde, Symonds, George Moore, and Arthur Symons, all of whom were influenced by Swinburne. Pater carried the intense aesthetic experience to its heights; Wilde enjoyed making the expression of the critic's sensibility a form of fine art; Symons looked for the exact personal quality, "a quality of nerves," in Rossetti, Swinburne, and the French symbolists; Moore and Symonds both tried to elicit specific moods from literature and art. With the single exception of Pater none of these men was as sensitive as Swinburne to the risks involved. The greatest was the temptation to neglect the traditional offices of contrast, analysis, and judgment for an arbitrary recording of one's direct responses. As Swinburne's first published essay, the paper on Marlowe and Webster—*Undergraduate Essays*, 1858—demonstrates, he realized from the beginning that criticism must be demanding and eclectic. Another danger was the loss of perspective, the tendency to consider criticism as the equal of creation. Even at its best, said Swinburne, criticism was but a "handmaid of the higher arts" and always "more or less imperfect, impotent, and faulty, when measured by the size and value of a great book" (*VH*, 178-179). The "flaccid scrawl of some boy's pencil on the margins" (*VH*, 169) was the metaphor he chose to make the telling point. For example, criticism was unable to provide a satisfactory distillate of lyric poetry. "There is something too rough and hard, too faint and formless, in any critical language yet devised, to pay tribute with the proper grace and sufficiency to the best works of the lyrical art" (*WB*, 60).[21]

> The test of the highest poetry is that it eludes all tests. Poetry in which there is no element at once perceptible and indefinable . . . may have every other good quality . . ; if all its properties can easily or can ever be gauged and named by their admirers, it is not poetry—above all, it is not lyric poetry—of the first water. There must be something in the mere progress and resonance of the words, some secret in the very motion and cadence of the lines, inexplicable by the most sympathetic acuteness of criticism. (*W&B*, 215)

In *William Blake* Swinburne attempted to convey the exact effect of poetry. He began with comparisons: Blake's songs reminded him of

Beaumont and Fletcher, and in their "tender supremacy of style and noble purity of perfection" of Tennyson. He decided to "drop comparison and cease looking back or forward for verses to match with these" (*WB*, 60). A different slant was required; in seeking it he matched the intensity of his critical instrument against the intensity of Blake's poems. With a peculiar nervous force he distinguished shades of softness, sound, odor, and color. Groping towards synaesthesia, he alluded to music and painting:

> They have a fragrance of sound, a melody of colour, in a time when the best verses produced had merely the arid perfume of powder, the twang of dry wood and adjusted strings; when here the painting was laid on in patches, and there the music meted out by precedent; colour and sound never mixed together into the perfect scheme of poetry. The texture of these songs has the softness of flowers; the touch of them has nothing metallic or mechanical, such as one feels in much excellent and elaborate verse of this day as well as of that. The sound of many verses of Blake's cleaves to the sense long after conscious thought of the meaning has passed from one: a sound like running of water or ringing of bells in a long lull of the wind. (*WB*, 61)

The modern critic may adopt an idiom fresher, more inventive, and less stylistically encumbered than Swinburne's; but he must eventually support his responses with critical ideals which, in their broad outlines at least, will resemble Swinburne's. Our favored analytical approach cannot alone capture the elusive magic of great art. Swinburne was keenly aware of art's paradoxical mute palpability. With typical astuteness he said: "If we insist on having hard ground under foot all the way we shall not get far" (*WB*, 152). Freedom rather than rigidity, flexibility rather than a stereotyped approach, provide criticism with its best chance for success.

CHAPTER III

ART, FORMULAS, AND MORALITY

No aspect of Victorian art is more widely known than its didacticism. The picture of bearded poet- and painter-saints declaiming religious truths and social shibboleths from various eminences has become a stereotype: Tennyson singing out from Farringford; Browning instructing youth and age in mysteries of the soul distilled from Renaissance life and art; Carlyle, a poet in prose transmitting apocalyptic thunder from a writing loft in Chelsea; Arnold despairing over beauty and life and advising a private, stoic rigor; Elizabeth Barrett crying for the children; William Morris penning socialistic ballads, broadsides, and utopian dreams; Holman Hunt painting sermons; Ford Maddox Brown extolling work. While one must laud the humanitarian impulse and the "involvement" of these people, one has the impression of an immense dulling weight.

Swinburne was unavoidably caught up in the question of morality and art, at times rebelling and at other times as feverish with didactic purpose as his most rabid contemporary. In his prose he frequently considered the role of the artist as prophet and the appropriateness to art of social, political, and religious themes.[1] Since he favored a modified aestheticism, he has been interpreted as a complete aesthete—wrongly, I think; his final allegiance was, as he himself declared, to the artists "on the side of the stars," to the men who stand for "brotherhood," "mercy," "right," "freedom," and "absolute truth." These were those few geniuses whose dedication to art was so complete that all themes were theirs to command. They were no hack propagandists slighting the requirements of their art for the sake of a social or religious message. Beauty first and then truth was Swinburne's principle, and ideal art was an energetic fusion of both. For this his models were Aeschylus, Plato, Shakespeare, Ben Jonson, Milton, Dryden, Blake, Hazlitt, Shelley, and Ruskin.

This principle and related ones were framed against his own vivid struggles with the Philistines, whose moral standards cast an immense pall, he felt, over all of the arts and whose tastes were unhappily reflected in the popular papers and journals. Swinburne, like Whistler, despised the Tom Taylors and the Prudhommes; and the Ruskins and Tennysons, too, when their interest in the general welfare grew excessive and patronizing. The fault of the British is that they have proceeded "by the rule of thumb," suppressing all that was "inconvenient to them" not through an appeal to reason "but always, if possible, to some precedent, or form, or letter . . . which saved them from the necessity of recurring to general principles." Heine, in a comment on English narrowness (*"ächtbrittische Beschränktheit"*), declared that he would have considered spending his exile in England except that he could not abide two things: coal smoke and Englishmen. Of all peoples, Arnold said, the English have become

> the most inaccessible to ideas and the most impatient of them; inaccessible to them, because of their want of familiarity with them; and impatient of them because they have got on so well without them, that they despise those who, not having got on as well as themselves, still make a fuss for what they themselves have done so well without. But there has certainly followed from hence, in this country, somewhat of a general depression of pure intelligence: Philistia has come to be thought by us the true Land of Promise, and it is anything but that; the born lover of ideas, the born hater of commonplaces, must feel in this country, that the sky over his head is of brass and iron.[2]

The uproar which greeted the *Poems and Ballads* in 1866 acquainted Swinburne all too quickly with the Philistine critics. The details of that book's reception, which so frightened the Moxon publishing house that it suppressed the trial edition, have been told often enough. Still worth mentioning, however, is Swinburne's adroit *Notes on Poems and Reviews*, written to prepare the way for J. C. Hotten's new edition of the offending volume. The manuscript of the pamphlet, now in the Huntington Library, contains a handful of passages which were never printed. Since they did not appear in the original publication, their suppression was apparently with Swinburne's consent (the Bonchurch version is an exact reproduction of the pamphlet). The first deleted passage, originally intended to conclude the opening paragraph, contains a veiled hint that Moxon risked a lawsuit because of the broken contract:

> Nor was I willing to bring forward any matter which would concern myself, had not others assumed the right to make it their affair. With equal silence & equal scorn I had hoped to pass by the scurrility of this man & the treachery of that. Others, not I, may be curious to inquire whether a breach of contract were spontaneous or suggested. It is enough for me, on conviction of a man's unworthiness of trust to decline any further dealing with such an one & withdraw from his hands on any trust, all property of mine which they [the publishers] had hold of. Exposure could hardly discredit those who court detection; & the makers & breakers of contracts may be left to fatten on the fruits of their furtive audacity. I pass on to things, however contemptible, yet for the moment of more importance than such as these. (p. 2)

Swinburne shook his fist at public virtue, "a rank and rapid growth, barren of blossom and rotten at root," and at middle-class critics, "moral milkmen" who travel the streets crying their wares, "the requisite fluid," he said, that "fresh or stale, sour or sweet . . . runs from a sufficiently copious issue" (*NPR*, 363, 364).

His vituperative attitude was sustained by his reading of the Elizabethan George Chapman, who had been as contemptuous of the obtuse in his day as Swinburne was in his. In an essay written in 1875, he quoted Chapman:

> "Such is the wilful poverty of judgments, wandering like passportless men in contempt of the divine discipline of poesy, that a man may well fear to frequent their walks. The profane multitude

I hate, and only consecrate my strange poems to those searching
spirits whom learning hath made noble, and nobility sacred."
(*GC*, 142)[3]

Swinburne followed this passage with a biting analysis of the common
Elizabethans, the "honest English citizen" of average mind and in-
clination. Of course the analysis works as an indictment also of the
Victorian Philistine. The occasion was a satiric play, *Two Wise Men
and the Rest Fools*, generally attributed to Chapman (wrongly, Swinburne thought, though he willingly proceeded with his examination
of it). The theme of the play was the despicable "average of opinion"
found among "honest English citizens of the middle class." These
citizens

> were jealous of change, suspicious of innovation, indignant at the
> sight of rascality which they were slow to detect, much given to
> growl and wail over the decay of good old times and the collapse
> of good old landmarks, the degeneracy of modern manners, and
> the general intolerability of things in an age of hitherto unknown
> perversity; men of heavy-headed patience and heavy-witted hum-
> our, but by no means the kind of cattle that it would be safe for
> any driver to goad or load overmuch. (*GC*, 181)

Swinburne's position reflects an insight which, so far as I know, no
critic of nineteenth-century art has sufficiently examined. The issue is
the paradox of the artist who contemptuously rejects a mass audience
and at the same time desires its adulation. It is an issue germane to any
discussion of nineteenth-century aestheticism with its many authenti-
cated cross motives and contradictions.[4] Irving Babbitt has described
an apostle of beauty disturbed and even angered by the hostility and
insensitivity of the world around him. "The aesthete who assumes an
apocalyptic pose," he wrote, "is an especially flagrant instance of the
huddling together of incompatible desires. He wishes to sport with
Amaryllis in the shade and at the same time enjoy the honors that
belong only to the man who scorns delights and lives laborious days."[5]
Again, Chapman is apropos. Swinburne read his "acrid tone of angry
contempt" for "common readers" as a mixture of haughtiness and
petulance: it "had in it," Swinburne said, "some salt of sincerity as
well as some underlying sense of conscious failure in the pursuit of

that success on the image or idea of which he turns and tramples with passionate scorn. It is not usually till he has failed to please that a man discovers how despicable and undesirable a thing it would have been to succeed" (*GC*, 142-143).

Something of this spirit had also colored the *Notes*, which were written as much to persuade Philistine readers as to scold them. Swinburne's main purpose, to declare the special inverse morality of his flamboyant ballads, revealed no small fraction of Babbitt's "huddling together of incompatible desires." With rather showy contempt he argued that "Laus Veneris," "Faustine," "Dolores," and "Hermaphroditus" are stages in the symbolic experience of grand mortal souls in spiritual torment. He admitted that except by contrast the morality of the poems was quite remote from mid-nineteenth-century standards of propriety, of which he pretended complete ignorance, and he was to dismiss the matter in *John Ford* with the remark, ostensibly a quotation, that the ears of this generation "are the chastest part about them" (*JF*, 373).[6] Swinburne had only contempt for writers and painters who let themselves be cowed by Philistia, and in another essay warned those who were still free that the beast will "swallow your honey-cake to no purpose; if he does not turn and rend you, his slaver as he licks your hand will leave it impotent and palsied for all good work" (*WB*, 140). Those "who try to clip or melt themselves down to the standard of current feeling, to sauce and spice their natural fruits of mind with such condiments as may take the palate of common opinion, deserve to disgust themselves and others alike" (*WB*, 248). A school of poetry, Swinburne said, glancing toward a brave new world, "subordinated to any school of doctrine, subjugated and shaped and utilised by any moral idea to the exclusion of native impulse and spiritual instinct, will produce work fit to live when the noblest specimens of humanity are produced by artificial incubation" (*W&B*, 160).

In another essay, that on M. Prudhomme, he exposed the crude power of the bourgeoisie who pretended to an informed taste and spent their money to prove it. The bourgeois Prudhomme not only writes poetry but has established an art school. He officiates in his chasuble "at the shrine of a new and greater Diana." She is not of the Ephesians, however, but of the Philistines. Nor is this Diana the exclusive goddess of the French; since no people is so "hag-ridden, so bullied and beaten about, by the race of Prudhomme" as the English, she is their goddess too:

> We are born and baptized into the Church of Prudhomme, the most Catholic of all churches, outside of which there is no human salvation for us; and in that fold we must [as artists] die, or take up with the worst fate of the worst heretics.

In a description of Prudhomme's jaunt through a London gallery, Swinburne struck a neat riposte for the artist who surpasses Philistine comprehension. When Prudhomme denounced M. Leys, the Belgian painter whose works were on the gallery walls, sycophantic British officials removed the pictures and sent them back to Belgium where, Swinburne said, "we believe the artist . . . intends to dispose of them as tavern signboards; and failing that, to have them torn up and publicly burnt." While every moment in art produces its shoddy imitators, and the tide washes up "mere shingle and mud and broken spars" with "pearls of gold," the Philistine connoisseur rejects the works of value in favor of the showy worthless ones. These he lauds in his newspapers and persuades his friends to buy; works of merit may go unrecognized for generations, always "with the good leave of M. Prudhomme" (*PA*, 401-403, 407, 408).[7]

John Everett Millais, the Pre-Raphaelite, was for Swinburne and his friends an archetypal capitulator. After an extremely auspicious beginning—his early masterpieces, *The Blind Girl* and *Autumn Leaves*, were both exhibited at the Royal Academy in 1856—Millais devoted his career to slick conventional portraits and to saccharine literary scenes which proved so popular they earned him a knighthood and an income as large as a popular actor's. His *Bubbles*, a sparkling rendition of an over-dressed child blowing soap bubbles, was the zenith of conventionality. Pears Soap, Ltd., bought the picture, and it continues to sell their product, which has, according to the company, "enjoyed the highest reputation among the aristocracy since its invention in 1789." The picture remains a landmark in the history of mass advertising. Swinburne marked the beginning of Millais' deterioration in some suppressed passages in *Notes on the Royal Academy Exhibition, 1868*. He was uneasy about the slick touches in Millais' *Sisters* and *Pilgrims to St. Paul's* [See Plates 2, 5, 10, 11]:

The worst of these pictures, painted by a meaner man, would justly win notice and applause; but it is no small thing that a great man should do no greater work than some of this. The clear eye and the strong hand have not forgotten their cunning; it is a master whom we find too often at work fit only for a craftsman. Surely a painter who has done things so noble will not always be content to take for his battle-cry, "Philistia, be thou glad of me." (*NRA*, 34)

Arthur Symon's obituary of Millais (1896) contained a Swinburnian lament over the tragic waste of the painter's talent: his "respectability" was "a desecration of the spirit," for he "deliberately abandoned a career, which, with labour, might have made him the greatest painter of his age, in order to become, with ease, the richest and most popular." Symons took heart from a principle dear to serious writers and painters, one which Swinburne certainly would have endorsed: "The appeal of every great artist has been to the few; fame, when it has come, has come by a sort of divine accident, in which the mob has done no more than add the plaudits of its irrelevant clamour to the select approval of the judges."[8]

The frail value of public acclaim was clear, too, when Swinburne considered the artists who were spurned or ignored in their own day and later praised for their vision. Some of Swinburne's early sympathy for the Pre-Raphaelites developed because they had been among the host of the rejected. Blake was a prime example of one ignored and hence defeated by the Philistines. Much of Swinburne's zeal for Shelley and Charlotte Brontë sprang from his feeling that their greatness had been insufficiently appreciated by a recalcitrant world. Blake and Shelley, "mere artists," he explained, "were perhaps at root too innocent to do as much harm as they desired, or to desire as much harm as they might have done" (*WB*, 181). Implicit in this remark is a belief in the requisite estrangement of true talent from the practical world. Creation is a private act, mysterious, worthy of worship, all removed from the question of success or failure in the marketplace. Poets may have wings,

> but it is impossible that they should have feet to walk straight, eyes to see clear, hands to work hard on the common ground and in the common air of reality; they are fit only, as we all know, to be crowned and expelled by the same hands, waved off and wor-

shipped at due distance by the rational gratitude of their fellow-citizens. (*AV*, 431)

The artist's aloofness, Swinburne knew, enabled him to elude the threats of the Philistine. Art dedicated to itself deals with man's highest aspirations; the creative act is evidence of one such aspiration. When Swinburne adopted the tone and point of view of the aesthete he was underscoring a theme, a principle, a law which he felt had to be emphasized, even railed over and screamed about. "Let us hear no more," he said, writing of Blake [*See* Plates 6 and 7],

> of the moral mission of earnest art; let us no longer be pestered with the frantic and flatulent assumptions of quasi-secular clericalism willing to think the best of all sides, and ready even, with consecrating hand, to lend meritorious art and poetry a timely pat or shove. Philistia had far better (always providing it be possible) crush art at once, hang or burn it out of the way, than think of plucking out its eyes and setting it to grind moral corn in the Philistine mills; which it is certain not to do at all well. (*WB*, 139)

Art, he said, in a remark which became something of a battle cry for the aesthetes, can never be the "handmaid of religion, exponent of duty, servant of fact, pioneer of morality." And no artist will listen "to the blank bark of those porter dogs of the Puritan kingdom," the critics, "even when they fawn and flirt with tongue or tail" (*WB*, 140). The "business" of art is "not to do good on other ground, but to be good on her own. . . . To ask help or furtherance from her in any extraneous good work is exactly as rational as to expect lyrical beauty of form and flow in a logical treatise." She is "not like fire or water, a good servant and bad master; rather the reverse." She helps in nothing "of her own knowledge and free will: upon terms of service you will get worse than nothing out of her" (*WB*, 137). Swinburne complained that Shelley had spoiled his *Prometheus Unbound* by inserting "philanthropic doctrinaire views and 'progress of the species' " (*Letters*, I, 115). The lesson to be drawn? The man who "falls to artistic work with a moral purpose" shall lose "even that which he has" (*WB*, 138). The poet, Swinburne said in another place, is first of all "to write good verses and by no means to redeem the age and remould society" (*CB*, 417).[9] The following passage from *William Blake* reveals the special, largely Shelleyan ethic Swinburne considered indigenous to art. His idea that once technical matters are properly attended to other matters will take care of themselves is intriguing and indicates again the great importance he gave to technical achievement and how apprised he was of the latent moral power of art to operate firmly in the external world. In other words, he was not, in the strictest sense, an aesthete. A spiritual "advantage"[10] developed swiftly and automatically from a disciplined craftsmanship, one which far outranged the threats of conventional stricture and taboo. A dedicated, controlled art for art's sake is the first order of value; others follow of their own accord. Some ideas in the passage are reminiscent of Arnold's epochs of concentration and expansion and of William Morris' theories of culture:

> The contingent result of having good art about you and living in
> a time of noble writing or painting may no doubt be this: that
> the spirit and mind of men then living will receive on some points
> a certain exaltation and insight caught from the influence of such
> forms and colours of verse or painting; will become for one thing
> incapable of tolerating bad work, and capable therefore of rea-
> sonably relishing the best; which of course implies and draws with
> it many other advantages of a sort you may call moral or spiritual.
> But if the artist does his work with an eye to such results or for
> the sake of bringing about such improvements, he will too prob-
> ably fail even of them. Art for art's sake first of all, and afterwards
> we may suppose all the rest shall be added to her. . . . (*WB*,
> 137-138)

One writer who aimed too consciously for "improvements" was Walt Whitman. "Undigested formulas" too often marred his poetry, whenever the preacher had the upper hand his genius was choked and he became the "formalist," which for Swinburne meant "maker of formulas." In the *Leaves of Grass* were two warring voices: "Some-times in the course of two lines the note is changed, either by the collapse of the poet's voice into the tuneless twang of the formalist, or by the sudden break and rise of released music from the formalist's droning note into the clear sincere harmonies of the poet" (*UM*, 412). Whatever he says that is genuine, either about himself, or "a small bird's loss," or a great man's demise, or a nation's readying for battle, or "a child going forth in the morning," is well said; but when he speaks "not as though he must but as though he ought, as though it behoved one who would be the poet of American democracy to do this thing or to be that thing if the duties of that office were to be properly fulfilled, the tenets of that religion worthily delivered," he speaks badly. "Never before was high poetry so puddled and adulterated with mere doctrine in its crudest form." Nor was there "less assimilation of the lower dogmatic and the higher prophetic element" (*UM*, 411, 412, 413). Regrettable also were Whitman's random catalogs, his tumbling together the names "of all possible crafts and implements in one unsorted heap." To "sing the song of all countries is not simply to fling out on the page at random in one howling mass the titles of all divisions of the earth, and so leave them. At this rate, to sing the song of the language it should suffice to bellow out backwards and forwards the twenty-four letters of the alphabet" (*UM*, 414).[11]

In a long analysis of *Les Misérables* Swinburne again considered the relation of social theories to art. While few of these remarks have the "justice" of those in *Blake* and *Chapman*, they have interest as further examples of his polemical mode. The following remarks, direct and restrained until the third sentence, state the hypothesis:

> Any book above a certain pitch of writing must be taken first of all to be a work of pure art. For we can bring no man's work to a higher standard. All the excellence in the world will never serve for salt to a thing born rotten. (*VH*, 159)

Another passage, further intended to prick Philistine sensibilities, is grimly inhumane. The turgid, difficult style lacks the sinuosity of Swinburne's best prose. It is amusing that the remarks occur only one brief page after Swinburne has explained that humor "well mixed into a man's work gives balance and implies the power of abstinence and choice"; the man so gifted "cannot run to rant or relax into sentiment" (*VH*, 166). Here is the passage. The last sentence foreshadows Wilde's more characteristic apothegms.[12]

> ... we may reasonably grudge the time and labour—still more the faith and hope and fervent vigour of mind—lavished on social

subjects, and all kinds of actual wrongs and remedies; such of us at least as regard a good work of art as the first of all good deeds for an artist, and would consider a fresh Hamlet or a new Ruy Blas cheaply purchased by the hanging without trial of a dozen innocent men. . . .[13] Improve people beyond a certain point and they become an affliction to the unimprovable part of men. (*VH*, 167-168)

In the *Blake* Swinburne tried to dispose of the idea, glibly circulated by Carlyle and less glibly by Ruskin, that the noble life is better than the production of noble art. Swinburne held that the very creation of a noble work, regardless of the character of the artist, is itself the noblest of actions; only after we have confronted the work on its own terms do we consider the artist's personal character. Art is the apex of human experience, the point of the cone defining all else below it and encompassed within it. The problem is complicated.[14] Ruskin's equation of the noble and the aesthetic was not as simple as it might seem; like Carlyle he assumed a rising scale of values in all human experience, with aesthetic and ethical elements ascending together towards the ideal. The noble, to put it another way, had psychological overtones for Ruskin to which Swinburne was indifferent. In Ruskin's religious hero, as in his artist, there were various degrees of nobility and dedication, and for both, the highest nobility was Christian feeling. Ruskin saw, toward the end, that his ideas invited superficial interpretations; he railed, for example, at the sham Gothic buildings he had inspired.

> I have had indirect influence on nearly every cheap villa builder between this and Bromley, and there is scarcely a public-house near the Crystal Palace but sells its gin and bitters under pseudo-Venetian capitals copied from the Church of the Madonna of Health or Miracles.

And, he added, implying that his semi-seclusion was due in part to disillusionment, "one of my principal motives for leaving my present house is that it is surrounded everywhere by the accursed Frankenstein monsters, of, indirectly, my own making."[15]

Of course, it is always easy for the younger generation to see flaws in the older. Swinburne seems to have perceived the risks earlier than

65

Ruskin; free of the need to relate art to any formal religious dicta, Christian or otherwise, the matter was simplified for him. His task was to affirm the primacy of art. The aesthetic was always the support for social and ethical ideals.

> . . . if to live well be really better than to write or paint well, and a noble action more valuable than the greatest poem or most perfect picture, let us have done at once with the meaner things that stand in the way of the higher. For we cannot on any terms have everything; and assuredly no chief artist or poet has ever been fit to hold rank among the world's supreme benefactors in the way of doctrine, philanthropy, reform, guidance, or example: what is called the artistic faculty not being by any means the same thing as a general capacity for doing good work, diverted into this one strait or shallow in default of a better outlet. Even were this true, for example, of a man so imperfect as Burns, it would remain false of a man so perfect as Keats. The great men, on whichever side one finds them, are never found trying to take truce or patch up terms. Savonarola burnt Boccaccio; Cromwell proscribed Shakespeare. The early Christians were not great at verse or sculpture. (*WB*, 133-134)

The reference to these Carlylean great men helped Swinburne to his conclusion: "Men of immense capacity and energy who do seem to think or assert it possible to serve both masters—a Dante, a Shelley, a Hugo—poets whose work is mixed with and coloured by personal action or suffering for some cause" do not necessarily damage their art (*WB*, 134). Man's affections and allegiances are fleeting; art is permanent and resolved. This wisdom assists the hero-poet to maintain his integrity.

Swinburne's personal sympathies were with these creators embroiled like Blake, Shelley, and Hugo in the fiery issues of art and life, men who took as theirs the whole domain of human engagement. Man, they know, "is not wicked, and he is not good; by no means white as snow, but by no means black as coal; black *and* white, piebald, striped, dubious, sceptical" (*VH*, 237). These were the true "prophets of belief," the chain-breakers, the seers:

> . . . there must be somebody on the side of the stars! somebody to stand up for brotherhood, for mercy, for honour, for right, for

66

freedom, and for the solemn splendour of absolute truth. With all
their sublimity and serenity, flowers as they are of summer everlasting, the shining constellations have need that the world they guide
should bear them witness that they shine, and some man's voice be
raised in every age to reassure his brothers . . . across the night;
for nothing would be so terrible as an ultimate equality of good
and evil, of light and darkness, in the sight of the supreme and
infinite unknown world; nothing would bring so heavy an indictment against God as the mad and senseless waste of light
unprofitably lost and scattered about the hollow deep of heaven
without the direction of a will. This absence of will, this want of
conscience in the world, the prophet of belief refuses to accept as
possible. (*VH*, 238)

Swinburne's distaste was for those who would pervert art to narrow
ends. In his view, the conscious seeker after the didactic becomes immoral and grotesque. The inspired artist, "on the side of the stars,"
moves his audience, through beauty, to love the arts and to hate injustice.

Implicit all along in Swinburne's moral design is the corollary that
the artist who loses his integrity commits one of the worst "immoral-
ities" of all; and Swinburne expressed both regret and contempt whenever he saw an artist execute forms and develop themes uncongenial
to his real talent or forget that art must present the resolved experience
rather than the struggles and false starts along the way or, like Millais,
choose the slick and the facile for the sake of popularity and wealth.
The sculptor who is capable of carving works in ivory and gold should
never model "statues of snow" (*DGR*, 45). The artist true to his
vision is never "indecent"; "in the sight of art nothing is so foul as
falsehood" (*JF*, 382). These standards, delivered with some of the stale
diction of the conventional moralist, underlie Swinburne's views on
Philistinism, the didactic in art, and the ultimate ethical worth of
creative expression.

As a fashioner of idyls even Tennyson was vulnerable, as much
for having chosen so minor a form as for spawning a shabby host of
imitators. "We have idyls good and bad, ugly and pretty," Swinburne declaimed; "idyls of the farm and the mill; idyls of the dining-
room and the deanery; idyls of the gutter and the gibbet" (*NPR*, 371).

67

The trouble was that despite their occasional beauty these poems lacked the power of a vigorous genre art as well as the charm of ancient pastorals. *The Idyls of the King* aroused Swinburne's ire because the laureate had aimed too low. King Arthur is a "wittol" who is so moral that he is immoral, Guenevere is "a woman of intrigue," Lancelot a "co-respondent," Vivien "such a sordid creature as plucks men passing by the sleeve." The whole work lowered and deformed is "a case for the divorce-court," not for poetry (*UM*, 405-408). When Swinburne compared the poem with Malory's powerful work he concluded somewhat unfairly that Tennyson's poem was "home-made treacle" (*NCB*, 19).[16]

Like Tennyson, Byron at times miscalculated his own genius. He was no master of character and should never have published his attempts to be a playwright: "Manfred and Astarte are surely very inferior to Punch and Judy" (*Letters*, V, 73). This failing he shared with Wordsworth.[17] In drama he was "a thunderer whose bolt was forged most assuredly on no diviner anvil than that with which Dennis or Cibber is represented in the text or notes of the *Dunciad* as shaking the souls of his audience" (*W&B*, 175). Neither was he above pandering to the fashionable and popular. His choice of Eastern subjects for poetry seemed too adventitious. (This is now a fairly well agreed upon interpretation; Swinburne was one of the first to propound it.) Only in the *Giaour* do we detect some of Byron's "fiery sincerity" (*B*, 132); the other Eastern poems ring false. Neither their dramatic color nor their value as influences on the exotic strain in English poetry were enough to redeem their hasty workmanship and low-powered imagination.

When Arnold praised Byron for his choice of subjects it was at Shelley's expense, and this made Arnold himself a prey for Swinburne. Swinbure would permit no one to make light of Shelley, whom, as we know, he regarded as one of the most gifted lyricists of all time. It was Byron, Swinburne felt, who sometimes erred in choice of subject matter; Shelley did not spend his talent on inferior themes. Byron, Arnold said,

> threw himself upon poetry as his organ; and in poetry his topics were not Queen Mab, and the Witch of Atlas, and the Sensitive Plant, they were the upholders of the old order, George the Third, and Lord Castlereagh, and the Duke of Wellington, and Southey,

and they were the canters and tramplers of the great world, and they were his enemies and himself. (*W&B*, 198)

As he often did, Swinburne improvised upon well known phrases of his victim and sneered at this passage as "an instance of provincial and barbarian criticism" inspired by a "sour unreasonableness." "It is almost too contemptibly easy to retort in kind," he went on,

> by observing that when Shelley threw himself upon poetry as his organ, his topics were not Hours of Idleness, and Hints from Horace, and the Waltz, they were the redemption of the world by the martyrdom of righteousness, and the regeneration of mankind through "Gentleness, Virtue, Wisdom, and Endurance"; and they were the heroism of Beatrice and the ascension of Adonais, and they were the resurrection of Italy and of Greece, and they were the divinest things of nature, made more divine through the interpretation of love infallible and the mastery of insuperable song. (*W&B*, 198)

Another example of artistic immorality was the choice of fluctuating states of soul for subject matter. Arthur Hugh Clough was Swinburne's most worrisome example. Clough's religious poetry, veering, pathetic, and unresolved, expressed a "demi-semi-Christianity," (*DGR*, 22), aesthetically satisfying neither to Clough nor to his readers. There were already too many whines "of retrospective and regretful scepticism" in Victorian poetry, Swinburne said, too many "cobwebs of plea and counterplea" and "jungles of argument and brakes of analysis" (*MA*, 71) to add any more.

The often harshly treated Arnold was in this respect the model of all that was desirable. The philosophy of "Empedocles on Etna" was "solid . . . bare rock" in an age of "quaking ground."

> It is no small or common comfort, after all the delicate and ingenious shuffling of other English poets about the edge of deep things, to come upon one who speaks with so large and clear and calm an utterance; who begins at the taproot and well-spring of the matter, leaving others to wade ankle-deep in still waters and weave river-flags or lake-lilies in lieu of stemming the stream. Nothing in verse or out of verse is more wearisome than the delivery of reluctant doubt, of half-hearted hope and half-incredulous

faith. A man who suffers from the strong desire either to believe or disbelieve . . . is certainly worthy of pity, until he begins to speak; and if he tries to speak in verse, he misuses the implement of an artist. . . . We have had Christian sceptics, handcuffed fighters, tongue-tied orators, plume-plucked eagles; believers whose belief was a sentiment, and free-thinkers who saw nothing before Christ or beyond Judaea. To get at the bare rock is a relief after acres of such quaking ground. (*MA*, 66-67)

"Bare rock" was essential too in treating the actual processes of creation. The moral artist, in Swinburne's sense, knows that no matter how painful his creative struggle it must remain part of the undeclared substance of his experience, valuable if at all to himself alone. (Swinburne seemed to feel that a study of a poet's rough drafts would yield little.) He has no right to impose fluctuating and unshapen matter upon an audience. As Browning says in "Abt Vogler" the artist is obliged to transcend earth's "broken arcs" and convey the illusion of "heaven's perfect round." The workman, observed Swinburne,

> should see all sides of his work, and labour with all his might of mind and dexterity of hand to make it great and perfect; but to use up the details of the process as crude material for cruder verse . . . this no artist will ever attempt, no craftsman ever so perform as to escape ridicule. . . . (*WB*, 93)

One should work "supremely well" and disregard the "contingent consequences," public or private (*WB*, 139).

Another area unfit for art was that being explored by the naturalists; too few of their creative powers, Swinburne thought, were engaged in selecting, sharpening, and heightening. His responses here were more instinctive than rational, and his blindness to the new freedoms of theme and form supplied by these adventurers was one of his most serious weaknesses. He was ahead of his time in so many matters that it comes as somewhat of a shock when he is not; but he was too committed to the traditionalist view of decorum to give way on this. Whitman alone engaged him for a time; his attempts to allow for free verse poems show that he could be flexible; but, as was so true of him, he had first to be swayed emotionally by his subject. If he was impressed, he could adapt and modify; otherwise he could not. He seemed to expect that his readers would instinctively share his own fastidious horror of the naturalists and avoid the "troughs of Zolaism" that Tennyson too had warned against. The earliest passage on this appeared in 1857 in *Undergraduate Papers*, in the unreprinted essay on Marlowe and Webster. Swinburne theorized that the Elizabethans, despite their frequent displays of aesthetic tact, risked allowing "mere physical endurance" unrefined by any "sentiment beyond its own relations" to damage their plays:

> There is a truth in the old Greek theories which bade poets avoid all horrible exposure in their writings, and be careful of turning the exceptional into the repulsive. This dogma, pushed to the extreme, leaves us a tragedy bound in grave-clothes, with a nerveless whine for voice and a draped lay-figure for study; the clear eyes blinded with a fool's bandage, the mighty music and measured thunder as of the choral heavens, changed for an emasculated and sickly drawl. But poets far above the so-called "classic" school have erred as gravely on the other hand. Art is not dissection: nothing is more offensive than bare and sensuous horror. Spiritual suffering in every detail and symptom belongs to the large dowry of art; but not the details of the slaughter-house. The noble censure passed by Mr. Ruskin on the painters of foul and bloody scenes, the art whose place is in the kennel or the shambles, applies equally to the poet who defiles his power in the same way. (p. 11)

This theme appears also in *Under the Microscope*, that brilliant assemblage of mockery and good sense. In it Swinburne said that he did not object to "the presentation in art of an unchaste woman . . . [but] the creature presented should retain some trace of human or if need be of devilish dignity" (*UM*, 408). The difference between Dickens' *Oliver Twist* and the "literary patients of Dr. Ibsen" is that Oliver's "spiritual refinement" matters while Ibsen's characters remain, so Swinburne felt, debased and diseased with little hope of either moral or physical rejuvenation (*CD*, 58). One of Charles Reade's stage adaptations (Swinburne does not specify which one) is as dull as Zola's work; both of these "self-styled" naturalists base themselves on "documents" and, hence, are inevitably dull.[18] Swinburne was never afraid to beard lions in their dens; but he made the mistake of not realizing that Ibsen was a lion and in not perceiving the telling symbolic power of which Zola at his best was capable. The mine in *Germinal,* as it dominates both life and landscape, is one illustration. Swinburne's own efforts at fiction are rarefied treatments of a brittle aristocratic life, further narrowed to the country house set and based upon a comedy of manners. In their total obliviousness to a new climate of art they seem anachronistic to us now.

Several passages will help to clarify these formulas and provide firm statements on social-religious intention and art. "We are at one with the preachers of 'art for art' " and

> would give many patriots for one artist, considering that civic virtue is more easily to be had than lyric genius, and that the hoarse monotony of verse lowered to the level of a Spartan understanding . . . is of less than no value to art, while there is a value beyond price and beyond thought in the Lesbian music which spends itself upon the record of fleshly fever and amorous malady. (*VH,* 243)

It is not, he said, thinking on the page, that a fleshly record is the highest form of art; for beauty may as easily, and as appropriately, align (though not identify) herself "with moral or religious passion, with the ethics or the politics of a nation or an age." She must maintain her uniqueness and at the same time must deal effectively with the full life of man in society and with the whole nature of things (*VH,* 244).

One of his best passages illustrates his ultimate breadth of view and shows once again how demanding he was that the artist be "adequate" to his work. His topic was the appropriateness of ancient forms to contemporary art:

> If a poem cast in the mould of classic or feudal times, of Greek drama or mediaeval romance, be lifeless and worthless, it is not because the subject or form was ancient, but because the poet was inadequate to his task, incompetent to do better than a flat and feeble imitation; had he been able to fill the old types of art with new blood and breath, the remoteness of subject and the antiquity of form would in no wise have impaired the worth and reality of his work; he would have brought close to us the far-off loveliness and renewed for us the ancient life of his models . . . by loving and reverent emulation as of an original fellow-craftsman. No

form is obsolete, no subject out of date, if the right man be there to rehandle it. (*VH*, 247, 248)

Another vivid passage, published in 1893, praised Hugo's "Toute la Lyre" and provided Swinburne with an occasion for rebuking both the realists and the aesthetes. Hugo had made no effort to capture such " 'music' as may be attempted in the music halls of a 'new poetry' by the smashing of keys or the snapping of harpstrings," a poetry produced by subscribers to that "hoariest of impostures," an "artistic novelty or an aesthetic revolution." Only through an art of rules can poets avoid a sterile dilettantism and an offensive taste. The triad of absolutes with which Swinburne closed expressed once again his morality of art:

> . . . there is the sublime liberty of expression, the supreme perfection of utterance, which never . . . will be attained except by workmen in words . . . who can understand, accept, embrace, and rejoice in the rules and the conditions of their art: content in the recognition and happy in the acceptance of that immortal and immutable instinct whose impulse is for law, whose passion is for harmony, and whose service is perfect freedom. (*PVH*, 389)

These conclusions are tenuous; Swinburne sometimes had trouble separating aesthetic from programmatic elements, particularly if the artist in question were a great one. He was scarcely meticulous in the distinction he drew between the broad humanism of Shelley and the more exact allegiances of Byron; and his frequent discomfort over the aesthetes is further evidence of equivocation. He was aware, however, more aware than some of his critics have realized, of the widening split between artist and society; and his insistence upon the artist's cause was in all likelihood the result of his growing response to the chaos and drift about him. His efforts to set guidelines are among the few in their day to have force and intensity. He tried hard to keep something of a single world for both artist and public; he failed—we can hardly criticize him for not predicting the eventual immensity of the rift—but he assisted in preparing a twentieth-century tone. By 1900 the serious artist knew that a broad public was no longer his and that whatever order he found for his art would be his own, myth, aesthetics, and ethics all drawn from his private self.

CHAPTER IV

ON FIXITIES AND DEFINITES:
THE USE OF DETAIL IN ART

Swinburne had very nearly as much to say about detail in art, or about what Coleridge called "fixities" and "definites," as about Philistinism and morality; and with good cause. Verbal decoration, tortuous line and sentence patterns, pretty sceneries—in the Victorian world all seemed to proliferate endlessly. Amid this welter of gingerbread, a sense of the whole was in some danger of being lost, and Swinburne conceived it his duty not so much to invent new critical principles as to restore traditional ones: to remind his contemporaries, who fondly compared themselves, in vigor and imagination, to the Elizabethans, that the Elizabethans had paid a great deal of attention to overall design. His sources were as various as George Chapman, Ben Jonson, Coleridge, Blake, Hazlitt, Shelley, and Ruskin; he had absorbed not a little eighteenth-century and neoclassical air. What he fought for, and with considerable zest, was a use of detail subordinated to an ideal of the whole. The purple passage and nervously literal scene must not subtract from that whole; we must not be "vexed or fretted by mere brilliance of point and sharpness of stroke, and such intemperate excellence as gives astonishment the precedence of admiration: such beauties as strike you and startle and go out" (*MA*, 77). These topics and some presentation of background are the matters of this chapter.

A brief glance at some characteristic eighteenth-century work noted for its detail will serve to illustrate the change that took place between that period and the Victorian. On the whole, the earlier art, both of literature and painting, is more restrained, ordered, and given to "prospects": Pope's "Summer: the Second Pastoral, or Alexis" is an exercise in a classic form; Dyer's "Grongar Hill" is an arranged series of landscape scenes; Thomson's "The Seasons" is rarely overweighted with realistic detail and moves swiftly within its broader themes; Cowper's and Gray's poems are "a complete gallery, from which we may take down one detached picture after another";[1] Sir Joshua Reynolds' treatment of nature and objects is generalized and freely subordinated to the human subject; in George Stubb's paintings, sleek horses, phaetons, and their owners are simplified; and Thomas Gainsborough's muted personal art is swiftly rendered, conveying the illusion rather than the fact of controlled abundance. George Eliot's frequent use of the set framed scene in her first tale, *The Sad Fortunes of the Rev. Amos Barton* (1857), must have seemed old-fashioned even to her, for she abandoned the device in her next piece of fiction. What the Victorians supplied was no longer the typical catalog of trees, flowers and rivers, but gatherings of details, often in full color, drawn from actual nature, and demonstrating that the artist had observed with exhaustive care with little interest in prospects and, too often, too little regard for a sense of the organic whole. Victorian detail assumed some of the features of an artifact rather than of a picture.

For an image of the Victorian decorative spirit one has only to consult any of several studies of nineteenth-century taste, or to recall the homes of recent ancestors, to appreciate the bizarre and tortured forms this passion for opulence often took. The apotheosis of the impulse was reached in 1851 with the Great Exhibition, that predecessor of world expositions which exerted so strong an influence on English public taste. Grotesque furniture and machinery in Egyptian and Gothic modes vied for attention with equally grotesque *objets d'art*: silver compotes bearing lizards and toads as large as life ("The less of nature it contains," said Ruskin, "the more degraded the ornament. . . ."),[2] scrolled and flowered *papier-mâché* rockers and settees, sideboards complete with elaborate scenes from the hunt. John W. Dodds, the cultural historian of mid-century Victorian Britain, has praised the exhibition for its advanced machinery, its zest and energy, and its range and variety; indeed it was "a marvellous tribute to human ingenuity."

But from another view it was "a compendium of ugliness and bad taste almost terrifying in its effrontery."[3]

There was now in literature a verbal ormolu with tortured sentences and rampant language, which Swinburne related to the Gothic style of "intricate and grotesque traceries" (*MA*, 117). In the graphic arts the impulse appeared in painted records of nature's minutiae and in an unexampled rebirth of book illustration and engraving: the Victorian skill in rendering tail-pieces and letters of the alphabet, in designing books of which the formats were works of art and in which full page black-and-white illustrations teemed with detail and technical improvisations, has been compared to the skill of the Renaissance. A few specific references to some Victorian artists will indicate the scope of this enthusiasm, as well as the link with the scientific interests of the day.

There are the detailed journals and notebooks of William Holman Hunt and of Gerard Manley Hopkins (the latter's inscape-instress principle was supported by his intensive scrutiny of natural forms). There are Ruskin's elaborate descriptions of clouds, mountains, and vegetable species; Browning's eft-things, pompion-plants, oak-worts, gourd-fruits, honeycombs, and finches (Walter Bagehot selected Browning as the model for his poet of the *grotesque* imagination);[4] Tennyson's descriptions of the sword Excalibur, the landscape of "The Lotos-Eaters," Lancelot's image as seen by the Lady of Shalott, the departing knights of the Round Table on their quest of the grail; the spasmodic work of P. J. Bailey and Sydney Dobell; Marianne North's gallery of flower pictures [*See* Plate 8] painted in some of the most inaccessible places throughout the world; Arnold's flower stanzas in "Thyrsis" and "The Scholar-Gipsy"; George Meredith's nature descriptions, coloring both his poetry and his prose; Rossetti's sonnets; Swinburne's own detailed vignettes, particularly in "Laus Veneris," in the boar hunt sequence of *Atalanta in Calydon*, and in the battle scene in *Erechtheus*; Morris' jewel-like details and landscape insets, the wallpapers which transformed interior design, the elaborate types and decorations fashioned for the Kelmscott books; and Francis Thompson's convoluted gingerbread verse—in "Corymbus for Autumn" excessive metaphor nearly swamps the poem.

Richard Altick has provided a fascinating account of Hopkins' literalism, which he contrasts with Swinburne's.[5] Of the four poets,

Swinburne, Hopkins, Tennyson, and Robert Bridges, three viewed the effects of the Krakatoa eruption of August 1883 "with a double vision—the scientist's as well as the verbal artist's." The nonconformist was Swinburne, who utilized the material in a mannered "A New Year Ode to Victor Hugo." Hopkins sent a "scientific communication" describing the event to his friend Richard Watson Dixon. His exhaustive account of the sunsets caused by the volcano was a delicate blending of scientific description and aesthetic perception "in language of which few besides poets are capable." In a letter to Robert Bridges, Hopkins commented on Swinburne's poem: Swinburne "either in fact . . . does not see nature at all or else he overlays the landscape with such phantasmata, secondary images, and what not of a delirium-tremendous imagination that the result is a kind of bloody broth: you know what I mean. At any rate there is no picture." Swinburne would undoubtedly have read Hopkins' remarks as an obtuse confusion of the purpose of poetry and its relationship to nature, and have prided himself on the fact that he did write a poem about Krakatoa, something Hopkins never got around to doing. Hopkins knew what Swinburne's intentions were, but his irritation prevented his seeing that Swinburne's poetry, although different from his own, was equally legitimate. The miracle of Hopkins is that he so frequently transcended his own relatively narrow vision of poetry and the poet's role.

Swinburne would have found Tennyson's defense of the daisies in *Maud* equally uncongenial.

> I know the way she went
> Home with her maiden posy,
> For her feet have touch'd the meadows
> And left the daisies rosy.
>
> (*ll.* 432-5)

Challenged by critics, Tennyson explained that when one's feet disturb a patch of white daisies their rosy undersides *are* indeed exposed.

Swinburne couldn't have cared less about truth to nature as a test for his own imagery; he either shaped it according to an ideal, inspired by Pindar and Walter Landor among others, of the suggestive rather than the precise, or else he presented metaphors so controlled and heightened they foreshadow twentieth-century practices. In short, Swinburne's own images, except in the relatively few decorative moods of the early poetry, exist on a level of symbol and artifice seldom sought by Tennyson.[6] The sea in "Laus Veneris" (stanza 10) is barely significant as a real sea; it is a magnificent symbol of lust, a "panting mouth of dry desire" which suggests and intensifies Tannhäuser's tortured erotic state. A Forsaken Garden, almost ascetic in its details, symbolizes a total world beyond death and time realized through art alone; to appreciate Swinburne's economy one has only to imagine how Browning or Francis Thompson might have handled the theme.

Despite their differences, on at least one occasion Tennyson helped Swinburne to sharpen his own vision of the sea. The line appeared in "Lancelot and Elaine":

> And white sails flying on the yellow sea.

A painter, probably Edward Burne-Jones, brought it to Swinburne's attention.

> I could not but feel conscious at once of its charm, and of the equally certain fact that I, though cradled and reared beside the sea, had never seen anything like that. But on the first bright day I ever spent on the eastern coast of England I saw the truth of this touch at once, and recognised once more with admiring delight the subtle and sure fidelity of that happy and studious hand. There, on the dull yellow foamless floor of dense discoloured sea, so thick with clotted sand that the water looked massive and solid as the shore, the white sails flashed whiter against it and along it as they fled: and I knew once more the truth of what I never had doubted—that the eye and the hand of Tennyson may always be trusted, at once and alike, to see and to express the truth. (*T&M*, 340-341)[7]

Again, Tennyson's "finest image" revealed his scrutiny of the waters of the English Channel; he saw a "green-glimmering" wave "with all/ its stormy crests that smoke against the skies."[8] This was poetry to equal Shelley's "faithful subtlety" and Milton's majesty. Only Victor Hugo "can make words lighten and thunder like these" (*T&M*, 341). Swinburne always admired Tennyson for his craftsmanship and for his many splendid passages. It was in the occasional gaps between Tennyson's skill and content that Swinburne found matter for jest as well as painful regret.

He would have understood well Walter Bagehot's selection of

"Enoch Arden" as an ornate poem which "works not by choice and selection, but by accumulation and aggregation. The idea is not, as in the pure style, presented with the least clothing which it will endure, but with the richest . . . that it will admit."[9] The most offensive lines present the homely fact that Enoch is a fisherman:

> Enoch's white horse, and Enoch's ocean-spoil
> In ocean-smelling osier, and his face,
> Rough-redden'd with a thousand winter gales,
> Not only to the market-cross were known,
> But in the leafy lanes behind the down,
> Far as the portal-warding lion-whelp
> And peacock yew-tree of the lonely Hall,
> Whose Friday fare was Enoch's ministering.

On the other hand, while Swinburne admired the grace, radiance, and charm of "The Talking Oak" and "Will Waterproof's Lyrical Monologue" and the humor of "Northern Farmer" (Tennyson's "first and greatest provincial study"—*T&M*, 324), he reserved his greatest admiration for the majestic poems. Even the "Morte d'Albert, or Idylls of the Prince Consort" had an "exquisite magnificence of style" in many of the passages and contained "splendid flashes of episodical illumination." The description in "Lancelot and Elaine" of Arthur seated on his throne is Tennyson at his ornate best:

> . . . they found the clear-faced King, who sat
> Robed in red samite, easily to be known,
> Since to his crown the golden dragon clung,
> And down his robe the dragon writhed in gold,
> And from the carven-work behind him crept
> Two dragons gilded, sloping down to make
> Arms for his chair, while all the rest of them
> Through knots and loops and folds innumerable
> Fled ever through the woodwork, till they found
> The new design wherein they lost themselves,
> Yet with all ease, so tender was the work;
> And, in the costly canopy o'er him set,
> Blazed the last diamond of the nameless king.
>
> (ll. 430-442)

This one very long sentence is intricately built from a series of increasingly subordinate elements which develop like complicated interwoven vines about the spare, quiet, tender framework of the whole; the run-on effect of the central portion with its stress on a turning, "sloping," and dropping, complements the writhing pattern on the robe. The chair's design becomes chaotically involved before the golden dragons tumble down into a "new design." The effect is almost palpably descriptive; the subordinate clauses blend superbly with the visual matter they contain and are totally in its spirit. The appeal is both visual and tactile (this latter quality in Victorian art has been insufficiently understood); through the magic of style Tennyson provides his readers with a pleasure like that they might enjoy in moving their hands over elaborate wooden or ivory traceries. Such ornateness suits the conception of "Lancelot and Elaine," in fact, suits the entire epic, which moves from one elaborate, though not always artistically realized, conflict to another, and from one "baroque" dialog to another. The *abundance* that T. S. Eliot has praised as one of the qualities of Tennyson's greatness[10] is evident here, as is *exuberance*, an equally useful quality and a trait of Victorian art often overlooked by contemporary critics embarrassed and even appalled by its decorative and imaginative wealth. Not all Victorian exuberance was successful; this point I hope is clear; but when it was, it gave a certain effect not attainable by any other means.[11]

While there is no question that the Pre-Raphaelite painters Holman Hunt and John Everett Millais shared something of Tennyson's abundance, their exuberance was slighter. Both were guilty of substituting a meticulous fidelity for inspiration, and for this both were chastized by Swinburne. Hunt's *Hireling Shepherd* [*See* Plate 9], which demonstrates the evils of neglecting one's duty, holds us not so much by its message as by the literal renderings of weeds and costumes and by the death's-head moth which spreads its delicate, almost microscopically rendered wings across the shepherd's half-closed hand. His *The Awakening Conscience* is equally meticulous, and equally moralistic. In a setting washed with burning color, a woman of sullied virtue recalls her former innocence and, rapt by her recollection, rises from her master's embrace. Her dress and the oriental shawl draped around her hips are painted down to the last laborious detail. The lover's flesh and hair, velvet jacket, and shirt cuffs are rendered with extreme fidelity. The piano is as richly designed as an altar screen; the mangled bird with the sinister black cat hovering over it assumes a weird symbolic quality; and the carpeting, the elaborate view of the out-of-doors seen only in a mirror, and the very walls of the room create an opulent mood, so invitingly opulent, in fact, that we accept Hunt's didactic intentions with some difficulty.[12]

Millais was said to have sketched leaves and tendrils with the aid of a magnifying glass. (Robin Ironside has said of the Pre-Raphaelites in general that they were men who saw the world "without eyelids.")[13] Millais' *The Blind Girl* [*See* Plate 10] is a superb collection of details: a precisely rendered moth rests on the blind girl's shawl. Details of hair, clothing, birds, grass, flower forms, and rocks, and features of the town and field beyond, glow on the canvas with unmistakable reality. Lacking in most of Millais' best work, however, as in Hunt's, is the imaginative freedom which Rossetti's paintings have and which transcends the exercise of flawless technique. Ruskin had seen the risks Hunt, Millais, and some of the other Pre-Raphaelites were taking, told them that they were working too hard, and advised them to seek the large expansive freedom of Turner. In too many of their pictures sight had "failed for weariness, and . . . the hand refused any more to obey the heart."[14]

Swinburne also criticized Millais' glossy effects and Hunt's minutiae. In Millais' *Sisters* there is "no lack of graceful expressive composition" and "no stint of ribbons and trimmings," but there is

> a bitter want of beauty, of sweetness, of the harmony which should hang about the memories of men after seeing it as an odour or a cadence about their senses: and this beauty, this sweetness, this harmony, all great and all genuine pictures leave with us for an after-gust, not soon to pass or perish.

The *Pilgrims to St. Paul's*, though informed with noble sentiment, is cheapened by a slick treatment [*See* Plate II]:

> perhaps the knack by which the light is arranged so as to strike out severally from each pane of the glass lantern is too like one of those petty feats which are as lime-twigs laid to catch the eyes and tongues of the half-trained sight-seers who jostle and saunter through a gallery, pausing now and again to "wonder with a foolish face of praise." (*NRA*, 34)

Time has borne out Swinburne's suspicions of Millais; and when he chose not to reprint this passage in *Essays and Studies* nine years later he acted out of imagined fairness to a painter whose early genius he had much admired.[15]

His criticism of Hunt is in a letter to Francis Waugh. Swinburne coupled Hunt with Meredith:

> How very noble is most of Meredith's 'Vittoria'; but of late he has been falling or tripping rather here and there into his old trick of over refining. Art must dispense with hairsplitting; and he can so well afford to leave . . . [the] vexatious and laborious error of microscopic manipulation of minutiae to such artists as Holman Hunt. . . (*Letters*, I, 202)

The painters Swinburne preferred were those who, like Turner, Blake, Rossetti, and Whistler, had captured "the wider sense of things." One of these, the landscape artist John Crome, suggested a fine parallel with Charlotte Brontë's modelling of Shirley Keeldar on her memories of her sister Emily. The painting, one Swinburne had known all his life but does not name, displayed

> a wild sad track of shoreward brushwood and chill fen, blasted and wasted by the bitter breath of the east wind blowing off the eastward sea, shrivelled and subdued and resigned as it were with a sort of grim submission to the dumb dark tyranny of a full-charged thunder-cloud which masks the mid heaven of midnoon with the heavy muffler of midnight, and leaves but here and there a dull fierce gleam of discomfortable and deadened sunlight along the haggard sky-line or below it. (*NCB*, 36-37)

Against the austere and brooding sky of Charlotte Brontë's "tragic genius and stoic heroism" Shirley Keeldar gleams like a bleak but fierce flash of light, providing us with a portrait of Emily. But for this study we should have only the stark facts of Emily's painful life and the intimations of herself in *Wuthering Heights*:

> We should never have seen with the eye of our imagination any other than a misconceived and mutilated portrait, a disfigured and discoloured likeness of Emily Brontë; one curtailed of the fair proportions, if not diminished from the natural stature of her

spirit; discrowned and disinherited of its livelier and gentler charm of living feature. . . . (*NCB*, 38)

Charlotte worked best, Swinburne observed, "when painting more or less directly from nature"; Emily, however, like Blake, found such models "impossible"—they would have diminished her insight and disabled her hand (*NCB*, 38).

James McNeill Whistler, who for a time was a good friend of Swinburne, was not as successful as he thought in emphasizing the abstract—this despite the sharp witticisms he directed against detailed art. He had the Pre-Raphaelites in mind when he referred to the popular "art of anecdotage." Swinburne took up the question of Whistler's "principle of artistic limitation," according to which a canvas becomes a purely visual "arrangement" or "harmony" of colors, lines, and masses, and wrote some amusing irony at Whistler's expense. Said Swinburne [*See* Plate 12]:

> It is true, again, that Mr. Whistler's own merest "arrangements" in colour are lovely and effective; but his portraits, to speak of these alone, are liable to the damning and intolerable imputation of possessing not merely other qualities than these, but qualities which actually appeal—I blush to remember and I shudder to record it—which actually appeal to the intelligence and the emotions, to the mind and heart of the spectator. It would be quite useless for Mr. Whistler to protest—if haply he should be so disposed—that he never meant to put study of character and revelation of intellect into his portrait of Mr. Carlyle, or intense pathos of significance and tender depth of expression into the portrait of his own venerable mother. The scandalous fact remains, that he has done so; and in so doing has explicitly violated and implicitly abjured the creed and the canons, the counsels and the catechism of Japan. (*WLA*, 23-24)

Swinburne assumed that the quality of higher idea in an art work relates finally to what we might call "readings" of subject matter. Nature can never be entirely denied. The literal element, in a modified sense, does figure as part of the total impact; and here he was closer to Carlyle than to Whistler, who had simply overstated the case. There is, Swinburne maintained, a "loveliness in distinct outline" and a "grandeur in luminous clearness" (*WLA*, 24). At the same time he would also have insisted on the vast difference between the outlines of a Blake and Whistler and those of a Hunt and Millais.

Walter J. Bate has traced the "protest on behalf of *concreteness*" to the late eighteenth-century, where it began as a rejection of a dominant search for the universal in art and life rather than the particular.[16] This is true, and Professor Bate nicely develops the ramifications. There are, however, subtleties beyond a simple preference for the particular over the universal which make Victorian literalism unique. To understand these is, I think, to comprehend better the appeal of the baroque to the Victorians as well as the close affinity between art and religion maintained by so many of the writers, theorists, and painters. The roots of the matter have to do with the relationship of profane senses to spiritual ones, of the earthly to the transcendental, a relationship which seems to have found its way into Victorian thought mainly through Thomas Carlyle.

That there are two levels of sense experience is an ancient concept. The lower one consists of those impressions received through the five senses. The higher contains those vivid but abstract feelings (special senses) aroused by art, love, patriotic feeling, religious ecstasy, and the idea of freedom. Carlyle preached that the traditional dualism between sense and spirit, body and soul, earth and heaven is far too distinct. The seventeenth and eighteenth centuries, with their mystic and mundane realms, their division of reason from intuition, and their chains of being lowered from some remote balcony of the stars to span the universe all failed to allow sufficiently for the dynamic sparks of god, of over-soul, in all living forms and, hence, for the divinity of all living forms. The Romantics had seen this split and had tried to draw these divided worlds closer together. Coleridge, Pater was to note, had a "singular watchfulness for the minute fact and expression of natural scenery" and saw external nature not for its mechanics but as an "animated body informed and made expressive, like the body of man, by an indwelling intelligence."[17] Coleridge had said that the imagination has the "gift" of "reducing multitude into unity."[18] His distinctions between subject as "mind or sentient being" and object, required by mind for its realization—distinctions reminiscent of those made by Kant and Hegel—and his theory of "the necessary correlative of the object," later advanced by T. S. Eliot, assisted in the development of the new aesthetic. Shelley had subscribed to an ideal of "difference without discord." Keats's *empathy* was a refinement of similar values. Ignoring Samuel Johnson's advice, writers and painters were finding the streaks of the individual tulip far more exciting than any generalized image of the species.

But while the Romantics had rediscovered a passionate nature and described it unforgettably, they were still inclined to separate the spheres. In their epiphanies the earth is usually left behind. Manfred and Harold, to maintain their sanity, require a transcendence of the self and an absorption into abstract universal energies symbolized by the elements. Wordsworth, complained Arthur Hugo Clough, failed to look "directly at an object" and to consider it "as a thing in itself"; he took the "sentiment" produced by the fact as "the important and really real fact." He sentimentalized over sentiment.[19] When Thomas Carlyle set about completing the task, through Teufelsdröckh, he admonished the reader to "close thy *Byron*; open thy *Goethe*."[20] To adopt, that is to say, Faust's knowledge that the eternal moment transpires here in this physical universe while one is undertaking some mundane or grubby task—like reclaiming portions of the sea for farmlands—rather than Childe Harold's quest for ecstatic reverie. All specifics, said Carlyle, human beings as well as the lowliest huts they build, bear "visible record of invisible things." In the physical universe, this "small prose domain of sense," all details are "symbols" which lead us to the absolute where the finite blends with the infinite.[21]

> Fool! the Ideal is in thyself, the impediment too is in thyself: thy Condition is but the stuff thou art to shape that same Ideal out of: what matters whether such stuff be of this sort or that, so the Form thou give it be heroic, be poetic? O thou that pinest in the imprisonment of the Actual, and criest bitterly to the gods for a kingdom wherein to rule and create, know this of a truth: the thing thou seekest is already with thee, "here or nowhere. . . ."[22]

While this idea occurs frequently in Carlyle, its most complete statement is in *Sartor Resartus*. His juxtaposition of nature and the supernatural was by design: "Facts are engraved Hierograms," he said, "for which the fewest have the key."[23] When we share in Carlyle's celestial moments we rarely forget the object inspiring us or the earthly roots. Even his style as it drops suddenly from the elevated to the colloquial supports this idea. His contribution was that he sought to merge the natural and the supernatural so smoothly that real gradations become all but imperceptible. In this ideal state man continues to enjoy the pleasures of the natural and specific which are intensified through their fusion with the transcendental. The range of the spirit is in no sense restricted but is, rather, enriched.

This attachment is apparent in the work of more than a few Victorian artists. Every rift of ore in Holman Hunt's painting was intended to reflect divinity. Tennyson's cosmology was so arranged that a sense of physical rapport with the transcendental was a requirement for pastoral consolation (See *In Memoriam,* XCV).[24] For Browning, an element of dross present in all art gave a better indication of the artist's genius as transmitter. Rossetti's transfigurations of sacred and profane love occurred through the ecstatic blend (a "soul-sense") of the concrete and the abstract. Here Edward Burne-Jones and Simeon Solomon were like Rossetti. All of Solomon's work particularly Swinburne was inclined to read as treatments of various aspects of the two kinds of love. Solomon's design, *My Soul and I* [*See* Plate 13], which he created introduced his prose fragment, *A Vision of Love Revealed in Sleep*—Swinburne told Solomon that the work required more pictures—sets the keynote of the entire work.[25] Arnold, again, provided a clearer expression of this mystical idea. The "grand power" of poetry, he observed, is "interpretative";

> by which I mean, not a power of drawing out in black and white an explanation of the mystery of the universe, but the power of so dealing with things as to awaken in us a wonderfully full, new, and intimate sense of them, and of our relations with them. When this sense is awakened in us, as to objects without us, we feel ourselves to be in contact with the essential nature of those objects, to be no longer bewildered and oppressed by them, but to have their secret, and to be in harmony with them; and this feeling calms and satisfies us as no other can. Poetry, indeed, interprets in another way besides this; but one of its two ways of interpreting, of exercising its highest power, is by awakening this sense in us.

He concludes with a quietly elegant statement of the superiority of poetry to science:

The interpretations of science do not give us this intimate sense of objects as the interpretations of poetry give it; they appeal to a limited faculty, and not to the whole man. It is not Linnaeus or Cavendish or Cuvier who gives us the true sense of animals, or water, or plants, who seizes their secret for us, who makes us participate in their life; it is Shakespeare . . . Wordsworth . . . Keats . . . Chateaubriand . . . Senancour. . . .[26]

It is not surprising to find Ruskin voluble on this topic. In his serious way, and following Carlyle's example, he invested his enthusiasm for the ever shifting variety of nature with Christian values, writing of the morality of all art and of true and false ideals in painting and literature. In his *Pre-Raphaelitism* he said: "The man who can best feel the difference between rudeness and tenderness in humanity, perceives also more difference between the branches of an oak and a willow than any one else would. . . ." He praised the artist who has mastered the facts of nature and retained so deep a sense of religious awe that his work bears "witness to the unity of purpose and everlastingly consistent providence of the Maker of all things." Such an artist in depicting nature would retain

a fidelity to the facts of science so rigid as to make his work at once acceptable and credible to the most sternly critical intellect, [and] should yet invest its features again with the sweet veil of their daily aspect; should make them dazzling with the splendor of wandering light, and involve them in the unsearchableness of stormy obscurity; should restore to the divided anatomy its visible vitality of operation, clothe the naked crags with soft forests, enrich the mountain ruins with bright pastures, and lead the thoughts from the monotonous recurrence of the phenomena of the physical world, to the sweet interests and sorrows of human life and death.[27]

For the painter who lacked the talent to produce such exalted effects, but who had a skill for the literal, Ruskin had an ingenious thought. His remarks are a striking instance of a Victorian thinker's dedication to the value of natural detail and to the importance of the artist's social conscience. The government, Ruskin said, should encourage all second-rate artists then busy with fashionable insipidities to paint thoroughly accurate renditions of "the plants and animals, the natural

scenery, and the atmospheric phenomena of every country on earth."
He contemplated with special fervor and regret the grand addition to
human knowledge if such records had been kept during the preceding
two hundred years. Such an endeavor, he was certain, would more than
compete with science; it would surpass science and, perhaps, photog-
raphy, on its own grounds. Geological diagrams would be "no longer
necessary," he assumed. The artist's renditions of topographical features would supply the requisite accuracy and would have the additional power of stimulating the mind and the aesthetic sense. Scientific
art would especially further knowledge among "the common people,"
who apparently would be led through visual appeals to consider facts
which their ordinary brains would otherwise ignore. Aroused, Ruskin
flung this morally-tinged challenge at the non-literalist painter: every
artist "knows that when he draws back from the attempt to render
nature as she is, it is oftener in cowardice than in disdain."[28]

Ruskin's comments reveal another aspect of the Victorian preoccupation with detail and the sense that all human endeavor is one.
I referred earlier to the link between the use of detail and the currently
popular interest in science, a link which Ruskin had helped to forge
by the example of his own elaborate descriptions and the advice on
these matters he loved to provide. This aspect, implicit in my analysis
all along, is a matter of the artist's response to science and his efforts
to keep in step with the ever expanding worlds of the botanist, the
zoologist, the geologist, and the physicist. However, the term *science*
usually represented for the Victorian writer, painter, and critic little
more than an easy label for the use of naturalistic detail and the presentation of direct transcriptions and "documents" from life. George
Eliot (Swinburne attacked her for her "cheap science") found a useful
parallel between scientific method and the writing of fiction, crediting
the scientist with transcendental aims that he seldom had. Her attempt
at a synthesis is vaguely off-center, although she does manage to convey some of the excitement felt by the Victorian scientist intent upon
discovery. She announced that in fiction her own observations of human character ought to share with science the "highest striving . . . after
the ascertainment of a unity which shall bind the smallest things with
the greatest." She discerns "nothing petty" or shallow in the mind
possessing "a large vision of relations, and to which every single object
suggests a vast sum of conditions."[29] She is partially right, of course,

when she relates her own attention to detail with the procedures of the scientist; but when she equates artistic vision with scientific hypothesizing she misses the mark. No dedicated artist or scientist could object to the statement about conditions and relations; but there is, I suggest, something too inclusive in a statement on art and science which Blake, Shelley, and Rossetti—and Swinburne—could support as readily as Faraday, Galton, or Brunel. John Addington Symonds, whose father was a doctor and the kind of general scientist still possible in the nineteenth century, saw the Victorian genius as *scientific* rather than *artistic.* He too was not using the term *science* quite as we use it today, but in his equation of self-analysis, or psychology, and science he was speaking for a new point of view. Victorian poetry, he noted, fails to project the nation's soul; its forte is the subtle analysis and delineation of thoughts and feelings agitating society. "In such an age poetry must . . . be auxiliary to science. . . ."[30]

As we might expect, Swinburne was quite unwilling to make any accommodation for science; and he took his usual firm stand for the traditional and superior position of art:

> Admit all the implied pretensions of art, they remain simply nothing to science; accept all the actual deductions of science, they simply signify nothing to art. The eternal "Après?" is answer enough for both in turn. . . . Poetry or art based on loyalty to science is exactly as absurd (and no more) as science guided by art or poetry. . . . To art, that is best which is most beautiful; to science, that is best which is most accurate; to morality, that is best which is most virtuous. (*WB,* 144)[31]

On another occasion he was somewhat more devious and simply adapted the term to suit himself.

> There is a science of verse as surely as there is a science of mathematics: there is an art of expression by metre as certainly as there is an art of representation by painting. To some poets the understanding of this science, the mastery of this art, would seem to come by a natural instinct which needs nothing but practice for its development, its application, and its perfection: others by patient and conscientious study of their own abilities attain a no less unmistakable and a scarcely less admirable success. . . . (*Wh,* 310)

When he offered some advice to poets who might think sweet-sounding rhyme more important than the discipline of meter, rhythm, and cadence, humorous references to science helped him make his point:

> The question whether your work is in any sense poetry has no more to do with dulcet rhymes than with the differential calculus. The question is whether you have any more right to call yourself a poet . . . than to call yourself . . . on the strength of your published writings, a mathematician, a logician, a painter, a political economist, a sculptor, a dynamiter, an old parliamentary hand, a civil engineer, a dealer in marine stores, an amphimacer, a triptych, a rhomboid, or a rectangular parallelogram. (*Wh*, 311)

Finally, in a letter to Watts-Dunton to cheer him into better health, Swinburne improvised upon his lack of rapport with science in general and physiology in particular:

> My knowledge of anatomy, being limited to what I learnt last year from Randall Holme's book on heraldry, is rather "peculiar" than "extensive," and does not tell me what I hesitate to ask any member of this household—whereabouts "the bladder" is: though I do know from Dr. Moliere on which side is the liver. I hope you will soon be all right again as regards both. (*Letters*, VI, 88)

Imagination and fact, art and science, must remain forever separate, Swinburne maintained, and without apologies. Imitating Blake, he framed a useful metaphor of conflict: there is an old war "between the imagination which apprehends the spirit of a thing and the understanding which dissects the body of a fact" (*WB*, 143). Blake had said: "we impose on one another; & it is but lost time to converse with you whose works are only Analytics."[32] There can be no poetry or art based on a blind loyalty to science and the manipulation of facts under the guise of art; neither discipline is able to "coalesce with the other and retain a right to exist" (*WB*, 144). Art deals with beauty, and science with accurate, measurable detail. Aesthetic values are paramount. Art, to quote Swinburne again, can never be the "handmaid of religion, exponent of duty, servant of fact." Her business is to be good on her own, secure alike from the encroachments of science and of convention. In a judgment of Webster he turned once again to attack the realists. Webster had initiated the cheapening of Shakespeare's grand manner by desiring a heightened veracity, a greater natural truth, and was thereby

> misguided out of his natural line of writing . . . and lured into this cross and crooked byway of immetrical experiment by the temptation of some theory or crochet on the score of what is now called naturalism or realism; which, if there were any real or natural weight in the reasoning that seeks to support it, would of course do away, and of course ought to do away, with dramatic poetry altogether: for if it is certain that real persons do not actually converse in good metre, it is happily no less certain that they do not actually converse in bad metre. (*JW*, 309-310)

There was, perhaps, more prophecy in these remarks than Swinburne was aware of at the time; dramatic poetry has largely disappeared from the scene.

Organic imagery springs inevitably from true poetic genius, much as the flowers of the woods and fields grow quite naturally "under inevitable rains and sunbeams of the atmosphere which bred them." The statement reminds us of one Keats made in a letter to John Taylor: "the rise, the progress, the setting of imagery should like the Sun come natural . . . to him [the poet]." If "Poetry comes not as naturally as the leaves to a tree it had better not come at all."[33]

Although his essay on Keats is one of his shortest pieces devoted to a major writer, and is sketchy and conjectural, it testifies to Swinburne's ability to suppress some of his passion in favor of quiet judgments and analyses. Keats's special *virtue,* or excellence, was his gifted mastery of detail, a "divine magic of language applied to nature" (*NTS*, 379). In the depiction of flowers, for example, wherein he evoked "the hand of M. Fantin," the French painter, Keats displayed a "faultless force" and a "profound subtlety" of "cunning instinct for the absolute expression of absolute natural beauty" (*K*, 301). The parallel with Fantin may sound precious; what Swinburne meant was that Keats's detail provides more than "engaging sceneries," supplies rather what Pater admired, a poetry of literal fact with "a sort of a soul in it." "Clearness of impression" is a phrase Swinburne used for this quality, one manifest in "La Belle Dame Sans Merci" and "Lamia" (*K*, 300). Also, Keats was well advised in not continuing "Hyperion," a "triumph" but one without a "substantial subject" (*K*, 299). A rigorous clipping and pruning would have given the fragment a better organic structure. Finally, in the magnificent odes, particularly in "Autumn," Keats achieved an "exquisite contraction and completeness, within that round and perfect limit" (*NTS*, 380). It is to Swinburne's credit that he saw some of the problems in Keats's development. He was one of the first critics to assess Keats objectively.[34]

Swinburne felt that among the more ornate Victorian writers, only Dante Gabriel Rossetti achieved a consistent fusion of sense and ornament; and the *House of Life* prompted some critical remarks as complicated, as decorative, as aesthetically textured as the ornate sonnets themselves. Swinburne told Rossetti about the care he had taken with the article and wrote to John Morley, the publisher, that he had never taken "so much pains . . . with any prose piece of work" (*Letters*, II, 109). In it he admired Rossetti's "golden affluence of images and jewel-coloured words" which

> never once disguises the firm outline, the justice and chastity of form. No nakedness could be more harmonious, more consummate in its fleshly sculpture, than the imperial array and ornament of this august poetry. Mailed in gold as of the morning and girdled with gems of strange water, the beautiful body as of a carven goddess gleams through them tangible and taintless, without spot or default. (*DGR*, 7-8)

He had more to say on Rossetti's dedication, and particularly on his use of detail to convey "the physical charm of Christianity." Rossetti "belongs, if to any school at all, to the great Venetians," and shares Tintoretto's and Veronese's "thorough subjection of creed and history to the primary purpose of art"—like Titian, he works "with an equal hand whether the girl . . . be Mary or Ariadne." His "spiritual charm" is the direct result of his artistic integrity (*DGR*, 24).

It was with considerable delight, however, that Swinburne thought of Arnold's purposefully balanced use of detail. He was reviewing the *New Poems* of 1867.[35] "By some fine impulse of temperance" Arnold knows "all rules of distance, of reference, of proportion; nothing is thrust or pressed upon our eyes, driven or beaten into our ears" (*MA*, 77). His example tells us, as do the examples of all great poets, that adornment and thought must be "twin-born" and "wedded" in a vital harmony, in what Pater called "clear, orderly, proportionate form."[36]

Arnold's poetry, realizing this ideal, remains most "unfretted" by the "traceries" of the Tennysonians (*MA*, 117). Arnold's "triumph" is that of the lyre; he alone has refashioned this ancient instrument, symbol of traditional poetry, and in "a nation and in an age of luteplayers and horn-blowers." He has approached more nearly than any other poet of his time the "Greek" spirit in art, matching "against the Attic of the Gods this Hyperborean dialect of ours," and, Swinburne concludes, he has done so without earning "the doom of Marsyas" (*MA*, 80). Writers like Arnold (and Landor—*L*, 290-292)

> know what to give and to withhold, what to express and to suppress. Above all, they have *air*; you can breathe and move in their landscape, nor are you tripped up and caught at in passing by intrusive and singular and exceptional beauties which break up and distract the simple charm of general and single beauty, the large and musical unity of things. (*MA*, 77-78)

One difficulty faced by any critic who subscribes to principles of integral detail, and especially by an eclectic critic like Swinburne, is to show precisely how the separate details of a work of art contribute to an organic whole. In art, Pater declared, "structure is all-important . . . that architectural conception of work, which foresees the end in the beginning and never loses sight of it, and in every part is conscious of all the rest, till the last sentence does but, with undiminished vigour, unfold and justify the first—a condition of literary art, which, in contradistinction to another quality of the artist himself. . . I shall call the necessity of *mind* in style."[37] Implicit in these comments, which resemble Swinburne's and represent the best elements of Victorian aestheticism, is that duality at the root of much that I have explored in this chapter—the particular on the one hand, the encompassing whole on the other, and the difficulties of maintaining these in a meaningful aesthetic tension. One approach carried on by the late Victorians remained largely an experiment in interrelationship—the attempt to synthesize the several arts and to produce through synaesthesia a complex of the harmonized senses. A study of this approach occupies the next chapter.

94

CHAPTER V

SYNAESTHESIA
AND THE INTER-RELATED ARTS

Swinburne's emphasis on harmonic unity was directly related
to his use of synaesthesia and to his inherited conviction that the arts
have common areas of impact. That he employed considerable synaesthesia in his own poetry is well known; he is, in fact, one of the nineteenth-century masters of the device. Less well-known is the use he
made of such interrelationships to support his critical principles and to
frame judgments. One of his clearest equations of two arts, poetry and
painting, underscored his basic premise that the critic is obliged to
examine and to weigh details:

> It is empty to charge criticism with going hungrily into minute
> things and paltry questions of verbal or metrical quibbling. Upon
> these things depends the form of a poem; and upon the form de-
> pends the spirit; and upon these two depends the value of a man's
> work. The technicalities of metre, neither as yet verbally defined
> nor easily expressible in English without apparent pedantry of
> detail, are to poetry what the technical minutiae of combined
> colours are to painting. By the goodness or badness, the failure or
> success, of an artist's workmanship in these matters his entire
> achievement must be judged, if judgment be at all worth giving or
> having.

Moreover, "the formal side of the poetic art is no less predicable and definable than the formal side of the pictorial art." ("Look back again at that instance of the painter, always the closest parallel and surest touchstone you can bring for a man's verse.") The true artist knows that the "law of verse is that it shall be good verse; as surely as the law of painting is that it shall be good painting" (*CS*).

When Swinburne used synaesthesia to convey the precise flavor, or *virtue,* of a writer or of a particular work, he either blended the various physical senses, combining their separate appeals so that they emerged in unusual though often clouded contexts, or he interchanged the dominant sense appeal of one art with that of another. There seems never to have been a question in his mind as to the appropriateness of these methods.

The sources he drew upon are the expected ones. Blake, who figures so prominently in this study, was the prototype of the artist gifted in two arts; in discussing him, Swinburne freely interchanged critical observations about the poems with those of the designs and was among the few critics to see specific connections between Blake's two media. He confronted Rossetti's works with a similar ease and recognized that his friend's conscious subordination of pictures to poems and poems to pictures was an unusual gift, the well-known mystic vagueness the result often of the blending of aesthetic appeals. The "splendid quality" of Rossetti's painting, Swinburne said, "and the subtle faculty of verse gain glory from each other without taking, reign side by side with no division of empire, yet with no confusion of claims, with no invasion of rights" (*DGR*, 45-46). [*See* Plates 14 and 15]

Keats was again a forerunner. His use of participial adjectives and verbal compounds to stress and deepen some vital quality of a noun, "globèd peonies," "deep-delvèd earth," "warmèd jewels," "cool-bedded," "chain-swung," "sapphire-regioned," among others, served to heighten sense impressions. Richard Harter Fogle observes that Keats

> reinforces weak with strong sensation with great associative power; an odor image may merge with an image of weight, or a sound image take on an added sense of touch. These sensory effects, however, are merely incidental to fullness of meaning. Keats's fusions of sensation are only elements of more complex poetic processes. The life of his sense analogies lies in his power of

absorbing and humanizing his materials, a power exemplified in
the second stanza of the Nightingale ode.[1]

Taste provides the introductory appeal. "Country green" shifts to
"country dance," "dance" to "song," and "country," "dance," and
"song" blend into the condensed fusion of "sunburnt mirth."

In the letters too there are suggestions of rapport. A field of autumn
stubble "looks warm," Keats wrote to John Hamilton Reynolds, "in
the same way that some pictures look warm."[2] He wrote to John Taylor
of his desire "to diffuse the colouring of St. Agnes' Eve" throughout
an even longer poem "in which Character and Sentiment would be the
figures to such drapery."[3] In a criticism of Benjamin West's painting,
Death on the Pale Horse, he remarks that the arts have a common
ground in "intensity," a principle informing so many of Swinburne's
own views. Said Keats: "The excellence of every art is its intensity,
capable of making all disagreeables evaporate, from their being in
close relationship with Beauty and Truth."[4]

In the "Defence of Poetry" Shelley had discussed the interrelationship of the arts and, implicitly, of the various senses. The end of art
was the fusion into poetry of resistant materials from nature (the
artist's subject matter) and from the artist's imagination. Poetry, in
this abstract sense, was "the perfect and consummate surface and bloom
of all things; it is as the odour and the colour of the rose to the texture
of the elements which compose it. . . ." In its more restricted sense,
however, as a unique art form, poetry reveals through the medium of
language "the invisible nature of man" more successfully than the
other arts, so Shelley believed with some understandable bias. This is
not to say, he pointed out, that the great masters of sculpture, painting,
and music automatically fall short of the great writers. On the whole,
however, the other arts produce results as "unequal" to poetry as a
guitar is to a harp. His own poem, "To Jane: With a Guitar," sym-
bolically represents some of the unique and exalted properties of
verse. But apart from language "arbitrarily produced by the imagination" and relating "to thoughts alone," he held that "all other materials,
instruments, and conditions of art, have relations among each other.
. . ."[5] The way for the synaesthetist is open.

There are revealing instances of the fused appeal in Shelley's poetry. In the highly decorative "The Sensitive Plant," hyacinths fling out music and odor blends with sound and color:

> And the hyacinth purple, and white, and blue,
> Which flung from its bells a sweet peal anew
> Of music so delicate, soft, and intense,
> It was felt like an odour within the sense.
>
> (I:ll. 25-28)

Another passage, hardly one of his best, emphasizes the interpenetration of the senses through the metaphor of flowers and plants: each flower was interpenetrated

> With the light and the odour its neighbour shed,
> Like young lovers whom youth and love make dear,
> Wrapped and filled by their mutual atmosphere.
>
> (I:ll. 66-69)

In "Alastor" the soul's calm music holds the poet's "inmost sense suspended in its web / Of many-coloured woof and shifting hues" (ll. 156-157). In the last act of *Prometheus Unbound*, Panthea envisions a sphere where sound, color, and odor intermingle.

> With mighty whirl the multitudinous orb
> Grinds the bright brook into an azure mist
> Of elemental subtlety, like light;
> And the wild odour of the forest flowers,
> The music of the living grass and air,
> The emerald light of leaf-entangled beams
> Round its intense yet self-conflicting speed,
> Seem kneaded into one aëreal mass
> Which drowns the sense.
>
> (ll. 253-261)

Swinburne largely overlooked Baudelaire's place in the symbolist movement of the age, but he liked the aestheticism he found in his poetry. Counting *Les Fleurs du Mal* among his favorite books, Swinburne reported that the sound of the French poet's meters suggested "colour and perfume" (*CB*, 419). He particularly admired Baudelaire's delicate treatment of nature and his forceful intimations of universal meanings. "Failure and sorrow, next to physical beauty and perfection of sound or scent, seem to have an infinite attraction for him." His "faultless and studious simplicity" resembled Gautier's; "his manner of thought has a relish" like Marlowe's or Byron's on its "sincerer side." In addition, Baudelaire's universality transformed ugliness into beauty and made evil "moral"—but not moral, Swinburne emphasized, in the sense that a sonnet serves as "a moral prescription." The perpetrator of such "intellectual drugs" would be a wretched excuse for an artist, "a huckster and vendor of miscellaneous wares" (*CB*, 419, 420, 423).

It was Baudelaire's famous theory of *correspondances* that appealed to Swinburne in his own quest for new limits. Baudelaire had assumed a dualistic Neo-Platonic universe. The universe is a temple, he wrote in a sonnet that has become one of the best known in the twentieth century, a temple full of suggestive, half-concealed reflections of the real, raw materials for the fervent mind to transform into images of pure beauty divorced from the realm of physical nature. The sources of vision are the senses, the harmonizing agent is the imagination:

> La Nature est un temple où de vivants piliers
> Laissent parfois sortir de confuses paroles;
> L'homme y passe à travers des forêts de symboles
> Qui l'observent avec des regards familiers.
>
> Comme de longs échos qui de loin se confondent
> Dans une ténébreuse et profonde unité,
> Vaste comme la nuit et comme la clarté,
> Les parfums, les couleurs et les sons se répondent.
>
> Il est des parfums frais comme des chairs d'enfants,
> Doux comme les hautbois, verts comme les prairies,
> Et d'autres, corrompus, riches et triomphants,
>
> Ayant l'expansion des choses infinies,
> Comme l'ambre, le music, le benjoin at l'encens,
> Qui chantent les transports de l'esprit et des sens.

In a paraphrase of the poem, Swinburne noted that nature's "echoes" have the soft frail perfume of children's flesh, are as sweetly sounding as oboes, and as colorfully green as meadows; they suggest infinity and chant *"les transports de l'esprit et des sens."* For Baude-laire as for Blake and Shelley and for the Romantic artists in general, quests for aesthetic and spiritual truths were efforts to penetrate the enigmatic universal vastness. Enid Starkie has explained that for Baudelaire beauty was primarily "a spiritual reality" and that "art was the greatest and perhaps the only means of effecting beauty in this world, art inspired by this mysterious and undying attraction of the ideal."[6] The aims of art were unity and fusion, the harmonized aes-thetic and synaesthetic, and Swinburne felt, as did Baudelaire, that only those artists who had touched wings with an exalted passion could transmit to other men the truth of that encompassing mystery.

A critical passage by Swinburne on Blake comments on the synaesthesia and the fused properties of different arts. The *Poetical Sketches* "have a fragrance of sound, a melody of colour, in a time when . . . colour and sound never mixed together into the perfect scheme of poetry." The songs have "the softness of flowers" (*WB*, 61). This is a rather elusive observation. Sound, color, and scent were so allied in Swinburne's mind—he thought that they were in Blake's too—that the transposition of their separate properties seemed very natural indeed. He did not expect his reader to linger, testing for logicality, although he did assume a reader with an agile, informed mind who could move easily and with delight from allusion to allusion and from image to image. Stimulated by Blake, Swinburne announced that "the perfect scheme of poetry" results when color and sound mix together, something he thought Blake's contemporaries failed to realize. Since Swinburne was sensitive to painting and to the properties of color and visual design, he apparently had in mind some partially formed idea, based perhaps on what Shelley had taught him about synaesthetic fusions, that colors may suggest certain heightened properties ordin-arily considered indigenous to poetry. When he came to describe Ben Jonson's lyrics, he employed a variation of this theme. Rarely, said Swinburne, did Jonson achieve the "singing power which answers in verse to the odour of a blossom, to the colouring of a picture, to the flavour of a fruit" (*BJ*, 4). Despite its floridity, the announcement of Jonson's shortcomings as an impassioned lyricist is in general accurate.

The idea that the aesthetic experience for both creator and per-ceiver depends upon the vigorous interplay of the senses is a contrast to views which seek to divorce the experience of art from the transitory and the mundane in favor of an abstract transcendent ideal. At its best Swinburne's theory engages the total personality; out of this vital complex develop the mystical and the spiritual. "Kubla Khan" impressed him in this way and swept him into a Swedenborgian paradise "where music and colour and perfume were one, where you could hear the hues and see the harmonies of heaven" (*C,* 145). Marlowe contains "in his best verse all the light and music and colour and perfume proper to the dawn of so divine a day as opened with his sunrise" (*JF,* 400). Webster and Ford were able to fuse their "whole nature in one fire of sense and spirit" (*JF,* 400).

I am aware of no place in either the criticism, the letters, or the manuscript sources where Swinburne discussed the provocative psychological implications of these principles. Granted his times, this is probably too much to expect. But he clearly felt that a fervent experience in literature could be equated with one in the other arts and enriched thereby.

Edward Thomas traced Swinburne's first use of parallels between the arts as a critical device to the "Notes on Designs of the Old Masters at Florence" and to the *William Blake,* both published in 1868. By his "translations of pictures into words," Thomas observed, Swinburne "prepared for his own *Faustine,* for Pater's meditation on La Gioconda, for the metamorphoses of Dorian Gray."[7] Thomas might also have listed Wilde's and Henley's imitations of Whistler, Symons', Sharp's, and Davidson's borrowings from French Impressionism, and O'Shaughnessey's treatment of sculptural effects.

Swinburne had detected in *Les Fleurs du Mal* "a quality of *drawing*" resembling "the exquisite power" of Ingres and Flandrin. "Nothing can beat" Baudelaire's *"tes sourcils méchants"* as "a piece of beautiful drawing." It has "truth and grace," "ease and strength, the trained skill, the beautiful justice of manner" characteristic of *La Source* or of a Flandrin painting "under full soft hot light" (*CB,* 422). He compared the poet Collins with Corot and Millet:

> Corot on canvas might have signed his [Collins's] *Ode to Evening*;
> Millet might have given us some of his graver studies, and left
> them as he did no whit the less sweet for their softly austere
> and simply tender gravity. His magnificent Highland ode, so
> villainously defaced after his death by the most impudent inter-

polations on record, has much in it of Millais, and something also of Courbet. . . . (*Col*, 151)

A reference to Velasquez, and to Walter Scott, helped Swinburne to a criticism of Byron: "Set almost any figure drawn by Scott beside any figure of Byron's drawing, and the very dullest eye will hardly fail to see the difference between a barber's dummy and a living man fresh from the hand of Velasquez or of God" (*W&B*, 183). One of Swinburne's more original cross-comparisons equated Browning's *Sordello* with landscape painting:

> The poem, in short, is like a picture in which the background runs into the foreground, the figures and the landscape confound each other for want of space and keeping, and there is no middle distance discernible at all. (*GC*, 152)

In treating Albert Moore's picture *Azaleas*, [*See* Plate 19] Swinburne found allusions to Gautier useful. Moore's picture, he said,

> is to artists what the verse of Théophile Gautier is to poets; the faultless and secure expression of an exclusive worship of things formally beautiful. . . . The outlines of their work are pure, decisive, distinct. . . .

Moore presents a draped woman

> showing well the gentle mould of her fine limbs through the thin soft raiment; pale small leaves and bright white blossoms about her and above, a few rose-red petals fallen on the pale marble and faint-coloured woven mat . . . a strange and splendid vessel, inlaid with designs of Eastern colour; another—clasped by one long slender hand and filled from it with flowers—of soft white, touched here and there into blossom of blue. . . .

Like Gautier's poetry such a painting has no reason for being except its beauty, its "melody of colour" and "symphony of form" (*NP*, 198).

References to sculpture were useful in contrasting Dryden and Milton, in defending Marlowe, in presenting Chapman and Ford, and in explaining Watts's paintings. In defense of Marlowe Swinburne said that his "blocks of verse" are anything but unhewn. They held "some veins of rare enough metal to be quarried and polished by Shakespeare"

(*CM*, 272). Marlowe's *Hero and Leander* "stands out alone amid all the wide and wild poetic wealth of its teeming and turbulent age, as might a small shrine of Parian sculpture amid the rank splendour of a tropic jungle" (*GC*, 229). In Chapman's *The Conspiracy and Tragedy of Charles Duke of Byron, Marshal of France*, Charles and the king seem Michelangelesque. Their outlines are gigantic, "like two studies of a great sculptor whose work is never at its best but when it assumes the heroic proportion of simple and colossal forms" (*GC*, 195). Ford was a renowned sculptor of character, not a painter (*JF*, 373). Arnold's "Thyrsis," "placed beside much other verse of the time . . . shows like a sculptor's work [by] . . . an enameller's" (*MA*, 93). Watts's *Wife of Pygmalion* [*See* Plate 17], exhibited in 1868, was a "translation" of a Greek statue. The picture demonstrates how a painter may blend two arts so that they "become as sister arts indeed, yet without invasion or confusion; how, without any forced alliance of form and colour, a picture may share the gracious grandeur of a statue, a statue may catch something of the subtle bloom of beauty proper to a picture" (*NP*, 197).

Of course it is easy to see sculptural qualities in the draped semi-classical figures of Watts,[8] Leighton [*See* Plate 21], and Burne-Jones, particularly if the figures are set against neutral backgrounds, as they often are. The difficult task is to explain such paintings on their own visual grounds without references to sculpture, literature, or music. "No task," Swinburne admitted, "is harder than this of translation from colour into speech, when the speech must be so hoarse and feeble, when the colour is so subtle and sublime" (*NP*, 209). When he wrote of pictures he might have been more attentive to the genuinely visual problems of hues and tones, dispositions of line, foreshortening and perspective, arrangements and pattern and color, and the physical properties of paint; but he was better equipped to illustrate theories than to evaluate formal characteristics. For this reason, his art criticism, which suffers more than a little from an overabundance of assertion rather than demonstration, is less satisfactory than his literary criticism. The attitude too often supplants the insight. He was most at ease with the graphic arts of Blake and Rossetti, where he could discuss thematic qualities, very often in a literary framework.

Of the separate arts, he seems to have understood music least of all. Despite his frequent references to harmony, melody, and song, there is hardly any evidence that he was a competent judge of musical techniques and forms.[9] Nor does the fact that he composed parts of *Atalanta in Calydon* while listening to Mary Gordon practice Handel on the organ, and parts of *Tristram of Lyonesse* while "stimulated" by Wagner, reveal any genuine technical comprehension.[10] Edmund Gosse had to correct the editor of *The Spectator* for supposing that Swinburne "loved and understood music." Said Gosse: Swinburne was "remarkably devoid 'of ear'—that is to say, he lacked all capacity to appreciate and distinguish musical compositions by hearing them. . . ." If he knew generally what the composition was about and something of the composer's history, Swinburne "could genuinely believe himself to enjoy—and in a non-musical sense he did enjoy—a brief performance. But," Gosse concluded, "a deaf man could have done almost as much."[11]

As a result, nearly all of Swinburne's musical references are general, and too many are impressionistic. One example is a vague and obvious use of names: "Byron is as fit to be considered the rival of Coleridge and Shelley as Offenbach to be considered a competitor with Handel and Beethoven" (*W&B*, 162). It was when he turned to Whistler, the painter of musical effects, whose ear for music was also notoriously dull, that Swinburne most successfully defined some of the relationships of music to painting and writing. His first comments on Whistler's symphonies, nocturnes, harmonies, and notes were laudatory. Whistler must have been pleased with Swinburne's efforts to grasp some of his intentions. On a visit to Whistler's studio he was so inspired by *The White Girl* (1865) [*See* Plate 18] that he wrote a rather fine poem, "Before the Mirror (Verses Written Under a Picture)," which Whistler admired and exhibited, pasted to the frame of his picture.[12] Swinburne complained of the critic's inability to capture the qualities of a painting and decided that the musician and the poet do better justice to a painting than the critic, whose scanty efforts are apt to be "as a psalm of Tate's to a psalm of David's" (*NP*, 209-210). The conclusion, we assume, is that Swinburne thought his poem a more judicious rendering of *The White Girl* than a critical description could ever be. (In a wild moment he had remarked that Keats's sonnet on Chapman would remain "the final word of comment, the final note of verdict on Chapman's Homer" as long as "anything of English poetry shall endure"—*GC*, 226).

At any rate, after this modest prelude to Whistler's work he analyzed in prose three paintings from "The Six Projects" which he had seen at Whistler's studio [*See* Plates 22 and 24].[13] Metaphors from music abound. The pictures are themselves instruments: their "main strings" are "varying chords of blue and white, not without interludes of the bright and tender tones of floral purple or red." Whistler's is a "keynote" art. Vague motifs of color and shape are aesthetically arranged, not baldly and literally presented. In two of the "arrangements" the sea sets the dominant note, and in the second stretches out "wide and soft without a wrinkle of wind. The dim floor-work in front, delicate as a summer cloud in colour, is antiphonal to the wealth of water beyond. . . ." (*NP,* 210). Then Swinburne moved on to the human figures and their place in the scheme of the picture.

> [The] symphony or (if you will) the antiphony is sustained by the fervid or the fainter colours of the women's raiment as they lean out one against another, looking far oversea in that quiet depth of pleasure without words when spirit and sense are filled full of beautiful things, till it seems that at a mere breath the charmed vessels of pleasure would break or overflow, the brimming chalices of the senses would spill this wine of their delight. (*NP,* 210)

The idea of delicate amplitude suggests a nervous balance so swelling and tenuous that the merest displacement of color or form would destroy it.

Swinburne discerned musical qualities in Rossetti's paintings too. The *Lilith* has a "chief chord of stronger color" than appears elsewhere in the picture; in *Sibylla Palmifera* [*See* Plate 16] Swinburne admired Rossetti's arrangement of the main notes of color, finding their "cadence" splendid and simple (*NP,* 212, 213). Solomon's work, in which Swinburne took such a proprietary interest, also contained musical elements: "There is not . . . more of the painter's art in the verse of Keats than of the musician's in Solomon's designs." The painter has "wrought" his outlines "into perfect music" so well that " 'unheard melodies' " vibrate there (*SSV,* 444). The work which best conveyed an appealing music was the strange and mystical prose piece, *A Vision of Love Revealed in Sleep.* Solomon published the work in 1871, together with some designs, and Swinburne reviewed the work the same year. Two of Solomon's pictures, *My Soul and I* [*See*

Plate 13] and *Love Bound and Wounded* [*See* Plate 23] are included here as plates. They convey a sense of the tremulousness, as Swinburne called it, present in Solomon's work, a confusing sexuality in which the representative figures seem to be blent of male and female forms. Solomon's *Vision*, with its central theme that man and his soul undergo various loves to achieve Love, often reads like an exotic dream-fragment by a self-conscious prose poet steeped in Dante, Blake, Rossetti, and his own shadowy sexual preoccupations. Swinburne was aware of the work's disjointedness and as a result spoke carefully of the innate music which seemed to unify the parts. He also saw that the pictures helped to keep the work more or less together, and wanted even more designs than Solomon had initially provided. He said that *A Vision of Love Revealed in Sleep* had "a suffusion of music, a transpiration of light and sound, very delicately and surely sustained." The style "is soft, fluent, genuinely melodious"; its ease is at first deceptive, since only after one submits to the work does the "rhapsody" truly emerge (*SSV*, 446). Solomon's works "make music . . . in the dumb show of lines and colours." One group of his pictures take as their "living principle and moving spirit . . . music made visible":

> His groups of girls and youths [*See* Plate 20] that listen to one singing or reciting seem utterly imbued with the spirit of sound, clothed with music as with a garment, kindled and swayed by it as fire or as foliage by a wakening wind. In pictures where no one figures as making music, the same fine inevitable sense of song makes melodies of vocal colour and symphonies of painted cadence.

His colors "have speech in them" and are "full of large strong harmonies"; the "manifold mystery" of his allegorical figures "is audible" (*SSV*, 454-455).[14]

The French painter Legros' *The Refectory* struck Swinburne as a "cadence of colours":

> witness the red-leaved book open in one monk's hand on the white cloth, the clear green jug on the table, the dim green bronze of the pitcher on the floor; beside it a splendid cat, its fur beautiful with warm black bars on an exquisite ground of dull grey, its expectant eye and mouth lifted without further or superfluous motion. (*NP*, 201)

In these remarks, despite their inventiveness, terminology remains vague and reveals Swinburne's sketchy acquaintanceship with music.

Behind these efforts to provide a tool for both artist and critic lies the truth that while the arts overlap they must maintain their own attributes. The challenge to the theorizer is to delimit the areas of agreement which, at least in philosophical terms, help to make the various aesthetic experiences one. Few Victorian critics were equipped to discuss the matter with much acuteness. Pater was one of the few in Swinburne's own time.

Pater's famous analysis of synaesthesia borrowed from the Germans the term *anders-streben* to designate the tendency of one art to "pass into the condition of some other art." The arts become partially alienated from their own limitations and "are able, not indeed to supply the place of each other, but reciprocally to lend each other new forces." Music "seems to be always approaching to figure, to pictorial definition." Architecture, despite its own laws, "sometimes aims at fulfilling the conditions of a picture, as in the *Arena* chapel; or of sculpture, as in the flawless unity of Giotto's tower at Florence; and often finds a true poetry in those strangely twisted staircases of the *châteaux* of the country of the Loire. . . ." Sculpture "aspires out of the hard limitation of pure form" and moves "towards colour, or its equivalent." Poetry discovers its example elsewhere: analogies "between a Greek tragedy and a work of Greek sculpture, between a sonnet and a relief, of French poetry generally with the art of engraving," are, Pater declared, "more than mere figures of speech. . . ." These considerations led to his famous conclusion that "*all art constantly aspires towards the condition of music.*" [15] Music, or, as he said, "the principle of music" with its suggestions of the abstract and purified aesthetic state, is ideal, "representative" and "consummate" because it is the art in which form is indistinguishable from substance or matter. Theoretic implications of this symbolic "music" I will treat in the chapter on the harmony of art.

Swinburne undoubtedly saw here in Pater's statement principles which he himself had felt keenly and had helped to frame. The quest for the harmonized *virtues* of artists and for those shadowy areas of beauty where all differences of form "gather" together was always difficult. His own employment of synaesthetic figures was intended to illuminate these difficult areas at the same time that his general perceptivity and sense of aesthetic justice prevented his making of synaesthesia an end in itself. It was only one method among others. One of Blake's lyrics, for example, even if it contains no color references, may recall paintings. Pope's work had the perfection of Giotto's famous "O" (*CEP*, 138). Shakespeare's *The Comedy of Errors* was "embroidered on the naked old canvas of comic action" (*SS*, 33). We may question whether Swinburne's conceits and metaphors are symbolic of "the perfect scheme" of poetry, or really elucidate the complexities of a work. Sometimes, as in the quotation on Shakespeare, his figure gives forth more sparkle than light. But when he attempts to enlarge criticism by interfusing various sense appeals his method is fresh and striking. Here he is on fairly new ground as he strives to convey the synaesthetic qualities employed consciously by the artist as well as those which he, the critic, has experienced in the work. His aim at such times is to capture the multiple facets of powerful and elusive imaginations.

Despite the excesses of his manner he was aware of the problems in synaesthesia. He as readily condemned an art overweighted by sense blendings as he did an art deficient in emotion but long on technique and form. Also, he lamented that no critical language yet devised was smooth, fine, virile, or formed enough to treat lyrical art justly (*WB*, 60). Even his favored comparative method (by which, as we remember, he assessed Shelley in terms of Shakespeare, Keats in terms of Dryden) fell short, and there remained the difficult task of grasping the tone and atmosphere of the works being judged—a task so difficult, he found, that "we shall hardly find words to suit our sense of their beauty" (*WB*, 60-61). Synaesthesia, I suggest, was one of the devices he employed to resolve this difficulty. He was not averse to making a variety of exploratory trips to the citadels of art.

CHAPTER VI

PASSION AND TACT: CREATIVE TENSION

Blake's definition of artistic "execution" as the "chariot of genius" must have appealed to Swinburne's sense of the symbolic and the fanciful. The image of the chariot racing across the sky, scattering light with a dazzling force and requiring neither axle grease nor cotter pins, complemented the creative act, the ideal of a superbly fashioned art produced by genius. We might develop the metaphor further and imagine the chariot drawn by two puissant steeds, one symbolizing *tact*, or technical prowess, the other representing *passion*, or the animating and inspiring emotion. Genius at the reins keeps these creatures performing with the splendor one would expect of so allegorical a team, and the resultant *tension* supplies the energy driving the imagination along its celestial way.

This figure introduces a principle which lay at the very center of Swinburne's aesthetics: passion and tact, contrary forces of creation, must appear in all true works of art with a dynamic and vibrant strength. As this aspect of Swinburne's thought develops, similarities to Coleridge will no doubt suggest themselves. There is abundant evidence that he knew his Coleridge well. Swinburne had studied the *Biographia Literaria* and was schooled in Coleridge's Shakespearean criticisms, which he saw as the work of "the greatest though not the first great critic and apostle or interpreter of Shakespeare." He paired Coleridge's *Table Talk* and Eckermann's *Conversations with Goethe* as books which "will always hold their place among the most interest-ing and the most valuable of all our literary possessions . . ." (*PVH*, 284). He spoke of Coleridge's "exquisite critical genius" (*GC*, 151) and announced that he was of the "fathers that were before us" (*C*, 140) who have shaped the aesthetic and theoretical positions of many followers.

Like most of his contemporaries, however, Swinburne remained uneasy before Coleridge's much-remarked obscurity, and found the latter's talent as "fluctuant and moonstruck as the sea." Coleridge dis-coursed too often of events, circumstances, and accidents "which ex-tenuate this thing or qualify that" (*C*, 141); he seemed, in other words, incapable of realizing in his prose the very organicism he sup-ported so well in theory. Even his style was out of tune; it "stammers and rambles and stumbles" and "stagnates here, and there overflows into waste marsh relieved only by thick patches of powdery bulrush and such bright flowerage of barren blossom as is bred of the fogs and the fens—such a style gives no warrant of depth or soundness in the matter thus arrayed and set forth" (*C*, 153). His was a "marshlight theosophy (brighter indeed than the bedroom rushlights about it, but no star or sun)" based on "ghostly dialectics" and quite "distinct from his doings as a poet" (*NTS*, n.374).

Coleridge, we should note, had himself been sensitive to such crit-icism. "My prose writings," he said in the *Biographia Literaria*, "have been charged with a disproportionate demand on the attention; with an excess of refinement in the mode of arriving at truths; with beating the ground for that which might have been run down by the eye; with the length and laborious construction of my periods; in short with ob-scurity and the love of paradox." He found some comfort, however, in observing that none of his critics found his "compositions" trivial, or his mind "shrunk from the toil of thinking."[1]

Despite Coleridge's shortcomings, and Swinburne's failure to pro-vide any systematic critique of his thought, he proved of immense help to Swinburne in formulating his own theories. Passion, Coleridge had observed, operates not to create but to set the mind "in increased activity."[2] With this principle, obviously, Swinburne agreed. Coleridge had observed also that passion helps to arrange "new connections of thoughts or images," thoughts or images pre-existent in the artist's former conversations" which "are only collected and crowded together by the unusual stimulation." In defining passion Shelley had contrasted it with reason and emphasized its tendency to "act" according to its dictates alone: "The very word implies an incapacity for action, otherwise than in unison with its dictates. What is reason? It is a thing independent, inflexible; it adapts thoughts and actions to the varying circumstances, which forever change—adapts them so as to produce the greatest overbalance of happiness" (letter to Hogg, June 2, 1811).[3]

On the whole, Swinburne was less directly philosophical and psychological than either Coleridge or Shelley. His efforts to assess the degrees of tact (rigorous artistic control) in fusion with temperament (passion) were, as we shall see, almost always stimulated by an examination of specific poems, paintings, or sculptures. His thoughts flash out as insights and are superb when he hits the mark, distressing and silly when occasionally they miss.

Swinburne maintained that there were two kinds of passion, a distinction which provides some useful glimpses into the psychology of nineteenth-century figures. They were at a juncture of traditions, responding both to the fertile, detailed exuberance of the Elizabethans and Jacobeans and the reserved and controlled works of the late seventeenth and eighteenth centuries. Artists gifted with an unusual regard for concrete detail had what Swinburne thought of as the first kind of passion. Shakespeare, Keats, and Rossetti achieved their flights in direct proportion to their grasp of earthly reality, a grasp necessary before they could soar. Swinburne observed the second kind of passion in poets who, like Hugo, Blake, Coleridge, Shelley, and Byron, were universal and far-ranging. In their psyches passion began as an intuitive feeling, later dipped to touch nature, and then resumed its flight, inspirited and strengthened through contact with natural form. Their inspiration, in other words, was imposed on nature from without. What Swinburne said of one of their group applies to all: their main feature was a "love of dim vast atmosphere and infinite spiritual range" (*SSV*, 449).

Shakespeare's passion was expressed in life-like, detailed characters who were subordinated to the over-all designs of the plays. "Variety in unity," Swinburne observed, and a sensitivity to "the complex and diverse shades in a single nature" characterize Shakespeare's art at its best (*SS*, 59). To study Shakespeare's developing maturity is to study his increasing skill at creating many-faceted persons. The playwright's "new power" appeared first in the King Henry plays, where language shed its earlier "lyric and elegiac ornament" for a greater and more solid organic richness (*SS*, 57). The characters were no longer types of separate passions or thoughts; in their complexity and uniqueness these new personae demanded of their hearers the fullest exercise of the critical mind. There were similar developments in the comedies: Beatrice and Benedick are larger figures than Rosaline and Biron, and Philip the Bastard towers over Mercutio. Philip's many complexities were fused by Shakespeare into an "absolute unity of concord" (*SS*, 59). Swinburne's reading of *Hamlet* was particularly far-sighted since he was in disagreement with the prevalent critical practice of exaggerating Hamlet to the neglect of the play's total design. Irresolution, Swinburne decided, is not Hamlet's keynote. German commentators (particularly Goethe, before whom Swinburne refused to bend the knee) and "Gigadibs," Swinburne's archetype of the German-aping English critic, are quite misguided in their distorted and simplified interpretations (*SS*, 119). Look closely at the text, Swinburne advised. A "strong conflux of contending forces" exists there amid infinite complexity; no single "irresolution or hesitation or any form of weakness" explains the youthful hero (*SS*, 120).

In the brisk attack on critics who emphasized the sentimental aspects of Keats's life to the neglect of his poetry, Swinburne observed that Keats's "distinctive gift or power" was his "deep and cunning instinct" for an "absolute natural beauty" (*K*, 301). At its worst, Keats's hand was inept and sophomoric; at its best it was faultless and subtle. In the "Ode on a Grecian Urn" Keats transcended details; his passion was sufficient to capture "unheard melodies" of "a sense beyond the senses, perceived and enjoyed" (*SSV*, 444). Arnold had compared Keats's synthesis of nature and spirit with Maurice de Guérin's, a comparison Swinburne sneered at, though he should have admired Arnold's appraisal of Keats. Both Keats and Guérin, said Arnold, display a "perfect" natural magic; "when they speak of the world they speak like Adam naming by divine inspiration the creatures; their expression corresponds with the thing's essential reality." Arnold did, however, see an important difference: "Keats has, above all, a sense of what is pleasurable and open in the life of nature; for him she is the

Alma Parens: his expression has, therefore, more than Guérin's, something genial, outward, and sensuous."[4]

Like Keats, Rossetti masterfully informed the "concrete" with "spirit and thought." "The Woodspurge," "The Honeysuckle," "A Young-Fir-Wood," and "Sea-Limits" were particularly notable fusions of passion and theme. A "great gift of positive reality" explains "the vital, tangible, direct loveliness" of the *Poems*. An "inventive fidelity" joined with "whatever of fact is serviceable to the truth of art . . ." (*DGR*, 16). Even in the partly realistic "Jenny," much maligned by Victorian critics, there are touches of beauty, and "Sea-Limits" echoes "a living thing . . . beyond the reach of the sense, its chord of sound one part of the multiform unity . . . in which all things rest and mix . . ." (*DGR*, 13). Rossetti's paintings, too, earned Swinburne's praise for symbolic power derived from vivid detail passionately rendered. Swinburne's description of the *Sibylla Palmifera* [*See* Plate 16], despite a plethora of qualifying adjectives, is an interesting attempt to scrutinize a picture for both painterly and literary qualities:

> . . . a head of serene and spiritual beauty, severe and tender, with full and heavy hair falling straight in grave sweet lines . . . an imperial votaress truly, in maiden meditation: yet as true and tangible a woman of mortal mould, as ripe and firm of flesh as her softer and splendid sister [*Lilith*]. The mystic emblems in the background show her power upon love and death to make them loyal servants to the law of her lofty and solemn spirit. Behind this figure of the ideal and inaccessible beauty, an inlaid wall of alternate alabaster and black marble bears inwrought on its upper part the rival twin emblems of love and death, over the bare carven skull poppies impend, and roses over the sweet head with bound blind eyes: in her hand is the palm-branch, a sceptre of peace and of power. The cadence of colour is splendid and simple, a double trinity of green and red, the dim red robe, the deep red poppies, the soft red roses; and again the green veil wound about with wild flowers, the green down of poppy-leaves, the sharper green of rose-leaves. (*NP*, 213)

Shelley consistently led the poets in whom Swinburne discerned the second, the far-ranging, universal order of passion; and in comparing Shelley with Keats Swinburne revealed that his own sympathies were primarily with these cosmic vitalists. Keats's forte, an "exquisite contraction and completeness," a "round and perfect limit," was not Shelley's (*NTS*, 380). "The Euganean Hills" is "no piece of spiritual sculpture" stimulated by "the life of natural things." Shelley's passion, his "rhapsody of thought and feeling," was imposed upon nature; it was not, like Keats's, "born of the contact." Shelley's "soul" could synthesize everything and grasped "the things of the world," "all life of plants, and beasts, and men," and "all likeness of time, and death, and good things and evil." To Swinburne Shelley was an impressionist who aimed "to render the effect of a thing rather than a thing itself; the soul and spirit of life rather than the living form, the growth rather than the thing grown" (*NTS*, 380). Shelley never sought the experience of Keats's sparrow picking in the gravel, nor of his minnow flashing in the pool. Shelley's concern was with his own soul, integral and large, hovering over the earth, descending to earth for revitalization, and then resuming its transcendent flight. Like Byron, he was at ease with "the large motions and the remote beauties of space (*B*, 127).

In general, Swinburne was not so kind to Byron, and to a degree his reservations grew out of a mistrust of that poet's defective passion and subsequent confusion of rant with feeling. Byron's magniloquent ego narrowed his scope (unfortunately, Swinburne was rather like him in this) and made it difficult for him to give his whole mind and passion to anything, be it art, freedom, or "faith," that was not in tune "with his own spirit and senses." Because he lacked "passion proper" (*JF*, 399), he foamed too readily "at things and creatures not worth a glance or a blow" (*B*, 129). His genius was "imperative"; and he burned and stamped that genius into the persons and episodes of his poems. His single "radical emotion . . . deep as life and strong as death is that noble ardour of rage and scorn which lifts his satire into sublimity . . ." (*JF*, 399). His passion was negative and single: "In him Apollo was incarnate only as the dragon-slayer: he might stand so in sculpture with King George for Python, his arrow still quivering in the royal carrion. Of all divine labours that was the one which fell to his share of work; of all the god his master's gifts that was the one alloted him" (*JF*, 400).[5] His other passions are "skin-deep":

All his love-making from the first desire to the final satiety, may be summed up in that famous axiom of Chamfort which Alfred de Musset, his female page or attendant dwarf, prefixed as a label to one of his decoctions of watered Byronism (*JF*, 399).

The axiom appears at the beginning of "Chant Deuxième" of Musset's oriental tale *Namouna*: "*Qu' est-ce que l'amour? L'échange de deux fantaisies et le contact de deux épidermes.*"[6]

Byron's poetic technique, on the other hand, evinced a failure of tact. A feeble metrical sense was his "native and incurable" fault. "No poet of equal or inferior rank ever had so bad an ear. . . . His verse stumbles and jingles, stammers and halts, where there is most need for a swift and even pace of musical sound . . ." (*B*,127). Yet his "hand" had a "strong impressure," and his "indomitable and sleepless spirit" sought its complement in tempest and rebellion—or, as Swinburne superbly stated it, in "the magnificence of anguish" (*B*,128). When his "perfect . . . fierce and blind desire" ranged the exalted regions "of emotion and expression" he was unique and consummate (*B*, 126).

Of all Byron's works, *Childe Harold* best revealed his strengths and weaknesses. Deploring the fact that sections have been "mouthed and mauled by vulgar admiration," and excluding the first two cantos, which Swinburne felt were loosely constructed and marred by falsetto tones, Swinburne counted *Childe Harold* "among the choice and high possessions of poetry" (*B*, 129). The fourth canto is so nearly final that no line can be taken from it without damage to the whole. Its organicism, Swinburne explained, was due largely to Byron's passionate capturing of the "deep and glad disdain of the sea" for men and their works, a disdain which fills the canto "with a weighty and sonorous harmony grave and sweet as the measured voice of heavy remote waves" (*B*, 130). When "confronted with elements," Byron "casts the shell of pretence and drops the veil of habit." At such times his "scorn of men caught in the nets of nature and necessity has no alloy of untruth; his spirit . . . overlooks with a superb delight the ruins and the prayers of men" (*B*, 129).[7] Byron's passion was like Victor Hugo's in its response to "the higher things of nature," to "her large issues and remote sources." Characteristic of Swinburne's ambivalence toward Byron was the amusing compliment he paid the poet's energy and daring: "I never knew a man of better nerve: and I have known Richard Burton" (*J*, 247).[8]

Coleridge also, though within a smaller range than either Shelley or Byron, was at home in the cosmic sphere. He was the "reverse of Antaeus" since the "contact of earth" seemed to deprive him of strength. His political poetry, for example, was "weak of foot and hoarse of accent," a clear failure of the lyric voice (*C*, 142). An inept manipulator of "practical" creeds, he was, said Swinburne in a metaphor borrowed from Southey, "a footless bird of Paradise" who too often tried to walk on earth: "His gait was like a swan's on shore" (*C*, 143). Coleridge's development was very gradual and his genius moved "for some time over much waste ground with irregular and unsure steps." Yet "in its final flower" this "plant of strangely slow growth" was "perfect and wonderful" (*C*, 142). The "height and perfection" of his imagination, Swinburne concluded, earned Coleridge a rank with the major lyric poets.

By implication Swinburne included Blake, too, in this group of writers. Blake's mystic striving, his unworldliness, his fanaticism, are constant themes in Swinburne's study. For Blake, nature was a darkness out of which beings came [*See* Plate 25]. No materialist had "such belief in bread and meat as Blake had in the substance underlying appearance, which he christened god or spectre, devil or angel, as the fit took him . . ." (*WB*, 56):

> About his path and about his bed, around his ears and under his eyes, an infinite play of spiritual life seethed and swarmed or shone and sang. Spirits imprisoned in the husk and shell of earth consoled or menaced him. Every leaf bore a growth of angels; the pulse of every minute sounded as the falling foot of God; under the rank raiment of weeds, in the drifting down of thistles, strange faces frowned and white hair fluttered; tempters and allies, wraiths of the living and phantoms of the dead, crowded and made populous the winds that blew about him, the fields and hills over which he gazed. Even upon earth his vision was "twofold always"; singleness of vision he scorned and feared as the sign of mechanical intellect, of talent that walks while the soul sleeps, with the mere activity of a blind somnambulism. (*WB*, 91)

To describe Blake's rhythms Swinburne referred to the sea, that useful and familiar symbol of a creative passion and vast universals. Even in the short poems a rhythmic fall and turn echoes "the sudden weight and luminous motion of a strong long roller coming in with the wind" (*WB*, 181). Blake's rhythms recalled Milton from whose "long cadences and tempestuous undulations" Blake imbibed "a certain half-nervous enjoyment" (*WB*, 300). Blake's imagination is "clear," the air that breeds it is high, and the moisture that feeds it is pure. His speech was of "a far country" and "a lofty station." His passion was, in Swinburne's terms, ideally transcendent [*See* Plate 26].

Intense passion of either kind required the counterforce of a skilled technical control. Born of a sense of "right," this innate tact supplies organic tension and serves as a foil to an "unrefined passion." The superior artist knows unerringly how "to go the right way and do the right thing" (*WB*, 178). The "shaping spirit" of his imagination, the driver of Blake's chariot, "reforms of itself its own misshapen work, treads down and triumphs over its own faults and errors, renews its faltering forces and resumes its undiminished reign" (*GC*, 235-236). Such a touch is almost always infallible and excludes accident. This "soft fervour and faultless keeping of the poem give it that final grace of a complete unity of spirit and style which is the seal of sacred art at its highest" (*DGR*, 26). Marlowe, particularly in *Dr. Faustus*, had this gift of tone (*CM*, 272), as did Webster in *The Duchess of Malfy*.

Whenever such work fails there is usually an imbalance between passion and tact; and where one of these elements is too dominant there is miscarried effort. Ben Jonson, for example, erred through excessive tact; "in almost every instance," wrote Swinburne, Jonson's work "would have been better if the artist had taken less pains" (*BJ*. 6). Ford and Massinger, despite their excellences, lacked a final passion and hence are unable to make us feel. Ford's poetry is not like the sea:

> It might rather be likened to a mountain lake shut in by solitary highlands, without visible outlet or inlet, seen fitlier by starlight than by sunlight; much such an one as the Lac de Gaube above Cauterets, steel-blue and sombre, with a strange attraction for the swimmer in its cold smooth reticence and breathless calm. For

> nothing is more noticeable in this poet than the passionless reason
> and equable tone of style with which . . . he searches out the dark-
> est issues of emotion, the quiet hand with which he notes them
> down. At all times his verse is even and regular, accurate and
> composed; never specially flexible or melodious, always admir-
> able for precision, vigour, and purity. (*JF*, 372, 378-379)

Fletcher's work, on the other hand, was frequently blighted by an excessive passion: his general style is effusive and exuberant. Too anxious
to excite, he was wont "to goad and stimulate by any vivid and violent
means the interest of readers or spectators" (*B&F*, 418, 421).

Swinburne's idea of control reveals his fusion of a romantic impulse with neo-classical standards of form, a fusion in which discipline
is the combining force. (Recall Swinburne's early imitations of Pope's
couplets, Milton's ordered line, and Cowley's odes.) Artists possessing
"charm and clearness," resulting from control and forcefulness, have
a "natural light of mind" neither facile nor transparent, and "more
than brilliance, more than ease or excellence of style" (*MA*, 91).

Usually, for Swinburne, light symbolized imaginative power.
There is no obscurity in Browning's "lightning," he observed. There
is, instead, illumination which fires the reader's "apprehension" and
infects him with "spiritual interest." Browning irradiates by the
light of his "mind"; and he does not compel us first "to see with his
eyes, or with the eyes of the living mask which he assumes for his
momentary impersonation of saint or sophist, philosopher or malefactor. . . ." To create such an illusion there must be "brightness and
decision as well as subtlety . . . of genius"; and this is Browning's "supreme gift" (*GC*, 147-148; *NEP*, 107-108). This once-famous description of Browning's mind, still useful for its insight, appeared as a
digression in the study of Chapman.[9]

Swinburne had elsewhere adapted one of Matthew Arnold's
thoughts: this "light of mind" is "a quality begotten by instinct upon
culture, one which all artists of equal rank possess in equal measure"
(*MA*, 91).[10] Without pursuing the ramifications, Swinburne implied
that this quality is exact and gaugeable. An "instinct and a resolution
of excellence" enable the artist to suit his style to his subject matter, to
select an appropriate diction tonally uniform and pared of excres-
cences, to discern the proper scope and generic form for treating his

topic, and to complement his imagination with a technique mature and appropriate in all of its details as well as in its broadest outlines. The poet needs to experience "an ardent harmony" of his passion and his tact. In an image foreshadowing Yeats's recurring symbol of the dancer,[11] Swinburne declared, in an essay on Rossetti, that there must be "a heat of spiritual life guiding without constraining the bodily grace of motion" (*DGR*, 4). The spirit, like the artist's technical acumen, must be flawless and pure. Even the "least" work, if it is to merit critical attention, should have "charm and power," "sweetness" and "force." Its "bodily form" must "melt and flow by instinct into the right way." If keenness and force do not operate together, "if the handiwork be flawed, there must also have been some distortion or defect of spirit, a shortcoming or a misdirection of spiritual supply" (*MA*, 89).

According to Swinburne, art in tension between passion and tact generates delight from our surprise as we experience the emotion of a work, *i.e.,* the passion which through a process of identification becomes one with our own. (Keats had said that poetry "should strike the reader as a wording of his own highest thoughts and appear almost a remembrance.") Further, as we grow aware of the artist's resolution of very difficult matters of organization and form—in other words, as we appreciate his tact—we become increasingly impressed and are eventually awed. The Muses, Swinburne said with characteristic humor, bear children, and Apollo gives crowns only to those, the true artists, "who are able to win the crown and beget the child" (*MA*, 91). The route is rigorous and fraught with paradox; for the difficult way to a hard-won supremacy must appear effortless, the strokes of the chisel never visible on the form of the work itself.

Shelley was too uneven a craftsman to deserve continuous respect for tact. There were, Swinburne somewhat grudgingly admitted, "spots on the sun": the "Ode to Liberty" eventually "runs wild and falls to pieces"; the fault is "hasty laxity" and not "defective sense or taste . . ." (*NTS*, 353). His growth too was uneven. Swinburne described him in his early stage "as Hayley in the spangles of a harlequin"; it was evident that his "reasoning faculty was comparatively ripe before the imaginative or creative power had outgrown its greenest and sourest stage of crudity" (*W&B*, 194).

Thomas Lovell Beddoes seemed unable to acquire any real artistic tact. Though possessed of a "noble instinct" for poetry, he lacked the creative "mind" and was unable to produce more than "a few lofty and massive fragments of half-formed verse which stand better by themselves when detached from the incoherent and disorderly context. . . ." He failed to reduce "to any fitness of form his own chaotic and abortive conceptions . . ." (*GC,* 184).

The novelist Charles Reade also lacked "that last and greatest art . . . the art to veil." He was unable "to keep his hand close," but allowed "proclamation and ostentation" to have their way. His effects are too often labored; there is neither spontaneity nor real technical control (*R,* 352). George Chapman was guilty of similar errors. His volcanic energy and zest did not save him: his poems are a chaos "where grammar, metre, sense, sound, coherence, and relevancy are hurled together on a heap of jarring hurtling ruins." The grievous flaw—Swinburne insisted always that an artist must know what he is about—was that Chapman couldn't help himself; he "wanted skill or care to write better" (*GC,* 141) and he lacked an instinctive sense that his devices, particularly his fondness for inversion, were excessive. It was, of course, possible for him to create an ornate, involved poem which would at the same time be a significant work of art: it is not simply "the heavy and convulsive movement of the broken and jarring sentences, the hurried broken-winded rhetoric that seems to wheeze and pant at every painful step, the incessant byplay of incongruous digressions and impenetrable allusions" that reflect Chapman's main failure; the greater error is that he failed to provide a "perceptible centre towards which these tangled and ravelled lines of thought may seem at last to converge" (*GC,* 143-144). Swinburne spoke then of the difficulty met by the critic who hopes to translate such "crude and incoherent forms" into "some decent order and harmony." The task, sheer labor, is "as tough and tedious . . . for the mind as oakum-picking or stone-breaking" is for the body (*GC,* 144). Chapman was, of course, not always so disorganized. Swinburne praised his *All Fools,* "one of the most faultless examples of high comedy" in Elizabethan drama (*GC,* 165), for its beautiful and just display of tact—with the qualification that there was one slight blemish: the final discovery scene winds up too hurriedly (*GC,* 166-167).

With Keats, on the other hand, none of the many intricate revisions, corrections, deletions, and substitutions—"evident marks of the passage of the pumice-stone"—are obvious in the final form of his successful work. Keats and Wordsworth were among the few writers who consistently managed to convey the difficult illusion. They were "grinders," but

> There is no more sign of labour in the sensitive and subtle touch of the younger man than in the resolute and steadfast handiwork of the elder: a point perhaps even more remarkable in the genius of Keats than in the genius of Wordsworth. That exquisite and epicurean subtlety in expression of sensations impressed upon an exceptionally sensitive temper of mind and body, which was so specially characteristic of Keats as a student of nature, might have been supposed impossible of attainment without some sacrifice of simplicity and straightforwardness: yet, if the secrets of his workshop had never been made public, we could no more have felt certain that his work had not been thrown off at a jet, like Shakespeare's and Hugo's, than we should have dreamed of looking for the traces of the file on Wordsworth's. (*W&B,* 241)

Victor Hugo was not quite so easily assessed. Although Swinburne was convinced that Hugo was a genius, he was less sure of the giantism which made Hugo indifferent and even contemptuous of the attention to detailed character and object that was a hallmark of Shakespeare, Keats, and Rossetti. Hugo found it difficult to make his sense of artistic justice, or tact, conform to his intense feeling. Sometimes he seemed curiously remote from his work, interested in it chiefly insofar as it provided what Swinburne, echoing Ruskin, called a "background of gloom or glory." Great lives and events stimulated him, his passion grew out of "a catastrophic philosophy," out of an old geological theory drawn from a study of eras of revolution. As a result, Hugo was seldom content to allow his characters and incidents a gradual growth, and his people appear either in equilibrium or in revolt. The "infinitely little" that constitutes so much of life was to Hugo "morally absolutely zero." This was a pity, because his best efforts are those which strangely blend the infinitely great and the infinitely little. His strokes then "are the phosphoric flashes of the sea-fire moving on the depth of the limitless and living sea" (*VH,* 219).[12]

Many of Swinburne's best critical pronouncements derived from this criterion of an organic tensile balance. Alexander Pope failed both to control his passion, which in him took the form of anger and spleen, and to project a harmonized aesthetic feeling. Through an "excess of irrational impulse" this great writer suppressed principle and reason. The body was "as liable to misguide the mind, and emotion to get the start of reflection, as in the case of any hot brained lyrist—or even of any brainless athlete." Anger, Swinburne said, as appropriately of himself as of Pope, "is surely after all no less properly definable as a sensual passion than lust or gluttony" (*CEP,* 132-133).

Blake in the *Songs of Innocence* struck a fine balance between execution and feeling, one which contrasted favorably with the dominant poetry of his own day, which gave off "the arid perfume of powder, the twang of dry wood and adjusted strings" (*WB,* 61). In tact alone Blake was superior to the fashionable poets who were producing "metallic" and "mechanical" work, its "music meted out by precedent: colour and sound never mixed together into the perfect scheme of poetry" (*WB,* 61). Blake's "Infant Joy" struck a particularly responsive chord in Swinburne. Despite its informal design, it was "absolutely right." Any more formality, Swinburne decided, would destroy its "soft bird-like perfection of clear light sound" (*WB,* 161). Many of Blake's drawings were equally well-balanced. An illustration for Virgil [*See* Plate 28] had a "stormy beauty"; the "noble motion and passion" evident in all parts "are as noticeable as its tender sense of detail and grace in effect of light":

> Not a star shows about the moon; and the dark hollow half of her glimmering shell, emptied and eclipsed, is faint upon the deep air. The fire in her crescent burns high across the drift of wind. Blake's touch in this appears to me curiously just and perfect; the moon does not seem to quail or flicker as a star would; but one may feel and see, as it were, the wind passing beneath her; . . . likeness of the low-hung labouring moon, no blurred and blinking planet with edges blotted and soiled in fitful vapour, would have given so splendid a sense of storm as this white triumphal light seen above the wind. Small and rough as these half-engraved designs may be, it is difficult to express in words all that is latent, even all that is . . . in the best of them. Poets and painters of Blake's kind can put enough into the slightest and swiftest work they do to baffle critics and irritate pretenders. (*WB,* 115)

Wordsworth, that "great poet, perverse theorist, and incomplete man" (*MA*, 83), shared some of Blake's scope. While "meditation and sympathy, not action and passion, were the two main strings of his serene and stormless lyre," there were times when his "exalted and composed" verse "swelled into the strength of a rushing wind, and made the verses ring like storm-swept crannies of the crags and scaurs that nursed the spirit which imbues them" (*W&B*, 206, 237). Despite his wretched failures, among them "The Thorn," "The Idiot Boy," and "Lucy Gray" and despite his "inveterate and invincible Philistinism" (*MA*, 83), Wordsworth's best work fused powerful feeling and controlled form. Swinburne contrasted "Michael," "a beautiful success," with "Margaret," a failure because Wordsworth impaired the idyllic effect by using a "semi-dramatic form of narrative" (*W&B*, 220). The much admired "Ode on Intimations of Immortality" Swinburne rejected for its unfused technique and emotion; Wordsworth was unable technically and imaginatively to sustain the opening pitch; "a sense of incongruous realism and triviality" impairs the work. Swinburne preferred the "decisive" successes "Ode to Duty" and "Song at the Feast of Brougham Castle" (*W&B*, 223-224). "Glen Almain" and "The Reaper" are examples of Wordsworth's finest "metrical instinct" harmonized with "his peculiar tone of meditation," "a point," Swinburne ironically added, "of as much or as little importance to a poet's work as is the command of line and colour to a painter's" (*W&B*, 229). For similar reasons he far preferred The Prelude to The Excursion.

Swinburne singled out three poems by Coleridge for their demonstration of organic fusion: "The Ancient Mariner," "Christabel," and "Kubla Khan." "Kubla Khan" has "an exquisite instinct married to a subtle science of verse" and deserves a supreme place as a model of lyric music. "The Ancient Mariner" is organically "faultless after the fashion of a flower or a tree." It has an ease of finish and shows nowhere "on its smooth and spruce excellence" that "speckless and elaborate finish" which results from "the fresh rasp of file or chisel" (*C*, 145).

In a discussion of Shelley, Swinburne equated passion and tact with "inner and outer music," both "as divine as nature's [music] and not sooner exhaustible" (*NTS*, 376). (Harmony, incidentally, is a key term in Shelley's *Defense*.) In another place, passion and tact become passion and harmony: the "Ode to the West Wind" magically transforms external nature into "its highest pitch of harmony and passion" (*Sh*, 339). "Epipsychidion," notable for its tact and inventiveness, strikes a keen note of passion as it weaves its "wholly fantastic embroidery of partly imaginary emotion about . . . actual sensations of sympathetic and compassionate affection . . ." (*Sh*, 342). Here tension depends upon a nervous balance between two kinds of feeling, the imagined or artificial and the real or actual. Shelley blent these two feelings and imposed his weaver's technique so skillfully upon them that we are, in Keats's famous phrase, surprised by the fine excess.

Webster, to glance back to an earlier age, achieved a similar fusion of technique and emotion in *The Duchess of Malfy*. A "negative quality of noble abstinence, the utter and most admirable absence of any chaotic or spasmodic element, the chastity of a controlling instinct . . . rejects as impossible all hollow extravagance and inflation." With the skeptical reader in mind, Swinburne drew contrasts between Webster's play and *King Lear*: the Duchess' curse on her brothers is more temperate in its rage than Lear's on his daughters; also, there is nothing in any of Webster's plays to match the horror of Gloucester's blinding. The point is that Swinburne's admiration for Webster developed directly from his admiration for that dramatist's mastery of his materials; in a sense, the impact of the particular play is devastating because of the tension produced by a vigorous tact and a passion, violent but suppressed, straining against its bonds (*JF*, 403-404).

Morris and Rossetti, working in the Romantic vein, achieved a creative tension from a disciplined passion which continually threatened to break controls and free its wealth of imagery and emotion. Morris' artistic progress from the heightened but poorly disciplined "Defence of Guenevere" (1858) to the "Life and Death of Jason" (1867) was towards a greater tact imposed upon a teeming decorative impulse. Passion Morris had already demonstrated in sufficient measure. It was "Jason" which restored some of the romance and storytelling of ancient saga poetry to English literature and kept it under enviable control. Aware that powerful feeling is not the distinguishing feature of such poetry, Morris suited his flowing tale to "a potent passion," but one emitted, as Swinburne explained, "only by rare and brief jets" conveyed in a thoroughly suitable, direct, simple form of poetry. Morris' abstinence resulted from his English temperance and reserve, a respect, Swinburne jauntily remarked, "for good things as drags, but not as clogs." Morris' "descriptive and decorative beauties" are "always just and fit"; no note of form or tone of color is out of place; "no flower of the landscape is slurred, but no flower is obtrusive." Instinct and art have worked hand in hand (*M*, 56-8).

Rossetti created a coherent beauty from a rich texture of symbols, colors and tones, displaying at once "the grace of perfect force" and "the force of perfect grace." In this paradox, Swinburne suggested an ease both in the artistic rendering of passion and in the employment of a commanding technique. Rossetti's ideal grace, an ideal, incidentally, extolled by Pope and Hogarth, implies a fluent mastery. In the first phrase—"the grace of perfect force"—grace expresses Rossetti's knowledgeable handling of spirit and theme; in the second it evokes his equally capable handling of technique and design (*DGR*, 5). One of Rossetti's triumphs was "Sister Helen," which wholly fulfills the requirement for a first-rate tragic ballad: "There can be no pause in a ballad, and no excess; nothing that flags, nothing that overflows; there must be no waste of a word or a minute in the course of its rapid and fiery motion." A master of the ballad form must be "select in his matter and terse in his treatment." Only Meredith's "Margaret's Bridal-Eve" approaches the "tragic music" and "the swift yet solemn harmonies of dialogue and burden" of Rossetti's (*DGR*, 27). Another triumph was "The Blessed Damozel," which has "the charm of fluent force and facile power" plus a "grandeur of scale and sweep of spirit." There is a single intense impression. "No poem shows more plainly the strength and wealth of the workman's lavish yet studious hand" (*DGR*, 24). Further, Rossetti's "fine excess" reflected an uncommon "quality of nerves"—to use the phrase Arthur Symons was to find helpful in explaining Aubrey Beardsley and the French Symbolists,[13] a quality Swinburne had remarked faintly in Shelley's work and more distinctly in Victor Hugo's. In the *House of Life*, Rossetti had "finely" touched the subtlest "nerves." There is a "quiver and ache of soul and senses" which is "kindled and discoloured by half-morbid lights of emotion. . . ." The main melody of the cycle is like "a burning pulse." The "tremulous ardour" of "Penumbra" exposed "the finest nerves of life" (*DGR*, 12). In its shimmering suggestiveness, its many hesitancies and overlappings of the abstract and the real, Rossetti's most characteristic style does itself reflect this nervous quality; it exists not only in the subject matter but in the very texture of the poems and is the direct result, we infer, of Rossetti's admirable skill in adapting his sense of tact to the particular felt emotion.

As Swinburne understood the romantic artist and lived the role himself, during the stress of creation powerful feeling tightens until its pitch is feverish and drawn. At this point, the artist's effort to impose controls and subordinate emotion to design is apt to tauten nerves still further. In addition, an artist with a temperament like Rossetti's, who seeks to discipline highly specialized, often aberrational feelings of love, grief, and keenly rendered sensuous delights, complicates matters by choosing materials less susceptible to controls than more subdued, conventional subjects are apt to be. This is not to say—and certainly Swinburne did not believe—that the artist of "nerves" achieves more than the disciplined, classical artist; it is rather a difference of feeling and manner.

Among contemporaries, it was Matthew Arnold who fulfilled Swinburne's ideal handling of passion and tact, and in a classical sense. A "spontaneous temperance" is Arnold's "supreme charm." His "sense of right . . . bears no mark of curb or snaffle, but obeys the hand with imperceptible submission and gracious reserve" (*MA,* 76). He exactly fuses a technical with a spiritual beauty. There is here no flawed handiwork, Swinburne observed; nor is there "a misdirection of spiritual supply" (*MA,* 89). He is the poet of the day "most to be relied on": more than any contemporary "he unites personality and perfection," blending his classical temperament, his *virtue,* with a perfect form. He exactly fuses a technical with a spiritual beauty. "Above all he knows what as a poet he should do, and simply does that" (*MA,* 93). This is the direction Swinburne felt that great art should take: passion controlled by tact, the result a dynamic resolution of difficulties overcome, of all rigidities of feeling and of craftsmanship resolved. Arnold, Swinburne felt, was quite at home in the serene temples of the spirit.

CHAPTER VII

FORM

A central principle in Swinburne's system requires that the two kinds of form, inner and outer, largely determine the value of a work of art. This principle is not original; its utilization, with attendant moments of humor and insight, is. It was based to a certain extent upon Coleridge's principle of an organic whole of separate parts in balance and of a mystic transcendent force making for a whole greater than the sum of the parts. A difference is that in Swinburne's formalism individual temperament mattered more. Coleridge had declared that poetry is *generic*; it excludes *accident*, individual differences of "rank, character, or occupation," in favor of "the *common* attributes of the class," which are not "such as one gifted individual might *possibly* possess."[1] In his review (June 1888) of Whistler's "Ten O'Clock" lecture Swinburne praised the lecture's "dominant and central truth," the "principle of independence" by which the artist's first obligation is to his work. Despite his suspicion of Whistler's impressionism and his fondness for "distinct outline" Swinburne was of Whistler's view on the basic issue of individual genius, an issue which in several exaggerated forms came to dominate *fin de siècle* British art. There was in Swinburne's mind a specific connection between genius, even eccentric genius, and artistic form. We saw this in the last chapter in his defense of the artist of nerves.

There are relationships also between Swinburne's principle and Shelley's that are important to a full comprehension of Swinburne's organicism. Shelley's theory assumed an over-soul[2] consisting of the massed energy of all beauty human and divine, which hovered above the earth, dispelling its bits of radiance throughout the universe, coloring nature and the souls of inspired men. Swinburne retained much of Shelley's dualism but was on the whole less rhapsodic and inclined to base the creative leap more firmly on the realities of a difficult technique triumphantly overcome than on primary intuition. Emotion, though important as passion, could not entirely suffice. This difference as much as any other distinguishes Swinburne from his romantic predecessors. Further, there is a static quality in Shelley's theory absent from Swinburne's; Shelley's beauty seems, despite the ubiquitous images of wind, veil, and light invented to convey its power, somewhat too fixed in its transcendent abode, serene and remote among its clouds and trophies.

On its simplest and first level Swinburne's "form" refers to the traditional genres of poetry and painting: to epic, blank verse, lyric, and narrative poems, to the sonnet and the ballad, the novel—which he saw with some unhappiness as the genre of the age—,[3] and to historical, landscape, and portrait painting. In an essay on William Morris, he usefully contrasted Greek and English poetry. Both had their "lyric" and "tragic" schools; the English, in addition, have had the "subordinate schools, gnomic and idyllic, domestic and didactic." Neither Greek nor English boasts of many great "tale-tellers" or "sagamen"; and Morris, Swinburne rejoiced, is one of the select tradition which includes Homer and Chaucer (*M*, 56).

In addition to matters of genre, for Swinburne outer form involved questions of technique. When we consider Swinburne the poet, certainly none of his contemporaries except Tennyson was so adept at varieties of intricate verse forms. He spoke of the difficulty he met in writing foreign meters—he practiced complicated French lyric forms and extremely difficult classical ones. And as critic he praised Matthew Arnold's efforts to master the unyielding classic quantitative patterns: "It is hard to realise," he wrote, "and hopeless to reproduce the musical force of classical metres so recondite and exquisite as the choral parts of a Greek play."[4] Milton had failed, and Arnold had not succeeded (*MA*, 99). In the unpublished "The Chaotic School" he launched into Robert Browning for violating the form of the anapest:

Now if there is a small and simple thing in the technical line of metre it is the scheme of English anapests. That you shall not count anything but a foot of two long syllables equivalent to a foot of two short and a long, is surely no rigorous, no perverse, no perplexing rule. That you shall not allow the iambic substitute, which the facility of our lax English laws admits on sufferance as tolerable if illegal, to overcharge your verse, is as obvious and as requisite a law of common harmony as can well be conceived. Yet versifiers do continually violate these rules: but at least the run of such metrical Tarquins do not push their brutality beyond this simple crime of violation. Now as one of many specimens, read this line—which the context will show ought to consist of two rhyming anapæsts or their equivalent feet: *Stop veins I'd—have subside.* Actually the writer has made three long heavy full syllables—equivalent properly to a spondee and a half—serve as equivalent to a single anapæst. Let the schools consider that and "devise brave punishments for him" if they can; he has done it, and lives. This is a crime in the sight of any artist equivalent to murder in the sight of any judge: nay, to parricide under aggravating circumstances.

While an outer or "secondary" form is essential to perfection, it is not always "indispensable to the existence of art" (*M*, 52). At the outset of *A Study of Shakespeare*, Swinburne asserted that any criticism "which busies itself only with the outer husk or technical shell of a great artist's work," neglecting the inner force of spirit and thought, is inferior to the most rampant sort of critical impressionism. A study of externals—metrical form and "scheme of colours"—will help to reveal the "worth of a painter's or a poet's design," but a discerning critic will probe through the externals to the subtler characteristics of inner form, perceiving "the cause and the effect of every choice or change of metre and of colour" and "the reason and the result of every shade and of every tone which tends to compose and to complete the gradual scale of their final harmonies" (*SS*, 8-9). Implicit also in the observation about the dispensability of outer form is the theory that a work of art may exist which is so commanding in spirit that it transcends all flaws in its external design. By adapting, he could maintain his zest for the Brontës and George Chapman, and for the romantic genius generally.

A sampling of Swinburne's judgments will indicate the breadth of his organicism and provide an accurate frame of reference for the discussion to follow. His emphasis on a unified *Hamlet*, for example, was an excellent corrective to readings which stressed Hamlet's darkly introspective nature. In a just reading, Swinburne said, no "single person or separate passage" stimulates us to the exclusion of other persons or passages: "it is to the whole masterpiece that the mind turns at mention of its name" (*SS*, 52). Similarly, our comprehension of *Love's Labour's Lost* depends upon our sensitivity to the tone of the whole work (*SS*, 35). In another judgment, unusual for its day, Swinburne found Milton's *Paradise Regained* organically superior to *Paradise Lost*, since it transmits so successfully "the serene and supreme impression of the final whole" (*NEP*, 112).[5] He praised the clarity of impression created in "Lamia" and "La Belle Dame Sans Merci" and suggested that this was the result of Keats's unerring sense of the aesthetic whole (*K*, 300). Finally, the "consummating lines" of Tennyson's "Rizpah" cannot be "separately transcribed" or (Swinburne waxing precious) cannot be "wrenched out of their natural framework, or torn off the stem of thorns on which they set the topmost crown of tear-drenched and passion-coloured blossom" (*T&M*, 304).

Swinburne's more ambitious critical judgments are usually based on two varieties of inner form: the first is the "firm outline" (or the "just" and "chaste" form), the second, "gathering form." Rossetti's poems were special illustrations, for nearly all of his poetry displayed the two kinds of form. The source of Rossetti's "inborn sense of rule" and "tangible form and line" (*NEP*, 102) Swinburne traced to his Latin origins. In the most ambitious of Rossetti's works, *The House of Life*,

> Spirit and sense together, eyesight and hearing and thought, are absorbed in splendour of sounds and glory of colours distinguishable only by delight. But the scheme is solid and harmonious; there is no waste in this luxury of genius: the whole is lovelier than its loveliest part. Again and again may one turn the leaves in search of some one poem or some two which may be chosen for sample and thanksgiving; but there is no choice to be made.

While Shakespeare's sonnets have "a far more passionate and instant force," Rossetti's display "a nobler fullness of form, a more stately and shapely beauty of build: they are of a purer and less turbid water than the others are at times . . ." (*DGR*, 7, 8).

Although this high praise is to a certain extent supportable, Swinburne might better have engaged the skeptical reader if he had acknowledged the contrasts in Rossetti's cycle. The first sonnets, written in 1848, are less adorned and simpler in their verse argument than the later ones, the last written in 1881. Also, he might have accounted for the possible disruptions of the organic whole caused by "Part II. Change and Fate," which is shorter than Part I and something of a potpourri. The section oscillates around various themes: "transfigured life" (60), the artist's emotion (61), drifting moods (69), death (71-73), the challenge of the old masters (74-76), soul beauty and body beauty, contraries unresolved (77, 78), the seasons (82, 83), the sensitive soul who fails in his ambitions as poet and painter (91), and the finality of art (94). It is true that there are no startling fallings-off of hand and mind in the poem, no lapses of taste and idea such as those we find in "Maud" or "In Memoriam": "the meek, unconscious dove" of "In Memoriam," VI, is a lapsing into sentiment, particularly noticeable since it precedes the famous section on the dark house; also, the portions in which Tennyson's poets are the conventional shepherds of the pastoral elegy are out of place in a poem so informed with the direct and real conditions of men and nature. Swinburne was quite right: there are ways, and legitimate ones, of seeing coherence in *The House of Life* and discovering "the secret of its scheme." Here is one, for example, which would require little forcing: the issue of art, its creation, its qualities, and its final results, appears in all of the sonnets either directly or by implication. Perhaps his observation that the whole is lovelier than any part was meant to embrace variations in quality; since, however, he is not more precise in the treatment of Rossetti, he does appear overly enthusiastic.

In the same essay Swinburne praised other Rossetti poems for their unity. To pluck separate petals from "The Blessed Damozel" (called by Swinburne "the mystic rose") for "proof of its fragrance" or to tear samples from "Jenny" is to violate their beauty. In "Dante at Verona" an ardent verse forges "a memorial as of carven gold." Rossetti's translation of Dante's Francesca episode falls "of itself into a new mould, the exact shape and size of the first—to be poured from one cup into another without spilling one drop of nectar." In "My

Sister's Sleep" Swinburne discerns "the hardness of growing outlines." I cannot but feel that here again he might have offered us more by way of analysis. "Jenny" is a complex work, flawed by its author's indecision as to the appropriate tone for the whole; it is a curious blend of the sentimental and the naturalistic; its imagery, occasionally fine in its expressionistic vigor, is too often trite and sloppy. He is more convincing about "The Blessed Damozel," and his metaphor of the goldsmith introduces an ambitious discussion of the poem on Dante. But Swinburne was inclined to glide over some weaknesses in Rossetti, leaving us to assume either that he was blind to them or that he ignored them in order to support his partisan feeling for works disturbing and foreign to Victorian readers (*DGR*, 14-36, *passim*).

Swinburne's firm outline may seem reminiscent of neo-classical aims with their stress on a static proportion rather than a developing, growing organicism of the whole.[6] Swinburne's concept however is more kinetic than static. Despite the grounding of his theories in dissimilar traditions, he insisted repeatedly upon disciplined forms; as we shall see shortly, even his exuberant dynamistic theory assumed that, despite flaws, the genius of the artist must imbue the whole with an unmistakably single impact. In other words, he disagreed with Shelley's bits-and-pieces organicism. Shelley had announced in his "Defence of Poetry" that "the parts of a composition may be poetical, without the composition as a whole being a poem. A single sentence may be considered as a whole, though it be found in the midst of a series of unassimilated portions: a single word even may be a spark of "inextinguishable thought."[7] Swinburne disagreed also with Poe's notion (in "The Philosophy of Composition") that a long poem was "merely a succession of brief ones—that is to say, of brief poetical effects."[8]

Swinburne's position on the first variety of inner form is clear in a critical reading he gave to Morris' early poems. Finding them defective in form "in the abstract and absolute sense," he theorized that a work without an inevitable organic design wants "all." One of his favorite images for the complete work was the unmaimed classical statue; there can be no true work of art unless there is an unmistakable ordering, an inevitability, he implied, of parts harmonized and in balance.

Many able writers of verse whom no miracle could endow with competence to do such work [as Morris'] would have missed the faults as surely as the merits; would have done something where the poet has cared to do nothing. There is scarcely connection here, and scarcely composition. There is hardly a trace of narrative power or mechanical arrangement. There is a perceptible want of tact and practice, which leaves the poem in parts indecorous and chaotic. (*M*, 52-53)

Morris' early poems were ill clad: "their attire now and then" seemed "huddled on" and in need of "combing and trimming." "King Arthur's Tomb" has not been "constructed at all; the parts hardly hold together"; the work needed "joists and screws, props and rafters" (*M*, 52). But there were compensations allowable to genius, especially to a genius who seemed in narrative power and skill at rendering sharp detail a latter-day Chaucer. Morris was a poet of great future promise. Nine years later when the *Life and Death of Jason* appeared Swinburne saw none of the formal shortcomings he had noticed earlier. This new poem was "large and coherent" and "completed as conceived." There is a "simple sense of right," a graceful step, and a pure, just, and imaginative coloring (*M*, 55-56). This is obviously high but not extravagant praise; for Swinburne had subtly marked not only Morris' competence and charm but a telling evenness of style which, as it developed, Morris later seldom exceeded or fell far below:

> Here indeed there is not the stormy variety, the lyric ardour of the first book; there is not the passion of the ballads, the change of note and diversity of power, all that fills with life and invigorates with colour the artist's earlier designs. . . . (*M*, 55)

The cumulative effect of many of Morris' productions is lulling and finally repellent. They may not want for "practice," but they do lack what Swinburne called "narrative power" and vitality.

To explain the virtues of Byron's *Don Juan* and *Cain*, a perhaps unexpected coupling, Swinburne found useful a reference to Greek sculpture. (He regarded Hugo's *Torquemada* as being as flawless as a work of Sophocles or Phidias—*VH*, 104.) These works, he observed, are as "coherent and complete as trees or flowers; they cannot be split up and parcelled out like a mosaic of artificial jewellry." To "cancel or select a leaf" from *Don Juan* is to "injure the whole framework." Even the fragments of such a work

> are exquisite and noble, like the broken hand or severed foot of a
> Greek statue; but here as much is lost as there. Taken with their
> context, they regain as much of beauty and of force as the sculptured foot or hand when, reunited to the perfect body, they resume their place and office among its vital and various limbs. (*B*,
> 135)

In all likelihood, Swinburne enjoyed Byron's comparison of eighteenth and nineteenth-century poetry and his description of his own role in the Romantic movement. In a letter to John Murray, written from Ravenna, Feb. 7, 1821, Byron took W. L. Bowles to task for his commentary on Pope. Byron placed himself with those who firmly respect the classical virtues. The "poetical populace" who are against Pope

> have raised a mosque by the side of a Grecian temple of the purest
> architecture; and, more barbarous than the barbarians from whose
> practice I have borrowed the figure, they are not contented with
> their own grotesque edifice, unless they destroy the prior, and
> purely beautiful fabric which preceded, and which shames them
> and theirs for ever and ever. I shall be told that amongst those I
> *have* been (or it may be still *am*) conspicuous—true, and I am
> ashamed of it. I *have* been amongst the builders of this Babel . . .
> but *never* amongst the envious destroyers of the classic temple of
> our predecessor.[9]

Surprisingly, perhaps, it was Ben Jonson, some of whose opinions on these matters Swinburne said were "worth all Sidney's and all Shelley's treatises thrown together" (*BJ*, 9), who supplied Swinburne with an excellent, clear model: "The congruent and harmonious fitting of parts in a sentence," Jonson had said, "hath almost the fastening and force of knitting and connection; as in stones well squared, which will rise strong a great way without mortar."[10] Swinburne praised Jonson's *The Silent Woman* for its "combination of parts and the accumulation of incidents" (*BJ*, 36); *Every Man Out of His Humour*, however, gave the impression of a unity which in fact did not exist:

> And if it were not an inadmissible theory that the action or the
> structure of a play might be utterly disjointed and dislocated in

order to ensure the complete presentation or development, the alternate exhibition or exposure, of each figure in the revolving gallery of a satirical series, we could hardly fear that our admiration of the component parts which fail to compose a coherent or harmonious work of art could possibly carry us too far into extravagance of applause. (*BJ*, 12)

"Leading idea" was for Swinburne another way of describing this principal element of his prized organic design. The phrase lies buried in a passage of somewhat thickened prose. He is complaining that George Chapman and Fulke Greville were "the two most genuinely obscure in style" of all poets "upon whose works I have ever adventured to embark in search of treasure hidden beneath the dark gulfs and crossing currents of their rocky and weedy waters, at some risk of my understanding being swept away by the ground-swell—such a poet, overcharged with overflowing thoughts, *is not sufficiently possessed by any one leading idea, or attracted towards any one central point,* to see with decision the proper end and use with resolution the proper instruments of his design" (*GC,* 145; my italics).

Robert Browning, on the other hand, was endowed with the ability to see "the proper end" of many poems, and "to charge him with obscurity," Swinburne declared, "is about as accurate as to call Lynceus purblind or complain of the sluggish action of the telegraphic wire" (*GC,* 145). If he has a fault, it is that he is "too brilliant and subtle" for some readers, who cannot keep pace with his "spider-like swiftness and sagacity." Here Swinburne employed a striking image—"the animated line"—for the principal feature of a work's organic shape: Browning's spirit "leaps and lightens to and fro and backward and forward . . . along the animated line of its labour, springs from thread to thread and darts from centre to circumference of the glittering and quivering web of living thought woven from the inexhaustible stores of his perception and kindled from the inexhaustible fire of his imagination" (*GC,* 146).[11] More skillfully than any other contemporary poet, Browning focuses upon a central object and subordinates all "direct and vivid illustration" and "every symbol and every detail" to that central design. Few poets have displayed as splendid an imagination combined with a bright intellectual cunning (*GC,* 155). Through soliloquy, analysis, and apology Browning flung himself with all his heart and all his brain, with all the force of his intellect and all the strength of his imagination, into the assumed part of his client [he was "a great special pleader"]; to concentrate on the cause in hand his whole power of illustration and illumination, and bring to bear upon one point at once all the rays of his thought in one focus. (*GC*, 149)

In speaking of Simeon Solomon, Swinburne attempted a specific description of that elusive "filament," "connection," or "thread" (an image like the "animated line") which in its magical way gives firmness to the external elements of a work and is in itself "inner" in function and composition. Solomon's vision, Swinburne concluded, would have been more significant if his drawing had had more "body," more "shapeliness of thought," and, Swinburne added, stressing the importance of a tactile form, more "fixity of outline." This criticism recalls Swinburne's objection to Whistler's disregard of the precise line. Solomon's work requires a true form, "some thread of clearer connection, some filament, though never so slender, to link vision again to vision, some clue . . . to lead the reader's perception through the labyrinth of sounds and shapes" (*SSV*, 447-448). Solomon's defects are obvious to the most casual observer: a stumpy anatomy, an indifference to surface texture (*Meeting of Dante and Beatrice*—See Plate 26—is an exception), a pseudo-Botticellean sweetness of mood, and rendering of youths spoiled by an unsubtle hermaphroditic beauty. Swinburne might have handled this work severely; the note of hesitancy in his criticism of his friend's painting is perhaps understandable, though hardly to his credit. He is immediately freer once he is able to praise.

He was more straightforward in criticizing Edmund Spenser's shortcomings as an allegorist. Spenser lacked Rossetti's "inborn sense of rule and outline." His world was a "cloudy and flowery fairyland" marked with a "luminous and fluid nebulosity," and his "impersonated virtues and vices" lacked "tangible form and line":

> In Spenser the figure of a just man melts away into the quality of justice, the likeness of a chaste woman is dissolved into the abstraction of chastity. Nothing can be more alien from the Latin genius, with its love of clearness and definite limitation, than this indefinite and inevitable cloudiness of depiction rather than conception, which reduces the most tangible things to impalpable

properties, resolves the solidest realities into smoke of perfumed metaphor from the crucible of symbolic fancy, and suffuses with Cimmerian mist the hard Italian sunlight.

Swinburne concludes that on the whole Spenser's influence was regrettable:

> Allegory was no doubt a powerful factor to be reckoned with in casting up the account of English poetry before Spenser; but in the allegories of his most notable precursors down to Sackville there is surely as much more of body, of tangible and palpable outline, than in his, as there is less of it in any of his followers. I cannot, therefore, but think that the great influence of Spenser on succeeding poets whose lines of work lay outside the fields of lyric and dramatic verse was far from being good as well as great.

There was no poet until Milton "who could make head for a moment against that influence"—"unless a not very significant exception be claimed for Drayton and for Daniel" (*NEP*, 102, 103, 104-105).

Swinburne's second variety of inner form uses the most provocative of his critical terms, "gathering form." This term, an original one so far as I know, appeared first in his discussion of William Blake's *Songs of Experience*, where an image of the sea rather than some quiescent natural form was the symbolic complement of the idea. Blake's verse echoes "the long relapse of recoiling water and wash of the refluent wave" (*WB*, 164). As he continued the parallel, Swinburne employed alliterative effects to catch the heavy, prolonged motion of the waves. Blake's use of onomatopoeia and his alternation of masculine and feminine endings are effective. In "Earth's Answer," from *Songs of Experience*, Blake's third and fourth lines sink "as with equal pulses and soft sobbing noise of ebb, to climb again in the fifth line with a rapid clamour of ripples and strong ensuing strain of weightier sound, lifted with the lift of the running and ringing sea" (*WB*, 164). Several pages later he returned to this same image to explain the verse of some of Blake's songs. The poetry

> pauses and musters and falls, always as a wave does, with the same patience of *gathering form* [my italics] and rounded glory of springing curve, and sharp sweet flash of dishevelled and flickering foam as it curls over, showing the sun through its soft heaving

side in veins of gold that inscribe and jewels of green that inlay the quivering and sundering skirt or veil of thinner water, throwing upon the tremulous space of narrowing sea in front, like a reflection of lifted and vibrating hair, the windy shadow of its shaken spray. (*WB*, 179)

Despite the complex detail and the almost breathless evocation of effects, this passage through its many devices suggests the precise nature of dynamic or gathering form as Swinburne understood it. Particularly intriguing is the concept, realized metaphorically, that a gathering form sheds a collective brilliance upon itself as it proceeds; like the wave curling over, it reveals its accumulating beauty all the while it vibrates toward its total, shimmering consummation in the human mind.

In Swinburne's analysis of Hugo's style, already partially examined in Chapter II as an example of Swinburne's ability to reflect the manner of his subject, metaphors for gathering form are various and include the image of water. The theme supports Swinburne's idea that a work of literature gathers force and provides a sense of the direction taken towards resolution through details and parts in sequence. It deals not with the characterizing artist's mind but with the inner factors of tone and arrangement present in the work itself. Hugo's prose is a composite of effects ranging from the "tight-laced, short-breathed kind of march" to the "flexible, soft, sinuous" mood. Beauty "dilates every word and sentence to the full"; there is "a tremulous intensity of life." As the prose "expands and opens into vast paragraphs," the parts cohere "as water coheres," and thus the meaning "gets clothed and set out as suits it best" (*VH*, 169-170).

With less originality but similar conviction, Swinburne employed an image of the cloud to symbolize an art of "becoming": we should no more expect "solidity" in a cloud than we do in a shadow; the "confusion of molten outlines" is one of the glories of nature. But, he said, echoing Ruskin, even a cloud reflects "some law of form, some continuous harmony of line and mass, that only dissolves and changes 'as a tune into a tune' " (*SSV*, 447).

Swinburne's effort in the Blake passage to clothe his idea in a language and prose meter the beauty of which is itself an illustration of the idea, recalls Gautier's, Hugo's, Flaubert's, and Pater's strivings for

the precise word and phrase.[12] But most important of all, his statements are an impressive effort to come to grips with art's most elusive,
theoretical aspects; and this particular effort remains undated, despite
the twentieth-century critic's occasional belief that Victorian England
was a critical wasteland. Matthew Arnold is perhaps an exception; but
even he has not been everywhere graciously received.

Swinburne realized that before his theory of inner form could
prove meaningful and his role as critic be fulfilled, he had to resolve
the problem of the flawed work and its relation to a willful creative
genius. If he found little direct assistance, he must surely have delighted in Carlyle's polemic which appeared in his essay on Goethe.
"The 'critic fly,' " Carlyle said,

> if it do but alight on any plinth or single cornice of a brave stately
> building, shall be able to declare, with its half-inch vision, that
> there is a speck, and there an inequality; that, in fact, this and the
> other individual stone are nowise as they should be; for all this
> the "critic fly" will be sufficient: but to take in the fair relations of
> the Whole, to see the building as one object, to estimate its pur-
> pose, the adjustment of its parts, and their harmonious cöopera-
> tion towards that purpose, will require the eye and the mind of a
> Vitruvius, or a Palladio. But farther, the faults of a poem, or other
> piece of art, as we view them at first, will by no means continue
> unaltered when we view them after due and final investigation.

And Carlyle concluded, not very helpfully, that our final judgment of
such works should be based on "universal principles of poetic beauty,
not as they stand written in our text-books, but in the hearts and imaginations of all men."[13]

We might return here to Swinburne's limbless Greek statue, which
illustrated his concept of the organic whole. His implication that the
mutilated sculpture, like a severely edited poem, is a grotesque, deprived of its "context," relates not only to the problem of the flawed
masterpiece, but also to Swinburne's understanding of antique sculpture and to the nature of form.

Swinburne's references to Greek sculpture are always brief, usually no more than a mention contrasting the qualities of ancient art
with a modern work. Phidias is a recurring name, together with
Aeschylus, Sophocles, and Pindar; but Swinburne never treats in de-

tail any of the works attributed to Phidias, nor does he speculate on the aesthetics of sculpture itself. He left no published record of his responses to the Elgin marbles. His artist-friends were painters, and the interest in painting which they stimulated was never reinforced by a similar knowledge of the other medium. Thomas Woolner, the Pre-Raphaelite sculptor, hardly created original works; his portraits of Victorian notables supported the general pre-nineteenth-century English views of painting and sculpture as records of persons and their properties.

It is possible that Swinburne shared the generally pallid English attitude toward modern sculpture. One recalls the rather grim pre-Moore and Epstein statues adorning London malls and parks in celebration of kings and heroes, politicians and philanthropists, and such concepts as honor, industry, agriculture, and education. By contrast, the sensuous, non-didactic, frequently nude sculptures of Paris (the works arranged along the pebbled walks leading from the Luxembourg Palace, for example) are of a world and spirit which seem to have eluded the British and the Americans. George Eliot's Dorothea Brooke sits amid the treasures of the Vatican and is dimly aware that sculpture may work in some mysterious way its aesthetic wonders to perform. She recognizes, however, how ill-equipped she is for such responses, and begins shortly to reflect upon her marriage, the passing of time, and man's good fortune in not being able to hear the "roar which lies on the other side of silence." Art, for her, serves mankind in ennobling ways, with a modicum of the purely aesthetic.[14]

There are, of course, exceptions to these remarks. William Hamo Thornycroft (1850-1925), in his *Teucer, General Gordon, The Sower,* and *Cromwell,* was a sculptor of considerable strength and skill; Arthur Symons, perhaps because he formed many of his tastes at the founts of the avant-garde in Paris, had a keen appreciation of Rodin. Nor does it diminish the genius of Swinburne to show that his knowledge in some areas was incomplete. His comments on Greek sculpture, however, should be read with this in mind; and his response to the potential beauty of the flawed and incomplete work was limited. He hoped that Arnold might complete his "massive fragment" from "the chorus of a 'Dejaneira' "; "that must be a noble statue which could match" this work (*MA,* 97).

He found in the Greek marbles images of that ideal proportion and harmony he so admired in Aeschylus and, to a lesser degree, in Sophocles. Aeschylus he regarded as the purest, most refined, and most abstract of all dramatists; and his virtues of clarity and harmonious resolution of resistant materials, Swinburne felt, were also those of Phidias. Swinburne was aware, it should be said, of the grim subject matter of the ancients—the eye-gougings, pursuits by the harpies, murders, and suffocations. An artist's subject matter usually disturbed him less than the manner of treatment; and he waxed as passionate about violations of form among the ancients as among his contemporaries. Euripides he loathed—the word is not over-drawn—with some of the fervor he awarded Zola and the Ibsenites. Euripides had violated the ideal of the flawless work; roughnesses remained; his genius was subordinate to a gross subject matter; he was too flamboyant, unpoised, and incomplete. Of Euripides' psychological insights, unfortunately, Swinburne had little to say; this virtue was at best a gram placed opposite pounds of vice. Aeschylus, on the other hand, maintained complete control over grotesque themes and realistic materials. His work was finely executed with angularities and *bravura* touches. Swinburne would pay an artist no finer compliment than to compare him with Aeschylus.

Swinburne would, I feel, have little patience with our belief that a mutilated statue exhumed after centuries in the ground, cleaned and placed on a pedestal in a gallery, assumes a unique aesthetic appeal because of its age, associations, special patina, and fragmented power.[15] The torso of the Fitzwilliam Museum *Apollo* [*See* Plate 30] would have struck him, certainly, with the grace of its main curves and the strength of its magnificent chest and abdomen; but he would have hesitated to allow it much autonomous beauty in its present state. He would soon have regretted the mutilations, have begun to ponder over the longevity of art and the brutality of man, and would finally have lamented the spoilation of what was once a contained and noble whole.

An even fuller treatment of the question of genius and its relation to a flawed art and resistant difficulties overcome appeared in *The Age of Shakespeare*. It is one of the few times that Swinburne contrasts the Coleridgean facets of the mind: imagination, invention, and fancy. (He does not, I should point out, define the terms; they were largely common critical knowledge, since Burke, Hazlitt, and Shelley, besides Coleridge, had already discussed them.) He began by ranking Marlowe and Shakespeare above Chaucer and Spenser, declaring that the latter were "great writers and great men" who shared "between them every gift which goes to the making of a poet except the one which alone can make a poet, in the proper sense of the word, great." An exceptional ability to convey pathos, humor, or fancy cannot alone produce great art: we need to weigh the quality of the imagination, "as distinguished from invention or from fancy" (*CM,* 271). He theorized, apparently thinking as he wrote, that works of art approach perfection only insofar as their creators do; at their finest, a Shakespeare, a Shelley, or a Blake may give the illusion of having surpassed mortal limits, of achieving, as Pope said so well, that "grace beyond the reach of art."

Flaws in the works of genius continued to puzzle him, and he permitted himself this obvious but disheartening observation: "The faults and weaknesses of strong men seem usually an integral part of the character or the genius we admire for its strength" (*GC,* 233). The list of defects was long. Among them were Jonson's and Chapman's failures of style and tone; Blake's confusing symbolism, invented, Swinburne felt, in order to garb a deep rebellious anger (Blake lacked, Swinburne astutely observed, the full complement of ordinary imagery required for the sublimation of his mood); Hugo's inattentiveness to a rich middle area between extremes; Shelley's haste and untidy handling of the anapestic line (Swinburne's own favorite); Emily Brontë's failure to evolve a coherent total fictional pattern; and Tennyson's expenditure of flawless technique upon an impotent center of feeling. Yet each of these writers, Swinburne felt, was greater than his faults would indicate; the superior craftsmanship and inspiration of each made "their grave and frequent blemishes," as he said of Chapman, "bear manifestly more likeness to the deformities of a giant than to the malformations of a dwarf, to the overstrained muscles of an athlete than to the withered limbs of a weakling" (*GC,* 137).

When he wanted to refer to the apparently vast difference in art between technique and a transcendent result, he used the term "divided beauty." This concept had been a favorite of Blake and Gautier. Swinburne endowed it with symbolic flesh by employing the image of the hermaphrodite; thus he implied a psychic fusion of sexual differences representative of contrasting elements in art. He desired a unity between the harsh reality and the sublime ideal symbolized by Greek sculpture, specifically by the statue *Hermaphroditus* [*See* Plate 31], "this sculptured poem," which he had seen. In this statue the Greek sculptor had successfully shaped the two sexes (the two elements of divided beauty) into one perfect body:

> There is nothing lovelier, as there is nothing more famous, in later Hellenic art, than the statue of Hermaphroditus. No one would compare it with the greatest works of Greek sculpture. No one would lift Keats on a level with Shakespeare. But the Fates have allowed us to possess at once *Othello* and *Hyperion*, Theseus and Hermaphroditus. (*NPR,* 366-368)

Swinburne's series of four sonnets, "Hermaphroditus," was inspired by the statue and intended to symbolize in Shelleyan fashion—or so Swinburne argued—that beauty which like "ideal genius, dwells apart, as though by compulsion." The poem is also a study in sexual abnormality:

> Choose of two loves and cleave unto the best;
> Two loves at either blossom of thy breast
> Strive until one be under and one above.[16]

The marble statue itself reclines full-length on its couch, seeming to sleep; its left leg is raised, its right ankle displayed rather than at rest, its sleep very possibly an inviting pretension.

For the moment, at least, Swinburne the critic claimed to see in the sculpture the "sad and subtle moral" of the ancient myth of opposites, a moral anchored clearly in a flawed literal art: "perfection once attained on all sides is a thing thenceforward barren of use or fruit; whereas the divided beauty of separate woman and man—a thing inferior and imperfect—can serve all turns of life" (*NPR,* 366-368). And he found the concept an attractive aid not only for contrasting elements and styles in art but for symbolizing the artist adept in two media.[17]

The essay on Rossetti opens with an application of the hermaphrodite theme. Swinburne's immediate subject is the man of dual talents —Leonardo, Michelangelo, Blake, and Rossetti. Not only are such "double-natured" geniuses in danger of having one art subdue or spoil the other; they are also subject to dual attacks from critics, the weaklings and dullards who reject the presence of both "sunlight and moonlight in the same sky." Like that " 'sweet marble monster of both sexes' beloved of Shelley as of Gautier," the doubly-gifted man is unable to convince critics that he is not "sterile by excess of organs" (*DGR*, 3-4).

Single talents might be either male or female in their tone, or both. Keats was mainly feminine, as was Spenser. Arnold's "Thyrsis" has "all the accomplished and adult beauty of a male poem." "The Forsaken Merman" seems to be a composite; it resolves female elements with an expert male force (*MA*, 95). In Solomon's painting the contraries assume overtones of mystery, decay, and a blent sexuality. Swinburne's remarks anticipate similar ones made by critics trying, a few years later, to explain Aubrey Beardsley. Solomon created a "supersexual beauty, in which the lineaments of woman and of man seem blended as the lines of sky and landscape melt in burning mist of heat and light" (*SSV*, 453). *My Soul and I* contains both the idea of the separation of male and female qualities and their union as body and soul. Solomon loved "gorgeous mysteries": age and youth, boys and maidens, attraction and abhorrence, suffering and delight. His preoccupations suggest Baudelaire's, that "most loving of all students of strange beauty and abnormal refinement, of painful pleasures of soul and inverted raptures of sense" (*SSV*, 456). One of these abnormal works is *Bacchus* [See Plate 29]; another is *Heliogabalus*. These pictures, and others like them, have

> a fleshly glory of godhead and bodily deity, which holds at once of earth and heaven; neither the mystic and conquering Indian is this god, nor the fierce choregus of Cithaeron. The artist's passionate love of gorgeous mysteries, "prodigious mixtures and confusions strange" of sense and spirit no less than "of good and ill," has given him the will and the power to spiritualise at his pleasure. . . . (*SSV*, 453-454)

Walter Pater and Oscar Wilde included Leonardo and Botticelli among artists of this temper; Arthur Symons added Toulouse-Lautrec and Beardsley. When these divided elements are resolved, beauty is transcendent and bestiality transformed. Myth serves an organic art, at least as Swinburne envisioned it, by indicating the transcendent unifying beauty towards which all great art aspires; and it would seem that

Swinburne recognized also, as Browning had, the pathos of the human heart intent upon an unrealizable ideal.

William Empson is one of the modern critics who have been severe in treating nineteenth-century formalism. In his analysis he equates the common critical view that "some poetic effect conveys a direct 'physical' quality" with a vague "belief in Atmosphere." There seems to be in such effects "something mysteriously intimate, something like a sensation which is not attached to any one of the senses." Such effects may be "felt or thought; the two things are similar but different; and it requires practice to do both at once." At any rate, Empson suggests, the result is unnecessarily diffuse; he does not distinguish between Romantic and Victorian results.[18] Swinburne gave this very ideal an assured expression: poetry, he said, must possess an elusive mystical quality. Although it be "as nobly ardent and invigorating as the best of Byron's, or as nobly mournful and contemplative as the best of Southey's," if its several elements can be easily "gauged and named," it is not real poetry and especially not true lyric poetry: "There must be something in the mere progress and resonance of the words, some secret in the very motion and cadence of the lines, inexplicable by the most sympathetic acuteness of criticism" (*W&B*, 215). He reflects, of course, a favorite doctrine of his heroes Blake and Shelley. Blake believed, he said, that "only by innate and irrational perception" can we "apprehend and enjoy the supreme works of verse and colour" (*WB*, 85). And Shelley's poetry is sprinkled with direct and implied statements of the same idea.

The array of nineteenth-century writers believing in some form of mystic truth is impressive—Blake, Wordsworth, Coleridge, Shelley, Keats, Carlyle, Rossetti—and Empson, perhaps considering the formidable creative achievement of these men, retracts somewhat, declaring that while we may suspect the "formula" of tactile atmosphere and regret its unfortunate consequences for much nineteenth-century art, the formula is not therefore automatically "untrue" or "unusable." A critic, and especially a critic who is also a verbal analyst, must, Empson says, "remember about the atmosphere." This remark leads him to the not particularly fresh assumption that atmosphere "is the consciousness of what is implied by the meaning" of a poem. He believes, further, that this assumption is "profitable in many more cases than one would suppose."[19] His definition delivers us right back to the crux of the problem, and I can do no better than to present Walter Pater, the late Victorian specialist on this aspect of art. Pater's theory of atmosphere and integral form is still being debated.

The organic result of Pater's ideal of "mind,"[20] the annealing agent of style, closely resembles Swinburne's "hard outline." "Mind" also recalls Swinburne's "tact" (a term Pater frequently used) and the fusion Swinburne required between tact and passion. Mind, thoroughly integral to the work of art, is "architectural" in its force. It informs equally all elements of the parent work; in writing, its structural presence is discernible, so Pater felt, in the word, the phrase, the sentence, and the paragraph. (Shelley had said the same thing, and the concept is also Hegelian.)[21] An elusive quality, mind results from the artist's exactness in his handling of resistant materials, in his provision of a main skeletal framework for his subject matter, in his basic verse design, in his imagery and diction, and in his unique will and spirit, all combined into a "vital wholeness and identity, of the initiatory apprehension or view." "Insight, foresight, retrospect," the whole creative psyche, meet in a "simultaneous action." The result is the tensile work of art, or what Pater referred to as a "logical coherency." The phrase suggests Swinburne's mental rigor in combination with a harmonized technique. Pater described the organic ideal rather fully, at the same time presenting his famous theory of the integrity of the exact word:

> Such logical coherency may be evidenced not merely in the lines of composition as a whole, but in the choice of a single word, while it by no means interferes with, but may even prescribe, much variety, in the building of the sentence for instance, or in the manner, argumentative, descriptive, discursive, of this or that part or member of the entire design. The blithe, crisp sentence, decisive as a child's expression of its needs, may alternate with the long-contending, victoriously intricate sentence; the sentence, born with the integrity of a single word, relieving the sort of sentence in which, if you look closely, you can see much contrivance, much adjustment, to bring a highly qualified matter into compass at one view. For the literary architecture, if it is to be rich and expressive, involves not only foresight of the end in the be-

ginning, but also development or growth of design, in the process of execution, with many irregularities, surprises, and afterthoughts; the contingent as well as the necessary being subsumed under the unity of the whole.

In its emphasis on technique and inner structure, Pater's statement, despite its elaborate hesitations, advances one full step beyond Swinburne's organicism towards the twentieth century. The idea of "development or growth of design" and the "foresight of the end in the beginning" are facets of a principle of gathering form.

What William Empson tends to overlook in his assessments of nineteenth-century form are the changes in aesthetics brought about by the Victorians as distinct from the Romantics, and the relationships with the twentieth century. There are "profitable cases," to use his own words. To explain one case, by way of conclusion, I return to Swinburne's approach to the problem of the broken statue and the telling flaw. Earth and man wear the ideal down to their own imperfections. The broken work is *broken,* Swinburne would have felt, and is therefore less than itself. When the viewer, in his mind's eye, completes such a work and fits the torso with limbs, there results an object which is merely an echo of an original. So far as I know, Swinburne never saw Rodin's figures, many of them locked in marble in various states of bliss, vigor, suffocation, and dream. Nor did he fully appreciate Michelangelo's "incompleteness," which Pater found "puzzling" since it "suggests rather than realises actual form," but which he resolved in support of an advanced idea of form:

> incompleteness is Michelangelo's equivalent for color in sculpture; it is his way of etherealising pure form, of relieving its hard realism, and communicating to it breath, pulsation, the effect of life. . . . And it was in reality perfect finish. In this way he combines the utmost amount of passion and intensity with the sense of a yielding and flexible life: he gets not vitality merely, but a wonderful force of expression.[22]

In his "Notes on Designs of the Old Masters at Florence," an encompassing study of the drawings of several Renaissance masters, Swinburne makes no references to this quality of Michelangelo's art.

Swinburne felt that we must not deny the intentions of the artist. Our response to a work is never final until we have determined them. Nor have we a right to indulge in fantasy or to make readings which suit our own tastes. Art is not dream in this sense, but rather an experience of beauty transpiring at the center of all that is awake, objective, and graspable. Luminosity, or aesthetic vision, is for Swinburne always of two orders; the ideal rises out of the marriage of contrasting forces. He would, I am sure, look with immense disfavor on critics who develop elaborate myth systems, patterns of imagery, and total readings in support of critical suppositions and designs. In his concentration upon the final product and upon works completed, ideally at least, down to the last smooth detail, Swinburne relieves the perceiver of the need to share in the creative process. The three forces, artist, work, and audience, are all separate and distinct.

With the late Victorians, with Walter Pater and Oscar Wilde, and with the less influential Vernon Lee, who made a small but original contribution to English aesthetics by further developing Pater's ideas of the psychology of the viewer by blending them with ideas from German aesthetics, the role of the beholder becomes complex. By its very nature an art work is now considered incomplete until it engages a viewer, on whom it depends for its completion. There are, in theory, as many possible completions as there are responses. The work is therefore a fragment, its form latent, potential, smouldering. It assumes several final intensities and shapes, depending upon its inherent properties and the alertness, training, and sensitivity of the perceiver. The theory appeals since it implies a blending of the work and the perceiver in which art loses some of its customary autonomy as a transcendent entity to be approached with awe, a wingless vehicle blasting aloft through the empyrean of the soul. Now, man and art are more interdependent, both operating in an experience relieved of broad dichotomies and of ritual. In this aesthetics, a superior *form* is a dynamic fusion of energies transmitted from work to person and from person to work.

There is a corollary to this. The more engaged the perceiver, the more elusive, cryptic, and suggestive the artist is permitted to be. In this shift to obscurity we have, I think, although I merely note it, the aesthetic basis for much of the complexity and abstruseness of modern art. Assumed here is the trained layman, or, in esoteric terms, the initiate, member of a select, informed audience. Largely disappeared is the luxury, enjoyed by some of the major Victorians, of a huge middle-class public buying up poems and crowding the galleries to see contemporary works. The change in audience and the roots of the change in late Victorian England I have treated elsewhere in this book; and I have referred to ways in which Swinburne anticipated some of these things. He emphasized the separate integrity of the genius at work, subjecting the impulses he has received from vernal woods, celestial realms, or from recollections in tranquility, to a rigorous technique fashioned within the controls of his mortal hands and mortal brain. The demands on the beholder to evaluate form are therefore increased.

A frequent cry among lesser Victorian critics was that an intensive scrutiny of techniques and details would somehow sully the lofty beauty present in the work. Their responses were apt to be ecstatic and rapturous rather than informed and lasting. Beauty is mysterious still; but we are now, if somewhat self-consciously, willing to lock beauty, form, and harmony within the confines of the human brain. This is not to say that we have better critics than the nineteenth century had, or that our art is superior; but we are more aware of the complex relationships of artist, work, and audience.

*C*HAPTER *VIII*

HARMONY: THE SUPERNAL LOVELINESS

Swinburne's "music" of art, or harmony, had to do with aesthetic effects produced by a controlled technique balanced by emotion rather than with music as an art form (*See* Chap. V for Swinburne on music). Technique resulted in "external" music; "internal" music was based on ideas of nature and sublimity which proceeded by increasingly abstract stages to a "supra-sensual" state of pure aesthetic intuition. The general contours of this system[1] are, as the reader might guess, unmistakably indebted to Shelley, for whom man was

> an instrument over which a series of . . . impressions are driven, like the alternations of an ever-changing wind over an Aeolian lyre, which move it by their motion to ever-changing melody. But there is a principle within the human being, and perhaps within all sentient beings, which acts otherwise than in the lyre, and produces not melody alone, but harmony, by an internal adjustment of the sounds or motions thus excited to the impressions which excite them.

The Greeks alone had satisfactorily realized harmony through the arts: they had

> employed language, action, music, painting, the dance, and religious institution, to produce a common effect [in the drama] . . . ; each division in the art was made perfect in its kind by artists of

the most consummate skill, and was disciplined into a beautiful proportion and unity one towards the other.

As usual, Swinburne modified such concepts to suit himself. He began with a division of external music into two types. One was the manipulation of verse techniques, of meter, rhyme, rhythm, assonance, alliteration, and consonance—in other words, all of the constituents of "outer" form (*See* Chapter VII). Rhyme was the only one to prove troublesome. The spread of free verse, stimulated by Whitman's example, forced Swinburne to a reappraisal of his traditional view.

In 1867, writing on Matthew Arnold, Swinburne asserted that rhyme is an absolute "condition of verse in English" (*MA*, 98). A rhymeless lyric "is a maimed thing, and halts and stammers in the delivery of its message." "Message" referred to the emotion rather than to the didactic meaning. The fragments of Arnold's "Antigone" and "Dejaneira" were excellent, and the chorus of *Merope* dealing with Arcas and Callisto was "a model of noble form and colour." But, Swinburne, complained, "*Merope* does not fasten at once upon the memory like a song of Callicles, or like 'The Merman,' or like any such other." Arnold has thrown away "the natural grace of rhyme," abdicating "half the power and half the charm of verse" (*MA*, 98-99). "Variety of singing power"—this was in 1870—ranks with "imagination, passion, thought, harmony," the very highest qualities of poetry (*DGR*, 47). In 1872, when he turned to Whitman, he tried as usual to be fair to a recognized talent, and in a liberal gesture allowed that rhythm may produce an even greater flexibility than rhyme; a poet writing in free verse may have so skillful a rhythm that his poems may qualify as art. But, Swinburne was emphatic, "in rhythm he must needs sing." He apparently was still dissatisfied, for he continued the subject in one of his lengthiest and most elaborate footnotes.[2] He reminded himself that rhymed verse with its music had soared higher than any "human speech has ever done." Shelley's song of the earth from *Prometheus Unbound* was his example. Swinburne again seemed to be thinking aloud as he wrote, and for his own benefit juxtaposed this high praise of Shelley and rhymed lyric verse with his recognition of the transforming power of rhythm. The delay was brief. He embraced the fresh conclusion to which he had come, saying that he far preferred Whitman's rhythms to any "dulcet metres" produced by some "poeticule," some inept hack "curled up to snarl and whimper beneath the inaccessible vine of song"; and he dissociated himself from the sciolists and pedants who insisted upon rhyme. He advised his poet-readers to follow their own dictates in the matter, remembering that the intensity of their passion in balance with their controlled imagination would produce "triumph" equally well in either rhyme or rhythm (*UM*, 414-415).

There was another aspect of rhyme, not to be overlooked. Its presence in serious drama was a mark of the apprentice writer. The form might work splendidly in the lyric or in romantic comedy, but in tragedy it was shallow, "peculiar," and incapable of the lofty strains of a tragic harmony. The occasion for the remarks was Swinburne's 1875 analysis of Shakespeare's technical development. The early romantic comedies were written in rhyme. When Shakespeare turned to tragedy, rhyme became his "evil angel." Gradually, the angel yielded to the good angel, blank verse. In *King Henry VI, Part I* Shakespeare was at work "with both hands—with his left hand of rhyme, and his right hand of blank verse. The left is loth to forego the practice of its peculiar music; yet, as . . . the right grows freer and its touch grows stronger, it becomes more and more certain that the other must cease playing, under pain of producing mere discord and disturbance in the scheme of tragic harmony." The scene between the old king and his son "on the verge of desperate battle and certain death" was "the last and loftiest farewell note of rhyming tragedy." Rhyme persisted, however, both in *Romeo and Juliet* and in *Richard II*. In the former

> the river of verse has broken its banks, not as yet through the force and weight of its gathering stream, but merely through the weakness of the barriers or boundaries found insufficient to confine it. And here we may with deference venture on a guess why Shakespeare was so long so loth to forego the restraint of rhyme. When he wrote . . . his youngest tragedy he had not yet strength to walk straight in the steps of the mighty master [Marlowe]. . . . It is in the scenes of vehement passion, of ardour and of agony, that we feel the comparative weakness of a yet ungrown hand, the tentative uncertain grasp of a stripling giant. . . . Apollo has not yet put on the sinews of Hercules. (*SS*, 24-25, 26, 27-28, 34, 35)

It is in the garden and the balcony scenes (Acts II and III), both in blank verse, that we have the very heart and spirit of the play. With *Richard II* rhyme made its "last hysterical struggle" to hold its place in tragedy (*SS*, 31). Swinburne observed that it was inevitable and natural that Shakespeare should have moved from rhyme to blank verse. After all, he noted, tragic poets are first of all poets and not tragedians: "their lips have had power to sing before their feet had strength to tread the stage, before their hands had skill to paint or carve figures from the life" (*SS*, 31). External music could serve no finer office.

The second type of external music was the imitation in verse of the actual sounds of nature. Poets who achieved it either rendered these sounds as exactly as they could or evoked them by means of onomatopoeia. The reason Swinburne considered this form worth extended comment is that he felt these imitations were preludes to higher, more abstract harmonies. He borrowed a term from Pater to suggest that the poet's function was "mediatorial." The poet stands between the reader and those experiences in nature which he transforms into art. Blake's "sound," for example, echoes nature and remains "long after conscious thought of the meaning has passed from one: a sound like running of water or ringing of bells in a long lull of the wind" (*WB*, 61). "The Lamb" and "The Chimney-Sweeper" convey a "bird-like perfection of clear light sound"; their notes are more "like the notes of birds caught up and given back than the modulated measure of human verse" (*WB*, 161). Other passages from Blake recall the rhythmic swell of the sea, pausing, mustering, and subsiding "always as a wave does" (*WB*, 179).

Hugo, too, was able to capture the potent and climactic harmonies of the sea. One of his poems, "Une Nuit qu'on entendait la mer sans la voir," was a model of verbalized music; its oceanic tones led Swinburne to regret the absence of any similar work in English. He seemed to have in mind an imagistic treatment of the sea similar to his own "Hymn to Proserpine" with its superb symbol, the whitening wave of the world.

> We ought to have in English, but I fear—or rather I am only too sure—we have not, a song in which the sound of the sea is rendered as in that translation of the trumpet-blast of the night-wind,

with all its wails and pauses and fluctuations and returns. . . .
(*VH*, 29; see also 120, 349)

So important was Hugo's poem to Swinburne that he reproduced it in
its entirety.

Swinburne detected this external music in works conveying various natural moods even though the intent of the writer was not at all
to provide transcriptions. At its worst this device degenerated into a
frenetic word and emotion painting apt to jar the modern ear. At its
best it provided an additional tool for defining qualities. Marlowe's
Tamburlaine reminded him of a "simoom" blustering "through the
noisy course" of its "ten fierce acts" (*CM*, 271). This metaphor,
though mixed, is energetic and he might have done more to prove his
point if he had cared to. Marston's rambunctious art ran easily into
"brakes and jungles of crabbed and convulsive bombast," leaving the
reader struggling "as though he were compelled to push his way
through a cactus hedge: the hot and heavy blossoms of rhetoric blaze
and glare out of a thickset fence of jagged barbarisms and exotic mon-
strosities of metaphor" (*JM*, 356). Chapman was another who could
overwhelm a reader with his volcanic energy but who was unable to
soar. His poetry, to borrow from John Stuart Mill, is "heard" rather
than "overheard":

> His fiery and turbid style has in it the action rather of earthquakes
> and volcanoes than of the oceanic verse it labours to represent; it
> can give us but the pace of a giant for echo of the footfall of a
> god; it can show but the huge movements of the heaving earth,
> inflated and inflamed with unequal and violent life, for the in-
> numerable unity and harmony, the radiant and buoyant music of
> luminous motion, the simplicity and equality of passion and of
> power, the majestic monochord of single sound underlying as it
> were at the heart of Homeric verse the multitudinous measures of
> the epic sea. (*GC*, 228-229).

Dryden also possessed this vigor. The tone of his best satire, clear,
fresh, and brisk, more than compensated for his "various offences
against art and manhood, against duty and beauty alike" (*CEP*, 120).
But his verse invites comparison with nature's harmonic best. His
"wings make such mighty music of the most malodorous air that our

senses for the minute are conscious of nothing but the large and fresh delight of their passage and their sound" (*CEP*, 124).

Such parallels with nature, direct and indirect, have a limited appeal. And the artist who is struck by pretty accidents, by what Hazlitt ingeniously called nature's "idea deformity," may dwell on discrimination and contrast to the neglect, to borrow again from Hazlitt, of that more encompassing nature which rests on "harmony and continuity of effect."[3] Although Swinburne was not as self-conscious about these "ideal" qualities as Hazlitt, he was enough of a transcendentalist to assume that the artist would impose upon his materials the force of his own spirit, itself a partaker of universal harmonies.

As we would expect, in Swinburne's system "inner" music always transcends "outer," and to contrast the dual sounds (outer and inner) he opposed Shelley and Byron to Milton and Spenser, revealing again his preference for a passionate art inspired by elemental forms to a production fostered by rule and patterned according to an architectonics of the human brain. In the final act of *Prometheus Unbound* Shelley had demonstrated this rapport between elemental forms and emotion through images of the moon (the transcendental sphere) and the earth (the origin of specific beauty). The moon expresses its loving affinity for earth and declares that she must follow him:

> Drinking from thy sense and sight
> Beauty, majesty, and might,
> As a lover or a camelion
> Grows like what it looks upon,
> As a violet's gentle eye
> Gazes on the azure sky
> Until its hue grows like what it beholds. (ll. 481-487)

Milton's *virtue*, on the other hand, is "chiefly of sound." His majestic melodies exclude and supplant "all other motives of material beauty," all of the forces, in other words, of actual nature. Their main inspiration is technical, and their melodies inventions of the mind. We might wish that Swinburne had explored the technical values of a poetry like Milton's; for he could have argued that such work, freed of precise evocations, is aesthetically pure and thus more "harmonic" than verse taking its inspiration from a concrete nature. But he did not. Unlike Milton, Spenser lacked the "width or depth to receive and con-

tain" natural forces. "Despite his fertile and fluent ingenuity, his subtle and sleepy graces, the effeminacy of colour no less than the
monotony of metre," Spenser's "Tarpeian Muse" (*NEP*, 104) failed
to delight sufficiently in great outer things (*B*, 125). His immense
charm—and Swinburne recognized those qualities which Tennyson
and his followers caught up from the Elizabethan—rose from the deli-
cacy of his art, from a soft, misty music, "the sweet airs and tender
outlines and floating Elysian echoes . . ." (*GC*, 138).

Keats, Coleridge, and Wordsworth all took an insufficient delight
in nature's outer forms. Keats and Coleridge, Swinburne complained,
employed nature "mainly as a stimulant or a sedative," while Wordsworth saw her as "a vegetable fit to shred into his pot and pare down
like the outer leaves of a lettuce for didactic and culinary purposes"
(*B*, 126n). By contrast, Byron and Shelley were masters at transforming
hints from nature into mature art. They were

> not content to play with her [nature's] skirts and paddle in her
> shallows. Their passion is perfect, a fierce and blind desire which
> exalts and impels their verse into the high places of emotion and
> expression. They feed upon nature with a holy hunger, follow her
> with a divine lust as of gods chasing the daughters of men. Wind
> and fire, the cadences of thunder and the clamours of the sea,
> gave to them no less of sensual pleasure than of spiritual susten-
> ance. These things they desired as others desire music or wine or
> the beauty of women. This outward and indifferent nature of
> things, cruel in the eyes of all but her lovers, and even in theirs
> not loving, became as pliant to their grasp and embrace as any
> Clymene or Leucothea to Apollo's. (*B*, 126-127)

Swinburne might have supported his position by drawing attention
once again to Shelley's insistence upon the relationship between nature
and a universal harmonics. One of the semi-choruses of *Prometheus
Unbound* (II, ii, ll. 48-63) reveals a peculiar mystic chemistry which
seemed to produce the desired results. Its effervescence, I fear, has connotations lacking in Shelley's time. A series of tactile, visual, auditory,
and olfactory images provide what Swinburne called the "strength of
waters and winds." Songs originate from the depths of clear lakes and
pools (symbolic of lucent creative minds) as effervescent bubbles. As
they reach the watery surfaces, their confined energies burst, rise and

"flow like meteors," merging at last with other harmonies to create a
rush of Shelleyan music:

> And first there comes a gentle sound
> To those in talk or slumber bound,
> And wakes the destined. Soft emotion
> Attracts, impels them: those who saw
>   Say from the breathing earth behind
>   There steams a plume-uplifting wind
> Which drives them on their path, while they
>   Believe their own swift wings and feet
> The sweet desires within obey:
> And so they float upon their way,
> Until, still sweet, but loud and strong,
> The storm of sound is driven along,
>   Sucked up and hurrying: as they fleet
>   Behind, its gathering billows meet
> And to the fatal mountain bear
> Like clouds amid the yielding air.

Swinburne required, however, more than a Shelleyan description
of art's melodic transcendence. Implicitly, at least, he envisioned the
way to beauty's celestial reaches as a series of steps. The first, already partially discussed in the paragraphs on external music, involved
the manipulation of physical detail, colored always by the artist's passionate delight in what he has observed. This was a joy, paradoxically,
whose "divine force of meaning" (*C,* 147, 154) carried important overtones of the hedonistic and the sexual. Swinburne's passion, as it appeared in the remarks on Shelley and Byron quoted above, was a
"fierce and blind desire" for art, very much like a craving for the flesh.
His vocabulary emphasized the starkly sensuous: "holy hunger" and
"divine lust" of "gods chasing the daughters of men."

The idea of the sudden springing to life of the intangible world
via the concrete is basic, as we have seen, to much Victorian aestheticism. One of the most important influences on Swinburne and the other
Victorians was Hazlitt. According to Walter Bate, Hazlitt's principle
of "sympathetic identification" is the "one point of view which perme-
ates and colors many of his other principles and gives a certain unity to
his criticism. . . ."[4] In Hazlitt's psychology the artist grows so aware

of a striking physical object that he loses himself in the contemplation of it. The "ideal" expression of nature "satisfies and accords with the inmost longing of the soul. . . ."[5] In "On Poetry in General" Hazlitt claimed for poetry the power of "answering to the music of the mind, untying as it were 'the secret soul of harmony.' "[6] For Hazlitt the process was one in which a single sense excites "by affinity those of another," enabling the artist to grasp the physical object as a vital entity.[7] Bate discusses the relation between Hazlitt's sympathy and Keats's centering of "the various qualities of an object into a single apperception." The object, for Keats as for Hazlitt (and also, we should add, for Swinburne), "emerges as a totality with its several aspects resolved into an amalgamated whole."[8] In general, however, Hazlitt was more attentive than Keats to the broader ethical meanings of such swift permeating moments of harmonic truth. Disinterestedness is the great artist's state of mind; and "gusto" is the "chief force" liberating us from egoism. The "power or passion defining any object," said Hazlitt, serves to present whatever of expression or character exists in the "object," and "in the highest degree of which the subject is capable."[9] Such flexibility, Hazlitt assumed, lifts and expands the sympathies of the reader until he too shares something of the deeper harmonies of the universe.

An excellent Victorian statement on the relationship between "the irregularly constructed music of nature" and the higher harmonies was made by the aesthetician David Ramsay Hay. There is, he said,

> an almost endless variety of systematic arrangements of beautiful figures, often so perfectly symmetrical in their combination, that the most careful application of the angleometer could scarcely detect the slightest deviation from geometrical precision; while, amongst the masses of foliage by which the forms of many trees are divided and subdivided into parts, as almost amongst the hills and valleys, the mountains and ravines, which divide the earth's surface, we find in every possible variety of aspect the beauty produced by that irregular species of symmetry which characterizes the picturesque.

His central point is that picturesque beauty, devised by man, is based on a comparable universal symmetry:

for, as none of the irregularly constructed music of nature could be pleasing to the ear unless there existed in the arrangement of its notes an obedience, however subtle, to the great harmonic law of Nature, so neither could any object be picturesquely beautiful, unless the arrangement of its parts yields, although it may be obscurely, an obedience to the same law.[10]

On the whole, Hazlitt and Swinburne were perhaps not quite so imbued as Shelley with the grand abstraction, and saw first of all a physical nature broadening in time to encompass the grand Romantic universals of aesthetic, moral, and physical truth, making the realization of a harmonized beauty at least possible. The impelling emotion is a "supersensual" one; the condition when achieved, as Thomas Connolly points out, penetrates the very verse form to repeat the music and the pulse of nature.[11] This important step towards a consummating inner music remains highly colored by the temperament of the particular artist. When this occurs, a universality and breadth characteristic of great classic art is inextricably fused with individual tone. Said Swinburne,

> The nearer such an artist's work comes to this abstract perfection of absolute beauty, the more clearly will he see and the more gladly will he admit that it never can come so near as to close with it and find, as in things of meaner life, a conclusion set in the act of fruition to the sense of enjoyment, a goal fixed at a point attainable where the delight of spiritual desire may be . . . consumed in the moment of its consummation. (*GC*, 241)

In other words, the ideal remains elusive; the moments of complete transcendence are far rarer than the enthusiastic Shelley had supposed. Heaven, or "the supernal loveliness" (Poe's phrase), remains, and the struggle to arrive there is rarely won. The artist, Swinburne concluded, must be

> content to know and to accept the knowledge that ideal beauty lies beyond the most beautiful forms and ideal perfection beyond the most perfect words that art can imbue with life or inflame with colour; an excellence that expression can never realise, that possession can never destroy. (*GC*, 241)

Shelley's vivid, recurring image of the singer isolated is a familiar one. There is in Swinburne's principles enough Shelleyan regard for the consummate ideal to encourage artists to accept withdrawal and isolation as desired ends.

With nature again as the starting-point, and guided by Plato, Longinus, Hogarth, and Burke,[12] Swinburne moved another step towards the final harmony of an inner music. Through sublimity the artist may draw himself and his audience towards aesthetic purgation. In a review of Victor Hugo's *L'Homme qui rit* Swinburne saw the sublime in a crucial interplay between Hugo's characters and nature's enigmatic moods. In Hugo's novel *Les Travailleurs de la mer* the human beings caught by storm stimulate our imagination and contain the raw materials for catharsis. We detect in this powerful struggle "a new sense and a new sublimity added to the tempest by the remorse of men sinking at once under sin and storm, drowned under a double weight of deeds and waves." Wind and sea "gain strength and depth from the human figure set to fight them" (*VH*, 216). Elsewhere in the same work, Hugo achieves the sublime through his handling of the grotesque: he transforms the image of a mutilated child's face into a figure of heroic beauty; and in an execution scene ("that swinging of carrion birds with the swing of the gibbeted carrion"), through "a horrible charm" and a "shocking splendour of effect," he supplies "tragic awe and terror" (*VH*, 217). Hugo's mastery is here "divine." A static nature could also produce the sublime. Nature's "living affinity," as Swinburne called it, with bows to Carlyle and Ruskin, leads the contemplative man to a "joyous and terrible sense of his ephemerality." The creation of and the enjoyment of art enable him to purge his fear and transform it into aesthetic joy.

On an obvious level, the sublime included any subject generating fear and horror and accompanied by some form of delight or pleasure as the agent of purgation. More subtly, the sublime was achieved whenever the artist resolved the awesome and difficult techniques of his art. This higher aesthetics Swinburne equated with that "latent mystery of terror which lurks in all the highest poetry or beauty, and distinguishes it inexplicably and inevitably from all that is but a little lower than the highest" (*JW*, 295). As usual, he sought to turn the principle into a critical tool. He contrasted Shelley's sublime fervency with Wordsworth's "sublimity in tenderness." Marlowe's fusion of "terrible" subjects with a vigorous technique produced sublime effects (There were times, Swinburne knew, when Marlowe failed to produce this fusion—*CM*, 272; *JW*, 294), as did Webster's "sheer force of tragic and noble horror" (*JW*, 294). Tennyson's "Rizpah" transformed terror into beauty. And Charles Lamb was an effective drama critic because of his alertness to the sublime in Marlowe's Faustus, Marston's Andrugio, Tourneur's Vindice, Ford's Calantha, and Webster's Duchess (*L&W*, 284). There is a "delicate line," Swinburne observed in a remark that still maintains its truth, between "the impressive and the terrible," between "the horrible and the loathsome" (*W&B*, 176). For the most part these men were all able to draw it.

Sublimity was one of the final agents, then, of an exalted harmony. In two passages on Rossetti, one simple and direct, the other complex and baroque, Swinburne enumerated the traits of genius leading to what he called an "ardent" music or, to modify one of Shelley's concepts, a "heat of spiritual life." He discerned these essential traits: grace, motion, sweetness, and force which operate with "an instinct and a resolution of excellence" to produce the "heat" (tension) which in turn guides "without constraining the bodily grace of motion," prevents any "malformation of thought or word," gives "charm and power" to the work, and possesses a sweetness "that cannot be weak" and a force "that will not be rough."

> There must be an instinct and a resolution of excellence which will allow no shortcoming or malformation of thought or word: there must be so natural a sense of right as to make any such deformity or defect impossible, and leave upon the work done no trace of any effort to avoid or to achieve. It must be serious, simple, perfect; and it must be thus by evident and native impulse. The mark of painstaking as surely lowers the level of style as any sign of negligence; in the best work there must be no trace of a laborious or a languid hand. (*DGR*, 4-5)

In the more complex baroque passage Swinburne tests Rossetti's work by these standards:

> . . . besides that particular colour and flavour which distinguishes each master's work from that of all other masters . . . the general

qualities of all great poetry are separately visible and divisible; strength, sweetness, affluence, simplicity, depth, light, harmony, variety, bodily grace and range of mind and force of soul and ease of flight, the scope and sweep of wing to impel the might and weight of thought through the air and light of speech with a motion as of mere musical impulse; and not less the live bloom of perfect words, warm as breath and fine as flower-dust, which lies light as air upon the parting of lyric leaves that open into song; the rare and ineffable mark of a supreme singing power, an element too subtle for solution in any crucible of analysis, though its presence or absence be patent at a first trial to all who have a sense of taste. (*DGR*, 44)

These qualities are now grouped as contraries: "strength" is joined with "sweetness" or gentleness; "affluence" (which anticipates T. S. Eliot's "abundance") is paired with "simplicity," which in turn suggests economy, directness, and the elimination of what Pater called "surplusage"; "depth" finds its complement in "light," in airiness and briskness (the virtues for which Swinburne praised Arnold); and "harmony" with its connotations of a totally progressive arrangement is opposed by "variety." Massinger's *A Very Woman* succeeds in being "the flower of all his [Massinger's] flock" largely because of its "at once so delicate and so masculine" workmanship (*CS*, 287, 288). Each pair of values conveys tension, and the result, as Swinburne explained in the first passage, is "so natural a sense of right" that it excludes "deformity or defect."

It is in such complex works that the highest mode of inner music, "the great, single, aesthetic end of art" (*BJ*, 29), is achieved, and the " 'spirit of sense,' " a phrase borrowed from Shakespeare (*W&B*, 242), is at last secured. The "most inward and intimate effects" of "the sensuous and the meditative elements of poetry" in concert with imagination, fancy, passion, tact, gathering form, firm outline, and sublimity provide a synthesis of beauty superior to any of its elements and greater than the sum of their combinations.[13] These terms overlap, and a few brief concluding examples of Swinburne on writers who achieved this exalted music will show affinities also with his principles of organic form. Coleridge's "Christabel" is harmonized, and "Kubla Khan" reflects an "exquisite instinct" fused with "a subtle science of verse" in a "high and ample" music (*C*, 145, 146). Shelley surpasses Keats's "matchless refinement" and "singular intensity" and Wordsworth's sober harmonics to achieve art's "most inward and intimate effects" (*W&B*, 242). Arnold's songs of Callicles were perfect in their harmony and of a general and single beauty (*MA*, 78-79).

The unified outline, the connected purpose and "gathering form," and the series of graduated parts and details resolved and harmonized constituted a striking ideal in a day enamored of proliferation and baroque effects.

In a passage on Blake, Swinburne said that the critic has to know "what the workman was after." "Get well hold of the mystic, and you will then at once get a better view and comprehension of the painter and poet." If, however, "through fear of tedium or offence" the critic "refuses to be at such pains, he will find himself, while following Blake's trace as poet or painter, brought up sharply within a very short tether" (*WB*, 172). Elsewhere Swinburne said that "the essence of an artist is that he should be articulate" (*MA*, 89). To present Swinburne's articulateness, as well as the pains he took to serve creative power wherever he found it, has been my endeavor in this book. One of his acts of service was to expose and condemn the pretentious and the sham; another was to praise; and there was yet a third and difficult one: "to sift and test" genius "by proof of syllable and letter" (*NTS*, 373). To engage in this latter task, so painstaking and thorough in its demands, was to foreshadow a preoccupation of twentieth-century critics.

Swinburne's death on April 10, 1909, brought to a close an extremely productive life. Unlike Thomas Hardy, who "had done all that he meant to do," or Joseph Conrad, who was "not satisfied" (his work, he wrote, "is something—but not *the* thing I tried for"), Swinburne so far as we know left no statement as to whether he had, in fact, fulfilled his life ideal as artist and critic. Nor should we be particularly surprised: self-sufficiency was typical of him; his letters reveal little about what he thought of his own work either as he was writing it or as it appeared in print. His pen had moved surely, and the results, he would probably have said, were their own justification; it was not for him to make long-view judgments. Freedom, zest, scope of mind, and intensity of feeling are his hallmarks. Few critical efforts have been as innately stimulating, as pleasurable, and as consistently wise. He deserves his rank as critic not because he was always original but because he provided unique insights, reflected a broad interest in several cultures, fashioned an effective practical criticism from a synthesis of his several inheritances and, finally, gave us a style of marvelous virtuosity. Each reader reserves the right, of course, to withhold his approval of the prose; even from this distance of fifty-five years Swinburne dissuades those who seek the half-way position. His unabashed energy seems in these days of the casual style too intemperate, and one is never of Swinburne's party without knowing it. But those who may wish to join will find his effulgence, his humor and irony, even his cantankerousness, exhilarating, and his wisdom and commitment to the importance of art admirable. For these qualities, and for others named throughout this book, he himself may be said to wear one of those crowns reserved by Apollo for the dedicated and talented man. He belongs among the few truly vital critics of literature and art.

NOTES

CHAPTER I

1. *The Swinburne Letters*, ed. Cecil Lang (6 vols., New Haven, 1959-1962), I, xviii; hereafter cited as *Letters*. Since Swinburne was apparently unable to read German well and seemed generally out of sympathy with German literature and philosophy— he was of two minds on Goethe—the question of Germanic influence is at best of minor concern. Whatever affinities appear were probably absorbed through Coleridge and Carlyle, and possibly through Lamb via Crabbe Robinson. See Rose Egan, *The Genesis of the Theory of "Art for Art's Sake" in Germany and in England* (2 parts, Northampton, Mass. and Paris, 1921 and 1924), Part I, 13-16. C. E. Vaughan, *English Literary Criticism* (London, 1896), pp. ix-cii, deals with similar matters; pages lxxi-cii deal with Carlyle and the Germans.

2. Clyde Kenneth Hyder, *Swinburne's Literary Career and Fame* (reprinted, New York, 1963), p. 181, says: "In pleading for Chapman, he was something of a pioneer, as in his championship of Blake and the Brontës." Robert F. Gleckner, *The Piper and the Bard* (Detroit, 1959), pp. 33-34, opens his study of Blake by examining Swinburne's statement of the need to respect Blake's underlying organicism.

3. See Clyde Hyder's introduction to "Swinburne: Changes of Aspect and Short Notes," *PMLA*, LVIII (1943), 223-244, for conjectures on the dating. Hyder supplies energetic descriptions of Swinburne's invective and his "code for dealing with critics." He also agrees that Swinburne's changing attitude towards Whitman was "evolutionary rather than revolutionary"; it was the "Whitmanites" who distressed him. (*Ibid.*, p. 224).

4. The page references are to the manuscript in the Huntington Library Collections. I am grateful to Robert O. Dugan, Librarian, for permission to quote from this work.

5. ["Review of *A Note on Charlotte Brontë*], *Academy*, XII (1877), 234. When Swinburne attacked critics, Dowden gallantly raised no quarrel: "For one of us poor tribe . . . to be distinguished as a polecat, or an anthropoid ape, or even (if cheap science accept the term) as an aborted ascidian, may not seem a fate too severe."

6. By 1865, in addition to the 1853 preface to *Poems*, Arnold had published *On Translating Homer* (1861) and essays on the Guérins, Heine, Marcus Aurelius, Spinoza, Joubert, the influence of the academies, and the function of criticism. The professorship of poetry had begun in 1857. Swinburne attended Balliol College from 1856-1860. According to Edmund Gosse, Swinburne attended Arnold's first lectures, but was disappointed. Swinburne himself reported that his reactions on hearing Arnold deliver his Oxford lecture on the academies did not change: Arnold's subject was "merely fantastic" and his "process of deduction vicious and baseless" (*MA*, 113-114). Swinburne's admiration for Arnold's poetry had begun in 1849 and was never to cease. Gosse conjectures that Arnold's moderation and John Nichol's prejudice against Arnold in favor of Carlyle were responsible for Swinburne's coolness.—*The Life of Algernon Charles Swinburne*, Vol. xix of *The Complete Works of Algernon Charles Swinburne*, Bonchurch ed., ed. E. Gosse and T. J. Wise (20 vols., London, 1925-1927), pp. 50-51; hereafter cited as *Life*. I shall refer to the Bonchurch ed. as *Works*.

7. "The Chaotic School," hitherto existing in scraps—twenty-two blue foolscap

pages—scattered throughout various collections, public and private, and now assembled through the perseverance of Cecil Y. Lang, presents a fascinating problem in Swinburne criticism. Professor Lang has generously allowed me to read his unpublished introduction and to quote from it. Swinburne's view of Browning throughout these pages is negative, and contrasts greatly with the famous incidental passages on Browning in *George Chapman*. The difference is one of emphasis. In "The Chaotic School" Swinburne overstates the case, at times with engaging cleverness, making the essay one of his most humorous and most sarcastic forays, and at other times with lapses of taste and long-winded repetitions. And there are glimmerings of the panegyric he was later to publish on Browning's quality of *mind*. Cecil Lang places the work in the early sixties:

> The essay was composed between May 1, 1863, the opening date of the Royal Academy exhibition referred to, and May 28 (or a little later), 1864, the date of publication of Browning's *Dramatis Personae*, which is not alluded to (in an essay where nothing is overlooked, no opportunity lost) and which we know Swinburne to have read soon after its publication, probably within a fortnight (*Letters*, I, 100-01). The distance between these two terminal dates can probably be diminished a little.

8. There are several references to these poems in both the letters and the criticism. "Out of the Cradle Endlessly Rocking" was "the most lovely and wonderful thing" Swinburne had read "for years and years. I could rhapsodize about it for ten more pages, there is such beautiful skill and subtle power in every word of it. . . ." (Letter to Lord Houghton). In a letter to William Michael Rossetti about an edition of Whitman he regretted that Rossetti had chosen to omit "Sleep," "the lovely and most pleasurable poem on night and sleep and sleepers. . . ." "Camp of Green," from *Drum Taps*, was a "great idol of mine for its perfect classic (*not* academic but purely classic) beauty." The elegy on Lincoln—"a superb piece of music and colour. It is infinitely impressive when read aloud"—he first saw in the inscribed presentation copy of the fourth edition of *Leaves of Grass* Whitman had sent to him: "W. W. (by the by they are Wordsworth's initials—c'est joli) has sent me a copy of his last poems with inscription; they are very fine" (*UM*, 413, *WB*, 345, and *Letters* I, 58, 267, 268, and 204). Gay Wilson Allen, *The Solitary Singer: A Critical Biography of Walt Whitman* (New York, 1955), pp. 430-431, 445-446, 526-527, examines the matter of Swinburne's responses to Whitman and says that the importance of Swinburne's supposed "recantation" has been exaggerated by the biographers and critics.

9. *A Study of Swinburne* (New York, 1926), pp. 189-190.

10. "Walter Pater's Literary Theory and Criticism," *Victorian Studies*, I (1957), 32. Wellek says nothing about Pater's indebtedness to Swinburne, but this is a subject which has remained largely unstudied. Neither Gosse, *Life*, nor Thomas Wright, *The Life of Walter Pater* (2 vols., London, 1907), reports more than the merest scraps concerning their relationship, and nothing of any consequence on the matter of possible influences.

11. Swinburne rarely discussed his methods of writing prose. On one occasion, though, in an unpublished letter to John Addington Symonds, February 1, 1876, shortly after the appearance of his introduction to Charles Wells's *Joseph and his Brethren*, he described a revision. He had written the introduction to the play when he was at Oxford. He was unable to have it published at the time.

> Then I let the paper lie by for ten or twelve years, thinking it must be too crude and boyish for any use, rather thankful it was not in type to reproach me; till at last I took it up and pared it down and filled it out with hardly more than a

few sentences added and certain excesses curtailed—and the result is at last the resurrection of the book. I do hope it will now get a hearing.

I am grateful to Mr. J. Shum Cox, Librarian, Bristol University, for permission to quote from this letter, a copy of which was made by Symonds' daughter, Katharine Furse, and which is now part of the Bristol University Symonds collection.

12. *The Works of Matthew Arnold* (15 vols., London, 1903-1904), III, 5-6; hereafter cited as *Works of Matthew Arnold*. "The Function of Criticism at the Present Time," in which this passage occurs, was published first in the National Review, November, 1864.

13. *Byron 1824-1924* (Oxford, 1924), p. 6. According to Gosse, *Life*, pp. 156, 185-186, Swinburne "was not enthusiastic" about Taine. He reluctantly went to watch him receive an honorary degree from Oxford in 1871; to Sainte-Beuve, "whom he never appreciated," he "owed little or nothing."

CHAPTER II

1. There are many accounts of Swinburne's prolonged, sometimes nasty quarrel with Frederick James Furnivall to wrest Shakespeare from what he felt were the pedant scholars. Both men had devoted years of their lives to the study of Elizabethan literature. The most useful sketch of the relationship, supported by copious notes to the chief documents, is Clyde Kenneth Hyder's *Swinburne's Literary Career and Fame*, pp. 186-191. Professor Hyder says: "A confusion between what can be decided in criticism only by innate taste and what can be determined by mechanical methods has often led the man of genius to distrust the man of learning. Though destitute of neither the instincts nor the erudition of the scholar, Swinburne was perhaps so oversensitive to this confusion that he fell into the error of trespassing on the province of scientific method" (p. 186).

2. Swinburne complained also of Shelley's poor proficiency at Greek, drawing for support upon no less a classicist than Benjamin Jowett. Shelley's scholarship "was that of a clever but idle boy in the upper forms of a public school. His translation from Plato, as Mr. Jowett tells me, and his translation from Euripides, as I know by personal experiment, having carefully collated it with the original text, absolutely swarm with blunders, sometimes, certainly, resulting in sheer nonsense" (*Letters*, V, 122). I might remind the reader of Swinburne's charming portrait sketch, "Recollections of Professor Jowett," which conveys much sustained personal warmth. Swinburne praised most of Jowett's literary preferences, but confessed some slight disappointment over the Master of Balliol's tepidity towards Charles Lamb.

3. Poe's only other comment on the poem follows: "Although the rhythm here is one of the most difficult, the versification could scarcely be improved. No nobler *theme* ever engaged the pen of poet. It is the soul-elevating idea, that no man can consider himself entitled to complain of Fate while, in his adversity, he still retains the unwavering love of woman."—*The Achievement of American Criticism*, ed. Clarence A. Brown (New York, 1954), p. 211.

4. In his preface to "Adonais" Shelley had done as much as anyone to perpetuate the myth of a crucified Keats. William Michael Rossetti in his *The Poetical Works of Percy Bysshe Shelley: Including Various Additional Pieces from MS. and Other Sources* (2 vols., London, 1870), which Swinburne reviewed in his note to *NTS*, said that "Shelley was not alone at the time in supposing this, and it is still a popular tradition

among poetic readers. . . ." Lord Houghton (Richard Monckton Milnes) in his *Life, Letters, and Literary Remains of John Keats* (2 vols., London, 1848), had attempted to set the record straight.

5. See Professor Hyder's "Swinburne: Changes of Aspect and Short Notes" for conjectures on the dating.

6. *Ibid.*, pp. 225, 232, reviews Swinburne's excoriation of Tennyson over the art for art's sake matter, and quotes Tennyson's offending epigram, "Art for Art's Sake," published *Alfred Lord Tennyson: A Memoir by His Son* (2 Vols., London and New York, 1897) II, 92.

> Art for Art's sake! Hail, truest Lord of Hell!
> Hail, Genius, Master of the Moral Will!
> "The filthiest of all paintings painted well
> Is mightier than the purest painted ill!"
> Yea, mightier than the purest painted well,
> So prone are we towards the broad way to Hell.

7. Vernon Lee's French critic and novelist, André Marcel, who visits Yorkshire in order to study the Brontës, says to his companions Dorothy Orme and Mrs. Blake: "It is extraordinary how aesthetical questions invariably end in ethical ones when treated by English people; and yet in practice you have given the world as great an artistic literature as any other nation, perhaps even greater."—"On Novels," *Baldwin: Being Dialogues on Views and Aspirations* (Boston, 1886), p. 209.

8. For a lucid Victorian survey of historical critical principles see W. Basil Worsfold's *The Principles of Criticism: An Introduction to the Study of Literature* (London, 1897). In this now almost forgotten work, based on traditional theories, Worsfold is at his best in the chapters on Plato and Aristotle, three chapters devoted to Addison's contributions to aesthetics, a review of Arnold the critic, whose disciple Worsfold seems to have been, and a treatment of the novel as a literary form.

9. W. Brooks Drayton Henderson, *Swinburne and Landor: A Study of Their Spiritual Relationship and Its Effect on Swinburne's Moral and Poetic Development* (London, 1918), pp. 25, 26–27. To demonstrate affinities, Henderson uses a plethora of quotations; Landor's immense reading in several literatures, his zeal for freedom, his classicism, and his "Boythorn impetuosity of judgment" do seem to parallel Swinburne. Henderson's case seems overdrawn, though useful. Landor lacked, among other things, Swinburne's range of ironic and satiric effects and his enthusiasm for the Elizabethans.

It is worth noting that Addison in a *Spectator* paper (#291), on *Paradise Lost* says: "A true critic ought to dwell rather upon excellences than imperfections, to discover the concealed beauties of a writer, and communicate to the world such things as are worth their observation. The most exquisite words and finest strokes of an author are those which very often appear the most doubtful and exceptionable to a man who wants a relish for polite learning; and they are these which a sour undistinguished critic generally attacks with the greatest violence." The question of Addison's influence on Victorian aesthetics requires more exploration than it has received. Swinburne had read Addison but seems to have held him of little account as a direct influence on himself. Swinburne's biographers omit references to Addison from their indexes. W. Basil Worsfold calls Addison "the first genuine critic" to appear in England since the Renaissance and credits him with introducing "fresh considerations" which affected all genres of art—*The Principles of Criticism*, pp. 59–60.

10. Swinburne must have been pleased, however, to find Arnold's flattering use of his own phrases on Byron in the preface to *Poetry of Byron*, published in 1881.

"With the instinct of a poet Mr. Swinburne has seized upon" the "wonderful power" of Byron's personality: it lies in " 'the splendid and imperishable excellence which covers all his offences and outweighs all his defects: *the excellence of sincerity and strength.*' " *Works of Matthew Arnold*, IV, 145.

11. The comparative method was devastatingly parodied by Max Beerbohm in *A Christmas Garland* (London, 1912).

12. For the details of Swinburne's altercations with Austin, see Hyder, *Swinburne's Literary Career and Fame*, pp. 139, 160, 201-202.

13. The essay was an important moment in the Swinburne-Furnivall controversy, and provided Furnivall with a small triumph. Swinburne had assumed that certain words in the play were not used by Shakespeare; Furnivall, in two letters to *The Spectator* which he issued later as a pamphlet, proved that the words do occur in the plays. See Hyder, *Swinburne's Literary Career and Fame*, pp. 188-189.

14. While Swinburne rejected Little Nell, he was on the whole fond of portraits of children, waxing enthusiastic over George Eliot's and Mrs. Molesworth's depictions of the young (*R*, 367-368) and calling William Blake and Christina Rossetti the "high priest" and "high priestess" of "baby-worship respectively" (*VH*, 89, 190). Andrea del Sarto's "superb boy-baby . . . attempting to embrace his round fat knees with his fat round arms, and laughing with delight in the difficulty is a more triumphant child than ever painter drew before or since" (*OMF*, 194). Some of this fondness may have come from Landor, so W. B. D. Henderson, *Swinburne and Landor*, pp. 24-25, believes. Other possible sources I leave to the guesses of the literary psychologists.

15. *Swinburne* (New York, 1926), p. 188.

16. Swinburne refers to Thomas Medwin's *The Life of Shelley* (2 vols., London, 1847) and Thomas Jefferson Hogg's *The Life of Percy Bysshe Shelley* (2 vols., London, 1858), both untrustworthy accounts.

17. "Swinburne as a Critic," *The Sewanee Review*, XXXII (1924), 407. W. B. D. Henderson's phrase for this ability of Swinburne was "the power of emotional exegesis." Henderson said also that Swinburne "is a great critic because he was greatly temperamented, succeeding by force of genius in a school that counts its ephemera by the thousand."—*Swinburne and Landor*, pp. 46, 44.

18. Edmund Gosse, who confessed to an early hero-worship of Swinburne, described the effect of the new tone Swinburne achieved in the 1867 essays on Morris and Arnold:

> For the first time in English literature, an attempt was here made to produce a concrete and almost plastic conception of the work of an author, not minutely analysed or coldly condensed, but presented as if by an inspired neophyte. By all young aestheticians of that and the next few years, the advent of the *Fortnightly Review* with a critical article by Swinburne in it was looked forward to as a great event.—*Life*, p. 156.

19. Chaucer's special quality Swinburne expressed this way: he "was in the main a French or Italian poet, lined thoroughly and warmly throughout with the substance of an English humorist" (*NEP*, 98).

20. "John Addington Symonds: as a Theoretical and as a Practical Critic," Ph.D. Diss., University of Michigan, 1941, p. 169. E. K. Brown remarks that Swinburne's criticism rivals Symonds' "critical papers" in "zeal and verbosity." (Brown is excellent on Swinburne's poetry, but this particular equation is, I think, false. Symonds, in fact, expressed his own dissatisfaction with much of his prose. Zeal is hardly one of his characteristics; and his verbosity is of a far quieter, less original order than Swinburne's.)

Brown, "Swinburne: A Centenary Estimate" (1937), reprinted in *Victorian Literature: Modern Essays in Criticism,* ed. Austin Wright (New York, 1961), p. 307.

    21. Arthur Symons, *The Symbolist Movement in Literature* (new ed., New York, 1958), p. 48, echoes Swinburne: "The ideal of lyric poetry, certainly, is to be this passive, flawless medium for the deeper consciousness of things, the mysterious voice of that mystery which lies about us, out of which we have come, and into which we shall return. It is not without reason that we cannot analyse a perfect lyric." The explications of our own day Swinburne would have regarded as partial failures.

CHAPTER III

    1. By placing Swinburne in the Victorian hortatory tradition I am in disagreement with Newton Arvin who has said unequivocally that "Swinburne's criticism is exclusively aesthetic. . . . The rôle of the critic which allies him with the prophet is a rôle which Swinburne never fills . . ."—"Swinburne as a Critic," pp. 411, 412. Besides my own analysis, I am able to offer Ruth Child's "Swinburne's Mature Standards of Criticism," *PMLA,* LII (1937), 870-879, as further proof of Swinburne's prophetism. Arvin is aware, and rightly, that Swinburne's aesthetic *manner* is often hortatory, and then it is at its worst: "There are times when his speech falls into the monotonous liturgical drone of a half-transported priest: his gait becomes reverent and ceremonial and rhythmic like an acolyte's, and the air is heavy and sweet with incense of celebration" (p. 409). Miss Child, herself intentionally polemical, hoped to correct certain misconceptions about Swinburne, particularly the one that he is solely an impressionist critic. Although appreciative of Swinburne's aesthetic strain, Miss Child found the hortatory and moralistic strain more representative. Thomas E. Connolly, "Swinburne's Theory of the End of Art," *ELH,* XIX (1952), 277-290, provides a fuller historical explanation of Swinburne's criticism. His thesis is that Swinburne was all along of consistent mind, that he did not begin his career as a follower of art for art's sake, nor did he turn "to philanthropic or political ideals only when his own lyric inspiration waned." The flirtation with art for art's sake was merely a "temporary departure from his fundamental theory."

    2. It was Matthew Arnold, it should be noted, who in 1863 provided the initial gloss for Philistinism and gave tongue to a concept Carlyle had only mumbled. The essay was "Heine"; and since Swinburne had read deeply in Arnold's prose, may be helpful to review something of the substance and the tone of that presentation. The whole builds smoothly and includes slight touches of irony along the way. The final image is vigorous and keenly felt.

> *Philistinism!*—we have not the expression in English. Perhaps we have not the word because we have so much of the thing. At Soli, I imagine, they did not talk of solecisms; and here, at the very headquarters of Goliath, nobody talks of Philistinism. The French have adopted the term *épicier* (grocer), to designate the sort of being whom the Germans designate by the term Philistine; but the French term . . . is really, I think, in itself much less apt and expressive than the German term. Efforts have been made to obtain in English some term equivalent to *Philister* or *épicier*; Mr. Carlyle has made several efforts: "respectability with its thousand gigs," he says;—well, the occupant of every one of

these gigs is, Mr. Carlyle means, a Philistine. However, the word *respectable* is far too valuable a word to be thus perverted from its proper meaning; if the English are ever to have a word for the thing we are speaking of,—and so prodigious are the changes which the modern spirit is introducing, that even we English shall perhaps one day come to want such a word,—I think we had much better take the term Philistine itself.—*Works of Matthew Arnold*, III, 177-180. The essay first appeared in *The Cornhill*, VIII (1863), 233-249.

3. Swinburne was amused by the glossary of allusions Chapman appended to his first poem. Chapman had concluded that his "figures and similes . . . justify themselves, and prove sufficiently authentical to such as understand them; for the rest, God help them. . . . I cannot do as others, make day seem a lighter woman than she is, by painting her" (*GC*, 155-156). Ben Jonson also had his say, though in gentler terms: Jonson—and Swinburne quoted him—said that if his writing strikes a reader as obscure, and if it develops that the fault is "the hearer's or reader's want of understanding, I am not to answer for them no more than for their not listening or marking; I must neither find them ears nor mind" (*BJ*, 120).

4. For discussion of the complex nature of English aestheticism see Albert J. Farmer, *Le Mouvement esthétique et "décadent" en Angleterre*, 1873-1900; *Paul de Reul, L'Oeuvre de Swinburne*; Rose Frances Egan, *The Genesis of the Theory of "Art for Art's Sake" in Germany and in England*; Louise Rosenblatt, *L'idée de l'art pour l'art dans la littérature anglaise pendant la période victorienne* (Paris, 1931); Holbrook Jackson, *The Eighteen Nineties* (New York, 1914); Vida Scudder, *The Life of the Spirit in the Modern English Poets* (Cambridge, Mass., 1895); Mario Praz, *The Romantic Agony* (New York, 1933); Jerome H. Buckley, *The Victorian Temper* (Cambridge, Mass., 1951); and Helmut Gerber's "The Nineties: Beginning, End or Transition?" *English Institute Essays* (New York, 1959), pp. 50-79. I might also list my "The Salome of Arthur Symons and Aubrey Beardsley," *Criticism*, II (1960), 150-163; "Toward an 'Un-Definition' of Decadent as Applied to British Literature of the Nineteenth Century," *Journal of Aesthetics and Art Criticism*, XVIII (1959), 258-264; and "Athens and Troy: Notes on John Addington Symonds' Aestheticism," *English Literature in Transition*, V, No. 5 (1962), 14-26.

5. *Rousseau and Romanticism* (New York, 1959), p. 168. For a valuable discussion of the paradox in Swinburne and Shelley see William R. Rutland, *Swinburne: A Nineteenth Century Hellene* (Oxford, 1931), pp. 79f. For Keats see the letters of 23 and 24 August 1819 to John Taylor and John Hamilton Reynolds, *The Poetical Works and Other Writings of John Keats*, ed. H. Buxton Forman (8 vols., New York, 1938-1939), viii, 30-35; hereafter cited as *Works of John Keats*.

6. Harold Nicolson, *Swinburne*, p. 106, takes a lighter view of the *Notes*, I think, than Swinburne would have desired. Nicolson feels that they are largely disingenuous, "crackers fired impishly to startle his contemporaries out of the domestic idyll. . . ."

7. Swinburne continues his high-spirited attack:
Children themselves are inoculated with the spirit, and speak with tongues— the cloven tongues of the Pentecost of fools. The Rugby and muscular-Christian schools have pretty well infected the very race of boys with Prudhomme views —exquisite Prudhomme sentiment and "godly, manly" Prudhomme religion. But for these "earnest" and wonderful pedagogues, could mortal have realised the great conception, Prudhomme a boy? Prudhomme developing his muscles and morals at cricket or in the boats? Prudhomme—impossible and irreverent idea! —quivering from the recent birch? Human fancy reels backward aghast from

the godless and monstrous notion. Let the man be as moral and responsible as he will, could not the poor boy have been left at peace in his quiet honest animal condition? By no means; Prudhomme must have him too. Prudhomme walks among us as a man—as many men, for indeed he is everywhere; we brush against him in the street, sit close up to him in public places, and know not that our Master is there. He smiles on us, speaks to us, is gentle, tolerant, knowing, charitable, brilliant, pleasant—you would take him for any ordinary citizen; but the man has in him, as we said, something of the infinite and inscrutable force of nature—some fiery particle of the divine breath that makes and unmakes. For the Dunce is master of us all, and does with us what he will (*PA*, 402-403). Georges Lafourcade, *La Jeunesse de Swinburne 1837-1867* (2 vols., Paris, 1928) II, 326-342, treats Swinburne's responses to "*le puritanisme*" and "*le philistisme*" very well.

8. "The Lesson of Millais," *The Savoy*, III (1896), 57-58.

9. He chose Baudelaire to illustrate his point. The French were hostile to Baudelaire because he did not "break off on occasion in the middle of his proper work to lend a shove forward to some theory of progress . . ." (*CB*, 417).

10. Swinburne's emphasis on *spirit* provoked answers from at least two notable Victorians, one a critic and the other a poet. The critic was J. C. Shairp. Stimulated by Walter Bagehot's famous contrast between the pure and ornate styles, he regretted at some length the development during the seventies of a fashionable poetry of meretricious ornament, called it an "evil," and rather pompously cast his vote for the "pure style" of "high thinking and noble living." He seemed to detect in aestheticism a levelling and conformist element.—*Aspects of Poetry* (Oxford, 1881), pp. 157-158. The poet was Coventry Patmore. In his essay "Bad Morality is Bad Art," written in the nineties, he spoke for the conventional position and the "orthodox truth of humanity." As he cast a jaundiced eye at aestheticism's several guises, he lamented that truth was a maiden wearing garments so out of fashion that artists in tune with the *Zeitgeist* called her "old frump." Her whole wardrobe was "fallen . . . into decay." He longed for an artist who would provide the distressed maiden with new clothing and return art to healthier channels: "Happy is he who shall be found to have contributed even a ribbon or two towards the renovation of her wardrobe. . . ."—*Principle in Art* (London, 1898), pp. 19-20. Needless to say, Swinburne remained impervious to such agitations. Edward Dowden was a better known critic who appreciated the aesthetic position. In *Transcripts and Studies* (London, 1888), p. 224, he reprimanded readers and critics who judge art "merely by its ethical tendency." This is to judge "unjustly," Dowden says, "and the injustice is extreme in the case of Mr. Swinburne. He has widened the bounds of song; he has created a new music in English verse; he has enlarged the instrument of expression."

11. Wordsworth, whom Swinburne admired in so many ways, was also a calculating maker of formulas. He backed the Wanderer's "moral paces" and reinforced "the verbose reiterations of that inexhaustible itinerant with the yet more indefatigable infacundity [sic] poured forth upon 'the pensive Sceptic' by 'the philosophic Priest.' " Wordsworth was at his best "in his own far loftier land of natural contemplation," where he had little "prepense or fixed purpose." In "Resolution and Independence" "the lyrist is likewise a thinker"; there is "a breath of prouder music, a ring of keener sound, than we expect or admit in elegy . . ." (*W&B*, 231).

12. A. J. Farmer, *Le Mouvement esthétique et 'décadent' en Angleterre*, p. 155, says that in the *Blake* Swinburne "*emét à son sujet quelques réflexions épigrammatiques qui annoncent le ton de l'essai de Wilde.*" The essay is "Pen, Pencil and Poison."

13. Gautier's character in *Madamoiselle de Maupin,* ed. Adolphe Boschot (Paris, [1955]), p. 133, speaks of women, but his theme is art as well: *"Je préfère une jolie bouche à un joli mot, et une épaule bien modelée à une vertu, même théologale; je donne rais cinquante âmes pour un pied mignon, et toute la poésie et tous les poètes pour la main de Jeanne d'Aragon ou le front de la vierge de Foligno."*

14. In a charming but now forgotten piece of minor Victoriana, Sir Edward Strachey's *Talk at a Country House* (Boston and New York, 1894), the subject of theology and art occupies the attention of Foster, the guest at Sutton Court, and the Squire. Foster asks whether Tennyson had not "opened a new road in literature, in what he writes so freely as to another life, or rather as to our life after death?" The Squire agrees, but only if Foster is willing to "draw a line which shall put on one side Shakespeare, and on the other the New Testament, the Pilgrim's Progress, and all our Hymns of the Christian Church."

Foster says that that was his intention, but at the same time, if he were asked whether or not the writings of our great theologians were part of English literature, he "should hardly know what to answer."

The squire explains: "I think you are right. There is a real distinction, though it should be one of relationship, not of separation, between our thoughts of this life and of that which is to come. Poets and men of letters deal principally with the one, and preachers and theologians with the other; but Tennyson, while belonging to the former, has put himself in touch with the latter, with more openness and less of reticence than usual." The squire contrasts Wordsworth's "Intimations Ode" and Tennyson's "In Memoriam," perspicaciously noting Tennyson's dynamism: "The Idea, the Motive, underlying Wordsworth's Ode is that Man has in him another and truer life than that of Nature, of which he has indications in himself which seem like the recollections of a divine Mind whence he has come; while in Tennyson's poem the Master thought is going forward into a world to come" (pp. 112-113). We might wish that all Victorian squires had been capable of such discriminations.

15. In a letter to the *Pall Mall Gazette. Works of John Ruskin,* ed. Cook and Wedderburn, 39 vols., London, 1903-1912), X, 459.

16. Jerome H. Buckley, *Tennyson: The Growth of a Poet* (Cambridge, Mass., 1960), pp. 176f., rejects "Swinburne's complaint—echoed by many others," and explains that Tennyson used medieval models for his characterization of Arthur.

17. Macaulay had earlier made the same criticism of Byron:

Lord Byron, like Mr. Wordsworth, had nothing dramatic in his genius. He was indeed the reverse of a great dramatist, the very antithesis to a great dramatist. All of his characters, Harold looking on the sky, from which his country and the sun are disappearing together, the Giaour, standing apart in the gloom of the side aisle, and casting a haggard scowl from under his long hood at the crucifix and the censer, Conrad leaning on his sword by the watch tower, Lara smiling on the dancers, Alp gazing steadily on the fatal cloud as it passes before the moon, Manfred wandering among the precipices of Berne. . . . Ugo at the bar, Lambro frowning on the siesta of his daughter and Juan, Cain presenting his unacceptable offering, are essentially the same. The varieties are varieties merely of age, situation, and outward show.—*The Complete Writings of Lord Macaulay* (20 vols., Boston and New York, 1900), XII, 217-218.

18. Oscar Wilde, "The Decay of Lying," *The Complete Works of Oscar Wilde* (12 vols., New York, 1923-1927), V, 24-25, says: "I do not know anything in the whole history of literature sadder than the artistic career of Charles Reade. He wrote one beautiful book, *The Cloister and the Hearth* . . . and wasted the rest of his life in

a foolish attempt to be modern, to draw public attention to the state of our convict prisons . . . and lunatic asylums. . . . Charles Reade, an artist, a scholar, a man with a true sense of beauty, raging and roaring over the abuses of contemporary life . . . is really a sight for the angels to weep over."

CHAPTER IV

1. Vida Scudder, *The Life of the Spirit in the Modern English Poets*, p. 17. J. C. Shairp, *On Poetic Interpretation of Nature* (Edinburgh, 1877), p. 108, notes that "early poets hardly ever handle nature except to interweave it with human action and emotion, and as set off against the life of man." Thomson's *Seasons* is "the most striking example" of such poetry since the ancients. To regard nature "by itself, and as existing apart from man, is the mental attitude of a late and cultivated time, even though the descriptions may seem to be plain and unadorned." Shairp had the mid-Victorians in mind.

2. "Two Paths on Art," *Works of John Ruskin*, XVI, 325.

3. *The Age of Paradox: A Biography of England 1841-1851* (New York, 1952), p. 462. Dodds refers to the exhibition itself as "the Victorian paradox sheathed in glass."

4. "Wordsworth, Tennyson, and Browning; or, Pure, Ornate and Grotesque Art in English Poetry," in *English Critical Essays: Nineteenth Century*, ed. E. D. Jones (London, 1928), pp. 458f. Walter Pater's "Postscript" to "Appreciations" contains another notable discussion of the grotesque in art.—*The Works of Walter Pater* (8 vols., London and New York, 1900-1901), V, 241-261; hereafter cited as *Works of Walter Pater*. For an earlier and more informal treatment of the concept see Hazlitt's "On the Picturesque and the Ideal."

5. "Four Victorian Poets and an Exploding Island," *Victorian Studies*, III (1960), 249-260.

6. Critics have seldom realized, says T. E. Welby, that the influence of William Morris' color and archaisms on Swinburne was, though intense, of brief duration: "The Pre-Raphaelite phase was mainly an interruption in the natural development of Swinburne's genius."—*A Study of Swinburne*, p. 41. For an analysis of Morris' pictorial qualities see Graham Hough, *The Last Romantics* (new ed., London and New York, 1961), pp. 129-133.

7. For more praise of Tennyson's skill see *T&M*, 338-339.

8. These lines are also from "Lancelot and Elaine" (ll. 480-482). The complete passage reads as follows:

> They couched their spears and pricked their steeds, and thus,
> Their plumes driven backward by the wind they made
> In moving, all together down upon him
> Bare, as a wild wave in the wide North Sea,
> Green-glimmering toward the summit, bears, with all
> Its stormy crests that smoke against the skies,
> Down on a bark, and overbears the bark
> And him that helms it. . . .

9. "Wordsworth, Tennyson and Browning; or, Pure, Ornate and Grotesque Art in English Poetry," pp. 458.

10. The full comment is: Tennyson "has three qualities which are seldom found together except in the greatest poets: abundance, variety, and complete competence."— "In Memoriam," *Essays Ancient and Modern* (London, 1936), p. 175.

11. For example, I refer the reader to the Spasmodic poets, whose most representative poems are encumbered with detail and emotionally super-charged. See J. H. Buckley, *The Victorian Temper*, Chap. III, for an analysis of their place in Victorian literature. The prolific Lewis Morris was renowned for his word pictures, as was William Sharp.

12. One of William *Henry* Hunt's admirers was Marianne North, sister-in-law of John Addington Symonds, and herself an indefatigable painter of flowers whose trips in search of rarities took her throughout the world. She lamented that when she was ready for art school Hunt (1790-1864) was no longer taking pupils: "the only master I longed for would not teach," she said, "*i.e.* old William Hunt, whose work will live forever, as it is absolutely true to nature."—*Recollections of a Happy Life: Being the Autobiography of Marianne North,* ed. by Mrs. John Addington Symonds (2 vols., New York, 1892), I, 27. Hunt's still-life subjects were so much in demand that he had little time for the figure-studies of rustics he loved to do.

13. *Pre-Raphaelite Painters: With a Descriptive Catalogue by John Gere* (London, 1948), p. 13.

14. "Pre-Raphaelitism," *Works of John Ruskin*, XII, 388. Ernest Chesneau, *The English School of Painting, tr. by L. N. Etherington . . . Preface by Professor Ruskin* (London, 1885), pp. 197-198, rather severely dismissed the Pre-Raphaelites: "It may be that they succeed in gathering together the elements of truth in their infinity of detail, but the appearance of reality is always wanting to complete the faithfulness of their productions; they never arrive at a life-like harmonious *ensemble*." J. C. Shairp saw a similar danger: while modern science "by its contagion has stimulated the observing powers of the . . . poet" there is a tendency in poetry to go too far. Poets may make poetry "too microscopic and forgetful of that higher function which . . . ever spiritualises what it sees."—*On Poetic Interpretation of Nature*, p. 61.

These complaints have continued to our own day. Herbert Read, "Surrealism and the Romantic Principle" (1936), *The Philosophy of Modern Art* (Cleveland, 1954), pp. 135-136, includes the Pre-Raphaelites among nineteenth-century painters we should rescue "from the dustbin." He finds praiseworthy their encompassing philosophy of life which included painting, poetry, philosophy and politics; their conviction that most of their contemporaries were imbeciles in pursuing "the academic naturalism of the time"; and their willingness to experiment with sensations. But, Sir Herbert finds that they lacked a dialectic and the "real energy" to produce a revolution. "In a word, they were sentimentalists. They should have developed romanticism from the stage where Coleridge left it; instead, they developed nostalgia." Instead of reading the *Ancient Mariner*, Blake, and Keats they should have read the *Biographia Literaria* and Hegel. To contrast Morris and Marx is to measure "the failure of the Pre-Raphaelites and their followers." T. S. R. Boase, *English Art 1800-1870* (Oxford, 1959), pp. 292-293, wonders "how these men could have been so blind to much that Constable could have taught them. . . ." They did, however, break "a mannered tradition, and something survives of the vitality with which they did it." Graham Hough, *The Last Romantics* (See note 6 *supra*, pp. 40-67, has been more willing to see the complexity of the movement and the difficulties a critic has in summing up Pre-Raphaelite art. He calls for a full history of pre-Raphaelite painting in the light of modern taste. I suspect that the large subject pictures would do little to relieve the general sense of disappointment, but that many exquisite minor works would be revealed, besides a pervasive and beneficial effect on book-illustration and the smaller arts of design.—p. 66.

The following year, Denys Sutton, editor of *Apollo: The Magazine of the Arts,* devoted his December issue to Victorian art, hoping to stimulate a revitalized interest in the Pre-Raphaelites. He pointed the way by equating the "primitivism, implicit in Pre-Raphaelite doctrine" with that of Gauguin and remarked that "the hot colouring of the English artists was not all that dissimilar from Gauguin's."—p. 747.

15. Tennyson, according to his son, gave this advice to Millais, ironic when we consider Tennyson's own occasional fondness for allowing detail to take over: ". . . if you have human beings before a wall, the wall ought to be picturesquely painted, and in harmony with the idea pervading the picture, but must not be made obtrusive by the bricks being *too* minutely drawn, since it is the human beings that ought to have the real interest for us in a dramatic subject picture."—[Hallam Tennyson], *Alfred Lord Tennyson: A Memoir by his Son,* I, 380-381.

16. *Prefaces to Criticism* (New York, 1959), pp. 104-6.

17. *Works of Walter Pater,* V, 90. The astute Thomas Babington Macaulay had characterized Gray, Goldsmith, Beattie, and Cowper as poets dissatisfied with "the languid manner of their contemporaries." Their example of "mutiny against an absurd system" of eighteenth-century rules was more important than their actual thematic and formal departures. "They opened the house of bondage," said Macaulay, "but they did not enter the promised land." He said also that it was Byron, more than Scott, who contributed most to the revolution in poetry transpiring twenty years after Cowper's death.—*Writings of Lord Macaulay,* XII, 213-214.

18. *Biographia Literaria,* ed. J. Shawcross (2 vols., London, 1907), II, 14. Such a statement is only one step away from an aesthetics of the symbol. For a discussion of the ways in which both Coleridge and Carlyle anticipate twentieth-century symbolists, see Randolph Hughes, "Mallarmé: A Study in Esoteric Symbolism," *The Nineteenth Century,* CXVI (1934), 114-128, and my "Some Illustrations of Carlyle's Symbolist Imagery," *Victorian Newsletter* (1959), 31-34.

19. "On the Poetry of Wordsworth," *Prose Remains of Arthur Hugh Clough* (London, 1888), p. 315.

20. *The Works of Thomas Carlyle,* Centenary ed. (30 vols., London, 1899-1901), I, 153; hereafter cited as *Works of Thomas Carlyle.*

21. *Ibid.,* I, 175.

22. *Ibid.,* I, 156-157.

23. *Ibid.,* I, 161.

24. William A. Madden's excellent survey, "The Victorian Sensibility," *Victorian Studies,* VII (1963), 67-97, while it deals mainly with changing responses to religious absolutes and with the growth of a "private" voice in literature, treats the matter of detail briefly in relation to Tennyson. Tennyson objectified his "states of sensibility" in "the texture, shape, color, or motion of objects in the outer world in a way that Ruskin would later identify with the 'pathetic fallacy.'" See pp. 82-84.

25. For an important body of work based on the same themes, Evelyn de Morgan's brilliant paintings after Botticelli and Burne-Jones should be mentioned. It is unfortunate that so few of her paintings are in museums and galleries. Mrs. de Morgan was in general quite indifferent to selling her work. As a result, the walls of her former

home, Old Battersea House are covered with her striking canvases and provide a rare treat for anyone who goes to the trouble to arrange a visit. Since Old Battersea House now belongs to the National Trust it should eventually be open to the public on a regular basis.

26. *Works of Matthew Arnold*, III, 88-89.

27. *Works of John Ruskin*, XII, 371, 392-393.

28. *Ibid.*, XII, 349-350.

29. *The Mill on the Floss, George Eliot's Complete Works* (15 vols., Boston, 1888), X, 289.

30. *Essays Speculative and Suggestive* (3d. ed., London, 1907), p. 380.

31. Herbert M. Schueller, "John Addington Symonds as a Theoretical and Practical Critic," pp. 52-53, in commenting on this passage explains its departures from the ideas of the Romantic writers. Swinburne has further separated art and science and has changed the emphasis from "pleasure" to "beauty" and from "poetry" to "art."

32. "The Marriage of Heaven and Hell." Blake in another place named his enemies more specifically:

> The atoms of Democritus
> And Newton's particles of light
> Are sands upon the Red Sea Shore
> Where Israel's tents do shine so bright.

33. *Works of John Keats*, VI, 155.

34. As evidence of Swinburne's objectivity, we might point out that he did not rationalize Keats's failures: the "first book fell as flat as it deserved to fall"; *Endymion* contains "fulsome and liquorish endearments"; *Isabella* is "feeble and awkward in narrative . . ." (*K*, 296, 298). The many ramifications of the relationship of Keats to Swinburne have been fully explored by Georges Lafourcade, *Swinburne's Hyperion and Other Poems: with an Essay on Swinburne and Keats* (London, 1927).

35. This review pleased Arnold, Watts-Dunton reported in his preface to *Charles Dickens by Algernon Charles Swinburne; with Preface and Illustrative Notes by the Editor* (London, 1913), p. xiii. Arnold had spoken to Watts "with the deepest gratitude of Swinburne's appreciation of his poetry, and even went as far as to say that Swinburne's generous and glowing early essay had, at the time of its appearance, been the one thing needful to his being accepted as a poet first and a critic afterwards."

36. *Works of Walter Pater*, V, 258.

37. *Ibid.*, V, 21.

CHAPTER V

1. *John Keats: Selected Poetry and Letters* (New York, 1959), p. xix.

2. *Works of John Keats*, VIII, 49.

3. *Ibid.*, VIII, 128.

4. To George and Thomas Keats, *Ibid.*, VI, 102-103.

5. *See* Shelley's *A Defense of Poetry*, ed. Albert S. Cook (Boston and New York, 1890), pp. 38 and 37, and *Shelley's Poetical Works*, ed. H. Buxton Forman (5 vols., London, 1892), I and III.

6. *Charles Baudelaire: Flowers of Evil* (Norfolk, Conn., 1946), p. [ix].

7. *Algernon Charles Swinburne: A Critical Study* (New York, 1912), pp. 60, 61, 65-66.

8. Watts was adept at sculpture and pursued the art simultaneously with painting. He worked from 1873 to 1883 on an equestrian group commissioned by the Marquess of Westminster. An even more ambitious work, *Physical Energy*, was thirty-five years in the making. See *Paintings and Drawings of the Pre-Raphaelites and Their Circle* (Cambridge, Mass., 1946), pp. 113-114.

9. Cecil Lang (*Letters*, I, xxx) calls him "most unmusical of men."

10. See *Letters*, I, 93. Although Swinburne was aware of Wagner as early as the early sixties—Baudelaire had sent him a copy of his *Wagner et Tannhäuser à Paris* (*Works*, XIX, 86-87 and *Letters*, I, 87)—and wrote "The Death of Richard Wagner" and "Two Preludes" inspired by Wagner (published in *A Century of Roundels*, 1883), there is little proof that he was ever deeply influenced by Wagner's theories.

11. "Swinburne and Music," *The Spectator*, CXVIII (1917), 516. Incidentally, only one thoroughgoing effort, so far as I have been able to determine, has been made to draw exact parallels between Swinburne's poetry and musical techniques. Using a modification of Sidney Lanier's system of notation, Charles Edward Russell constructed bars of music to illustrate both melodic lines and sequences of chords inspired by the poetry. One example is his scoring of a line from "Laus Veneris," which he arranges with a main chord based on the sound of *W*, and which he calls the "chord of *W*". Changes in vowel sound supply the other notes, and, Russell says, "the effects are identical with changed chords in a dominant key in music, a device equally reasonable in poetry, and one that forcibly illustrates the essential unity of the arts. Taking note of the ingenious following of 'wings' with an allied sound in the first syllable of 'fingers,' something like this on a piano would be:

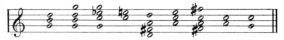

Wind's wet wings and fin - gers drip with rain."

Russell sees parallels with certain Wagnerian techniques, particularly the leitmotif. Since Swinburne was living when this piece appeared, it is interesting to conjecture whether he saw it and what his reactions might have been. Russell was convinced "that Mr. Swinburne has carried further than any of his predecessors a strictly musical view of poetry."—"Swinburne and Music," *North American Review*, CLXXXVI (1907), 427-441.

12. The poem was printed on gold paper and fastened to the frame. The fourth and sixth stanzas were printed in the *Royal Academy Catalogue*, 1865. Elizabeth and Joseph Pennell claimed that Whistler liked the verses better than his own painting. Swinburne supposedly disagreed and was ready at that time to stand up for Whistler against anybody, including Whistler himself. The Pennells reported also that Whistler was delighted with Swinburne's comments on his pictures in *NP*. See *The Life of James McNeill Whistler* (5th ed., Philadelphia and London, 1911), p. 92. Swinburne also based other poems on pictures. "Erotion" was "a comment" on one of Simeon Solomon's works (*SSV*, 453). His "Cleopatra," he reported to Gosse, illustrated a drawing by F. Sandys.—*Works*, XIX, 92.

13. The first picture is a sketch for *Variations in Flesh Colour and Green: The Balcony* (Freer Gallery, Washington). Whistler had begun the work by February 1864 and had worked on it intermittently, intending to produce a life-size version of it for the Salon. The sketch is now owned by the University of Glasgow. The second work, *Variations in Violet and Green*, is in a private American collection. There is a reproduction of it in E. R. and J. Pennell, *The Life of James McNeill Whistler* (Philadelphia

and London, 1908), facing p. 156. While the work recalls the Greco-Japanese sketches of the late sixties, the return to open air and water anticipates the "Nocturnes" of the seventies. For further notes on these first two pictures see the catalogue *James McNeill Whistler, an Exhibition of Paintings and Other Works, Organized by the Arts Council of Great Britain and the English-Speaking Union of the United States* (London and New York, 1960), pp. 46, 48. The third work, *Symphony in White and Red* (c. 1868), is in the Freer Gallery. I am grateful for the assistance of Bertha M. Usilton, Librarian, Freer Gallery of Art, in identifying these works.

14. For a record of Swinburne's friendship with Solomon see the Yale edition of the Swinburne letters, which includes some of Solomon's letters. There is no satisfactory study of Solomon the man and artist. Julia Ellsworth Ford's *Simeon Solomon: An Appreciation* (New York, 1909), valuable mainly for its reproductions and list of pictures, is otherwise sketchy and at best hints at Solomon's degeneration. Lionel Cambourne's study in progress should do much to fill this gap. Swinburne's review was, incidentally, not reprinted during his lifetime; it had originally appeared in the magazine, *The Blue*.

15. The quotations from Pater are from "The School of Giorgione," *Works of Walter Pater*, I, 133-135.

CHAPTER VI

1. *Biographia Literaria*, I, 149. Louise Rosenblatt, *L'idée de l'art pour l'art*, pp. 155-157, juxtaposes passages from Poe and Baudelaire with some from Swinburne to show that Swinburne found in these writers support for his views. It seems to me, however, that the influence of Coleridge was greater, with Arnold perhaps in second place. One essay which, at first, might seem important in this regard is Earl L. Griggs' "Swinburne on Coleridge," *Modern Philology*, XXX (1932), 215-216. Griggs limits his discussion, however, to the poetry and has little of value to say about Coleridge's theories or Swinburne's opinions of them.

2. *Biographia Literaria*, II, 42.

3. The action implied for the poet of passion is, obviously, the pursuit of beauty: The degree of one's passion, we infer from "The Sensitive Plant," equals the intensity of one's thirst for the beautiful. Shelley's plant, lacking the "radiance and odour" of other plants, "loves, even like Love. . . . It desires what it has not, the Beautiful!" (ll. 74-76). Swinburne, though very much influenced by Shelley, shows little direct influence of Plato. He preferred poets to philosophers, and found his chief Greek inspiration in Aeschylus, Sophocles, Pindar, and the lyricists. Samuel Chew, *Swinburne* (Boston, 1929), p. 271, remarks: "No other English poet of modern times and equal rank has been so little influenced by Plato."

4. *Works of Matthew Arnold*, III, 122.

5. As a letter writer, Byron was also the "dragon-slayer": his letters "are full of violence, insolence, bluster, affectation, hypocrisy, pretension, bullying egotism and swaggering nonsense: but no less certainly and unmistakably are they the letters of a man with a great gift for writing, a man of commanding genius, of indisputable and insuppressible powers." Here he is easily Shelley's superior. Shelley's letters "are in general very 'nice,' as women say . . . ; the letters of a candid and amiable young person who tries steadily to see for himself, without any great faculty of insight or capacity for getting away from his own subjective line of vision." If it were not for the poetry, only "a very few specialists who have almost a craze for the literature of 'Elegant Epistles' would dream of reading Shelley's . . ." (*W&B*, 199).

6. *"Oeuvres Complètes de Alfred de Musset"* (9 vols., Paris, 1922-1940), I, 418.

7. In 1828 Carlyle in his "Robert Burns," *Critical and Miscellaneous Essays*, I, 323, made somewhat the same assessment. Like Burns, Byron's "celestial element will not mingle with the clay of earth; both poet and man of the world he must not be. . . ." Byron's life "is falsely arranged: the fire that is in him is not a strong, still central fire, warming into beauty the products of a world; but it is the mad fire of a volcano; and now,—we look sadly into the ashes of a crater, which erelong will fill itself with snow!" See, also, Carlyle's "Goethe," *Ibid.*, I, 224-225. C. E. Vaughan, *English Literary Criticism*, pp. lxxxiv-cii, has a succinct treatment of Carlyle's contribution to nineteenth-century criticism.

8. Chew, *Swinburne*, pp. 258-259, has provided a helpful assessment of Swinburne's opinions of Byron. Chew compares the "Byron" of 1865, "a landmark in the history of criticism since it ushered in the revival of appreciation of the poet," with the "notorious" critique "Wordsworth and Byron" of 1884 and says that "if we disregard the violent phrases that overcloud" this essay "it will be apparent that the change from the essay of 1865 is one of tone and emphasis rather than of opinion." This strikes me as a sound estimate of the matter.

9. William Sharp, *Life of Robert Browning* (London, 1890), p. 106, writes this of Swinburne's comments: "Surely this question of Browning's obscurity was expelled to the Limbo of Dead Stupidities when Mr. Swinburne, in periods as resplendent as the whirling wheels of Phoebus Apollo's chariot, wrote his famous incidental passage" to the study of George Chapman. The image of the "whirling wheels" is particularly apt.

10. Swinburne was familiar with Arnold's emphasis upon "the power of the man and the power of the moment." Swinburne, however, seemed less willing than Arnold to explain an artist's shortcomings in terms of an impoverished cultural atmosphere. Arnold's "The Function of Criticism at the Present Time" first appeared in the *National Review*, No. 1, n.s. (1864), 230-231. See *Works of Matthew Arnold*, III, 6.

11. Frank Kermode, *Romantic Image* (New York, 1957), traces the dance theme to its culmination in Yeats.

12. It is refreshing to find Swinburne perplexed by some of his hero's faults; something towards a balance is provided, though one side of the scale still remains quite high. George Saintsbury, in 1889, gave his readers a catalog of Hugo's "remarkable gaps": defective logic; no "humourous contrast"; imperfect literary proportion—an ideal Swinburne insisted upon for most other writers; an insularity of view which placed France first, Paris second, and Victor Hugo third in his scheme; abuse of the sonority of proper names; inaccurate facts; an inept sense of measure; and childish politics. Saintsbury concluded, however, that Hugo's technical skill was still sufficiently astounding to produce converts; Hugo deserves the title of "the greatest poet hitherto. . . ." —George Saintsbury, *A Short History of French Literature* (Oxford, 1889), pp. 525, 526, 527. Swinburne's reaction to all of this doesn't seem to be on record. Hugo was such an overpowering figure in his century that it was apparently difficult for his contemporaries not to rank him higher than we do today. For a recent, succinct treatment of Hugo's faults see Emerson R. Marks, "Sainte-Beuve's Classicism," *The French Review*, XXXVII (1964), 411-418.

13. Swinburne made the audacious claim that Rossetti had more "traits of greatness" than any other poet of the day—which was not, in his terms, the same as saying that Rossetti was the greatest living poet. Despite the drastic treatment he gave to some of Tennyson's work, Swinburne would, of course, have awarded Tennyson the title. It

is surprising that Swinburne failed to comment on the nervous elements in Tennyson's "The Two Voices," "Maud," and *In Memoriam.*—See Harold Nicolson, *Tennyson: Aspects of his Life, Character, and Poetry* (new ed., New York, 1962), pp. 125-126, 301-304. Arthur Symons' *The Symbolist Movement in Literature* is a classic analysis of nerves in symbolist poetry. (Mallarmé had said that "poetry is the language of a state of crisis.") Following Swinburne and Pater, Symons remarked that Rossetti's nerves, as he sought a "strange, morbid, and subtly beautiful" world "became more and more his tyrant." In the essay on Balzac, Symons wrote of the belief of modern writers in "nerves and a fatalistic heredity." He spoke of Nerval's "illusions of the nerves, which he shares with every man of imaginative mind." At such moments the link, Symons said, "which holds our own faculties together in that sober health of the brain which we call reason" seems to wear down "to so fine a tenuity that the wing of a passing dream might suffice to snap it." La Forgue's art, similarly an "art of the nerves," is, Symons adds in a style reminiscent of Swinburne, "what all art would tend towards if we followed our nerves on all their journeys."—See pp. 13-14, 60, 106.

CHAPTER VII

1. *Biographia Literaria,* II, 33.

2. "Nothing in the world is single," Shelley wrote in "Love's Philosophy"; "All things by a law divine / In one spirit meet and mingle." In a letter to Hogg, January 3, 1811, he said: "I confess that I think Pope's *'All are but parts of one stupendous whole,'* something more than poetry. It has ever been my favourite theory, for the immortal soul, 'never to be able to die, never to escape from some shrine as chilling as the clay-formed dungeon, which now it inhabits'; it is the future punishment which I can most easily believe in." Also see "Adonais," ll. 466-468, "Euganean Hills," ll. 315-319, and "Prometheus Unbound," I, ll. 741-749.

3. He frequently refers to novels and devotes separate essays to Charles Dickens, Charlotte Brontë, Charles Reade, Walter Scott, Wilkie Collins, and Victor Hugo. In this array of works he does little actual theorizing about the form and, in fact, reveals frustration when he is unable to suit novels to the requirements of classical drama or high poetry. One of his most original treatments of novelists is his lengthy comparison of George Eliot, Mrs. Gaskell, and Charlotte Brontë (*NCB,* 6-26).

4. William Rutland, *Swinburne: A Nineteenth Century Hellene,* presents a thorough examination of Swinburne's use of Greek forms. Rutland's is one of the best written books on Swinburne.

5. He granted *Paradise Lost* supremacy for the "noblest episodes." Poe also had this opinion.

6. See Pope's *An Essay on Criticism,* Part I, ll. 69-71 and Part II, ll. 255-258, and Hogarth's "Of Uniformity, Regularity, or Symmetry" in *The Analysis of Beauty,* ed. Joseph Burke (Oxford, 1955), pp. 36-41. Pater's Marius relished Flavian's verse for "that firmness of outline" which he detected amid the rich "expression and imagery." —*Works of Walter Pater,* II, 117.

7. *Defense,* p. 33. Shelley did, it should be pointed out, accept a modified organicism: the mind he saw as "a fading coal" awakening to an inner brightness, which in turn like a flower "fades and changes" as it develops. And, he continued, emphasizing the organic mystery of creativity, "a great statue or picture grows under the power

of the artist as a child in the mother's womb; and the very mind which directs the hands in formation is incapable of accounting to itself for the origin, the gradations, or the media of the process."—*Ibid.*, 39, 40.

8. It is difficult to identify the specific influence of Poe's theories on Swinburne. Since he thought so little of Poe as a critic of poetry—"One of the very worst . . . that ever existed" (*Letters*, V, 72)—it is possible that he also thought little of him as a theorist. He refers to his other mentors frequently and to Poe very seldom. Samuel Chew, *Swinburne*, relegates a reference to Poe to a footnote, and that is of little consequence. George Lafourcade, *Swinburne: A Literary Biography* (London, 1932), p. 112, says that Swinburne in 1863 adopted a "theory of Art for Art's sake as laid down by Gautier, Baudelaire, and Poe"; but he says nothing further and excludes Poe from his index, as does Edmund Gosse in the *Life*.

All this is not to say that Swinburne underestimated Poe's poetic genius; he did not, and, in fact, seemed to regard him as America's best poet, after his enthusiasm for Whitman waned. When J. H. Ingram, future editor of Poe's *Works* and his biographer, asked Swinburne in 1874 to contribute to a fund for Poe's sister Rosalie, Swinburne gladly obliged, and suggested that Ingram raise money "among the admirers of Poe in Paris, if anything is left of the old set of artists and authors who learned of Baudelaire to enjoy the genius of his favourite" (*Letters*, II, 290). Also, see Swinburne's letter to Sara Sigourney Rice, director of the Poe Memorial Committee, who had also asked for contributions (Nov. 9, 1875; *Letters*, III, 84-85). Neither in this letter nor in the one to Ingram did Swinburne say anything specific about Poe's influence on him. For a survey of Swinburne's low estimate of American literature, see Edmund Clarence Stedman, *Victorian Poets* (Boston, 1876), pp. 402-404.

9. First published in March, 1821. *The Works of Lord Byron, Poetry*, ed. by Ernest Hartley Coleridge and *Letters and Journals*, ed. by Rowland E. Prothero (13 vols., London, 1898-1903), XII, 559.

10. In his comparison of Jonson, Sidney, and Shelley, Swinburne had in mind Jonson's remarks prefacing the first edition of *Every Man in His Humour*. The passage quoted obviously appealed (*BJ*, 119).

11. There is a very appropriate remark in Ben Jonson's *Discoveries*, quoted by Swinburne (*BJ*, 120), which seems identical to Swinburne's theory, both as it rejects verbiage and as it extols the clarity of intellect possessed by Browning, who keeps style and matter moving along the mind's skein:

> Whatsoever loseth the grace and clearness, converts into a riddle: the obscurity is marked, but not the value. That perisheth, and is passed by, like the pearl in the fable. Our style should be like a skein of silk, to be carried and found by the right thread, not ravelled and perplexed: then all is a knot, a heap.

Swinburne's remarks, especially in the section following the "animated line" image, are Shelleyan. I am thankful to Robert Gleckner for calling Hogarth's idea of "the serpentine line of beauty" to my attention and for reminding me of Blake's emphasis on the firm outline, acquired from his training as an engraver. Blake may have known Hogarth's principle. Sir Philip Sidney, in his clear civilized manner, would have enthusiastically supported Swinburne's organicism. In his "Defence of Poesie" he was highly critical of Spenser's *Shepherd's Calendar*, not only for its consciously archaic diction but for its lack of an inevitable informing design: "let but moste of the Verses bee put in prose," Sidney said, "and then aske the meaning, and it will bee founde, that one Verse did but beget an other, without ordering at the first, what should be at the last, which becomes a confused masse of words, with a tingling sound of ryme, barely accompanied with reasons."—*The Prose Works of Sir Philip Sidney*, ed. Albert Feuil-lerat (4 vols. Cambridge, England, 1912-1926), III, 37-38.

12. A classic statement of this ideal appears in Pater's "Style" (*Works of Walter Pater*, V, 32) where, incidentally, he declares his own admiration for Flaubert's sensitiv-ity to words in harmony with a main "architectural design." Flaubert himself reported that his procedure was delaying and painful. Pater conjectures that such meticulous craftsmanship "had much to do" with Flaubert's "diseased nerves."

13. *Critical and Miscellaneous Essays*, I, 259, 260.

14. Ruskin's position on the nude as a suitable subject for art is fairly well-known; but a sampling of comments from the eighth lecture he gave at Oxford, during Lent Term, 1872, in the series he called "The Eagle's Nest: Ten Lectures on the Relation of Natural Science to Art," will recall his ideas (the listing is mine). He announced that he was withdrawing anatomy from the course of study because:

1. The "habit of contemplating the human form . . . has been essentially de-structive to every school of art in which it has been practised."
2. The "study of the nude is injurious, beyond the limits of honour and de-cency in daily life."
3. "Scarcely any of the moral power of Greece depended on her admiration of beauty, or strength in the body. . . . The mere admiration of physical beauty in the body . . . conduced greatly to the fall of Greece. . . ."
4. That "a young boy, or girl, brought up fresh to the schools of art from the country, should be set to stare, against every particle of wholesome grain in their natures, at the Elgin Marbles, and to draw them with dismal applica-tion, until they imagine they like them, makes the whole youthful temper rotten with affectation. . . ."—*Works of John Ruskin*, XXII, 222, 223, 233, 235-236.

15. A powerful modern reading of such a sculpture—probably one in the Louvre —is Rilke's poem "Archaïsche Torso Apollos." W. L. Graff interprets the theme of the poem this way: "The torso is that of a God-Artist, more particularly the god of poetry and of orderly, disciplined music, in contrast with Dionysos, the god of ecstatic, intoxi-cating music."—*Rainer Maria Rilke: Creative Anguish of a Modern Poet* (Princeton, 1956), p. 156.

16. Rutland, *Swinburne: A Nineteenth Century Hellene*, pp. 294f., has a long analysis of the connections between Swinburne and Gautier. It was the famous ninth chap-ter of *Madamoiselle de Maupin*, he says, which led Swinburne to the *Hermaphroditus* in the Louvre. Swinburne also knew the stanza (36) on the hermaphrodite in Shelley's *Witch of Atlas* and Ovid's fable of the nymph Salmacis and her passion for the son of Mercury and Cytherea. See Swinburne's "Notes on Poems and Reviews." There is evi-dence in the tone of the "Notes" that much of what he said was said tongue in cheek. See also his letter to William Michael Rossetti, October 9, 1866 (*Letters*, I, 192f.).

17. He used the contrast of the mixed senses for satiric purposes also, sometimes unfairly: he referred, for example, to "the bisexual George Eliot" and called George Henry Lewes "George Eliot's morganatic wife." In better taste and more amusing is his description of George Sand, whom he chided for trying to arrange things both ways for posterity:

Before the final bar of posthumous opinion, even so illustrious a hybrid as Madame Sand must make up its mind to be judged either as Diana (let us say) or as Endymion, as a Faun or as a Dryad, as lover or as mistress: George or Georgette, Cephalus or Aurora, Salmacis or Hermaphroditus. And in this case

the ultimate verdict of judgment between these two literary lovers can in justice
be no other than that which I have already ventured to anticipate: that probably
he did not behave like a lady, but certainly she did not behave like a gentleman.
(*T&M*, 318)

18. *Seven Types of Ambiguity*, (New York, 1957), p. 21.

19. *Ibid.*, p. 22.

20. *Works of Walter Pater*, V, 21, 22.

21. When we note Pater's emphasis on style, on technique and craftsmanship, we
are in a different realm from Shelley's. Pater's mind is at the start less transcendent; it
is the human agent of control, structure, and form. Again, this difference marks a new
route from the Romantics; and the aestheticism of Yeats's formalist Byzantium poems is
not too distant.

22. *Works of Walter Pater*, I, 68-69. Anticipating a later aesthetics, Pater had also
noted that Michelangelo by leaving his works unfinished was trusting "the spectator to
complete the half-emergent form."—*Ibid.*, I, 76.

CHAPTER VIII

1. The most ambitious treatment of Swinburne's principles to have appeared thus
far is Thomas E. Connolly's "Swinburne on 'The Music of Poetry,' " *PMLA*, LXII
(1957), 668-688. Connolly separates Swinburne's main ordering of musical ideas and
touches on the related questions of the sublime as an element of art, of synaesthesia,
and of the meaning of music and form. Connolly has found, as I have, that Swinburne's
theories remained consistent throughout his career; and he too regrets that modern
critics have been so intolerant of both his style and his theories. Moreover, I am pleased
that he believes so firmly in the value of scrutinizing Swinburne's criticism. My own
study has led me to a reconstruction of Swinburne's principles along lines similar to
his. Swinburne's own definitions, though scattered, are fairly precise and determined
this approach. I might also point out that some of Connolly's ground was anticipated
by Ruth Child's "Swinburne's Mature Standards of Criticism." Paul de Reul's *L'Oeuvre
de Swinburne*, Chap., II, "Musique et Poésie," also treats the subject. The passages from
Shelley in the text are from the *Defense*, pp. 2, 16.

2. Thomas Connolly, "Swinburne on The Music of Poetry," p. 680, comments on
this passage on free verse but limits himself to Swinburne's main text and ignores the
ambitious footnote, which occupies nearly an entire page in the *Works*. As a result, he
makes Swinburne seem less coherent, more inconclusive, and more whimsical than he
really was. Connolly regards Swinburne's apparent shift from the merits of rhyme as
the result of a conscious inability to defend an earlier assertion that rhyme was essential to lyric poetry. But Swinburne never backtracked easily, and certainly never in
order to make his position more palatable to critics.

3. *The Complete Works of William Hazlitt* (21 vols., London and Toronto,
1930-34), VIII, 317, hereafter cited as *Works of William Hazlitt*. Hazlitt had explained how the inward effects of Claude's handling of nature achieved aesthetic fusion:
in a sky of Claude's, he said, "one imperceptible gradation is as it were the scale to
another . . . the broad arch of heaven is piled up of endlessly intermediate gold and
azure tints, and . . . an infinite number of minute, scarce noticed particulars blend and
melt into universal harmony" (VII, 39).

4. Walter J. Bate, *Prefaces to Criticism* (New York, 1959), p. 126.

5. *Works of William Hazlitt*, VIII, 320.

6. *Ibid.*, V, 12. In his later years, Swinburne lost some of his early enthusiasm for Hazlitt, at least as a critic of Shakespeare. In the essay on Lamb and Wither (1885) he wrote unflatteringly of "the Hazlitts prattling" at Lamb's heel, "the Dyce's labouring in his wake" (*L&W*, 285).

7. *Works of William Hazlitt*, IV, 78.

8. "Keats's Style: Evolution Toward Qualities of Permanent Value," *The Major English Romantic Poets: A Symposium in Reappraisal*, ed. by C. D. Thorpe, C. Baker, and B. Weaver (Carbondale, Illinois, 1957), p. 223. Shelley expressed his admiration for Keats's power to mould the separate senses into thought and sweet sound. See "Adonais," ll. 118-120.

9. *Works of William Hazlitt*, IV, 77. Hazlitt seems here to adopt Coleridge's terms, which is not surprising since his indebtedness to Coleridge was considerable.

10. *The Science of Beauty, as Developed in Nature and Applied in Art* (Edinburgh and London, 1856), pp. 12, 13.

11. "Swinburne on 'The Music of Poetry,' " p. 684.

12. Edmund Burke, *A Philosophical Enquiry into the Origin of our Ideas of the Sublime and Beautiful*, ed. by J. T. Boulton (London and New York, 1958), p. 73, demonstrated the connection of this idea with sublimity. "Infinity," he said, "has a tendency to fill the mind with that sort of delightful horror, which is the most genuine effect, and truest test of the sublime." While Burke seemed to have the arts in mind, his ideas were encompassingly philosophical. Joseph Burke, *William Hogarth, The Analysis of Beauty* (Oxford, 1955), p. lvii, calls Edmund Burke "the most influencial theoretician to take up Hogarth's ideas. . . ."

13. A passage from the final act of *Prometheus Unbound* (ll. 251-261) presents Panthea's vision of the sphere of harmony, a fusion of sound, color, and odor, which in its "elemental subtlety" "drowns the sense" of the perceiver. These lines once again reflect Shelley's characteristic treatment of the conjoined literal and the almost inexpressible abstract. *See* p. 98 *supra.*

BIBLIOGRAPHY

Allen, Gay Wilson. *The Solitary Singer: A Critical Biography of Walt Whitman.* New York, 1955.

Altick, Richard D. "Four Victorian Poets and an Exploding Island," *Victorian Studies,* III (1960), 249-260.

Arnold, Matthew. *The Works of Matthew Arnold.* 15 vols. London, 1903-1904.

Arvin, Newton, "Swinburne as a Critic," *Sewanee Review,* XXXII (1924), 405-412.

Babbitt, Irving. *Rousseau and Romanticism.* New ed., New York, 1959.

Bagehot, Walter. "Wordsworth, Tennyson, and Browning; or, Pure, Ornate and Grotesque Art in English Poetry (1864)," in *English Critical Essays: Nineteenth Century,* ed. E. D. Jones. London, 1928, pp. 430-491.

Bate, Walter J. "Keats's Style: Evolution Toward Qualities of Permanent Value," in *The Major English Romantic Poets: A Symposium in Reappraisal,* ed. C. D. Thorpe, C. Baker, and B. Weaver. Carbondale, 1957.

————. *Prefaces to Criticism.* New York, 1959.

Beerbohm, Max. *A Christmas Garland.* London, 1912.

Blake, William. *The Complete Writings of William Blake,* ed. Geoffrey Keynes. London and New York, 1957.

Boase, T. S. R. *English Art 1800-1870.* Oxford, 1959.

Brown, Clarence A. *The Achievement of American Criticism.* New York, 1954.

Brown, E. K. "Swinburne: A Centenary Estimate," in *Victorian Literature: Modern Essays In Criticism,* ed. Austin Wright. New York, 1961, pp. 295-310.

Buckley, Jerome H. *Tennyson: The Growth of a Poet.* Cambridge, Mass., 1960.

————. *Victorian Temper.* Cambridge, Mass., 1951.

Burke, Edmund. *A Philosophical Enquiry into the Origin of our Ideas of the Sublime and Beautiful,* ed. J. T. Boulton. London and New York, 1958.

Burke, Joseph. *William Hogarth: the Analysis of Beauty.* Oxford, 1955.

Byron, George Gordon, Lord. *The Works of Lord Byron.* Poetry ed. Ernest Hartley Coleridge. Letters ed. Rowland E. Prothero. 13 vols., London, 1898-1903.

Carlyle, Thomas. *Critical and Miscellaneous Essays.* 4 vols., Boston, 1861.

————. *The Works of Thomas Carlyle.* Centenary ed., 30 vols., London, 1899-1901.

Chesneau, Ernest. *The English School of Painting,* tr. L. N. Etherington, preface by John Ruskin. London, 1885.

Chew, Samuel. *Swinburne.* Boston. 1929.

Child, Ruth C. "Swinburne's Mature Standards of Criticism," *PMLA,* LII (1937), 870-879.

Clough, Arthur Hugh. *Prose Remains of Arthur Hugh Clough: with a Selection from His Letters and a Memoir edited by His Wife.* London, 1888.

Coleridge, S. T. *Biographia Literaria: with his Aesthetical Essays,* ed. John Shawcross. 2 vols., London, 1907.

Connolly, Thomas E. "Swinburne on 'The Music of Poetry,' " *PMLA,* LXII (1957), 680-688.

————. "Swinburne's Theory of the End of Art," *ELH,* XIX (1952), 277-290.

Daniel, Samuel. "A Defence of Rhyme," in *Elizabethan Critical Essays*, ed. G. Gregory Smith. 2 vols., London, 1950.

Dodds, John W. *The Age of Paradox: A Biography of England 1841-1851.* New York, 1952.

Dowden, Edward ["A Review of *A Note on Charlotte Brontë*"], *Academy*, XII (1877), 233-234.

————. *Transcripts and Studies.* London, 1888.

Egan, Rose. *The Genesis of the Theory of "Art for Art's Sake" in Germany and in England.* 2 parts, Northampton, Mass. and Paris, 1921 and 1924.

Eliot, George. *George Eliot's Complete Works.* 15 vols., Boston, 1888.

Eliot, T. S. *Essays Ancient and Modern.* London, 1936.

Empson, William. *Seven Types of Ambiguity.* New York, 1957.

Farmer, Albert J. *Le Mouvement esthétique et "décadent" en Angleterre (1873-1900).* Paris, 1931.

Fogle, Richard Harter. *The Idea of Coleridge's Criticism.* Berkeley and Los Angeles, 1962.

————. *John Keats: Selected Poetry and Letters.* New York, 1959.

Ford, Julia Ellsworth. *Simeon Solomon: An Appreciation.* New York, 1909.

Garrod, H. W. *Byron 1824-1924.* Oxford, 1924.

Gautier, Theophile. *Madamoiselle de Maupin*, ed. Adolphe Boschot. Paris, 1955.

Gerber, Helmut. "The Nineties: Beginning, End, or Transition?" in *English Institute Essays.* New York, 1959, pp. 50-79, 213-219.

Gleckner, Robert F. *The Piper and the Bard.* Detroit, 1959.

Gosse, Edmund. *The Life of Algernon Charles Swinburne.* Vol. xix of Bonchurch ed. of *Complete Works,* London, 1927.

————. "Swinburne and Music," *Spectator*, CXVIII (1917), 516.

Graff, W. L. *Rainer Maria Rilke: Creative Anguish of a Modern Poet.* Princeton, 1956.

Griggs, Earl L. "Swinburne on Coleridge," *Modern Philology,* XXX (1932), 215-216.

Hay, David Ramsay. *The Science of Beauty as Developed in Nature and Applied in Art.* Edinburgh and London, 1856.

Hazlitt, William. *Complete Works of William Hazlitt*, ed. P. P. Howe. 21 vols., London and Toronto, 1930-1934.

Henderson, W. Brooks Drayton. *Swinburne and Landor: A Study of Their Spiritual Relationship and Its Effect on Swinburne's Moral and Poetic Development.* London, 1918.

Hogarth, William. *The Analysis of Beauty*, ed. Joseph Burke. Oxford, 1955.

Hough, Graham. *The Last Romantics.* New ed., London and New York, 1961.

Houghton, Lord (Richard Monckton Milnes) *Life, Letters and Literary Remains of John Keats.* 2 vols., London, 1848.

Hughes, Randolph. *Lesbia Brandon: by Algernon Charles Swinburne*, commentary by Randolph Hughes. London, 1952.

————. "Mallarmé: A Study in Esoteric Symbolism," *Nineteenth Century, CXVI* (1934), 114-128.

Hyder, Clyde Kenneth. "Swinburne: Changes of Aspect and Short Notes," *PMLA,* LVIII (1943), 223-244.

————. *Swinburne's Literary Career and Fame.* New printing, New York, 1963.

Ironside, Robin. *Pre-Raphaelite Painters: With a Descriptive Catalogue by John Gere.* London, 1948.

Jackson, Holbrook. *The Eighteen Nineties.* New York, 1914.

Bibliography

James McNeill Whistler, an Exhibition of Paintings and Other Works. Organized by the Arts Council of Great Britain and the English-Speaking Union of the United States. London and New York, 1960.

Keats, John. *The Poetical Works and Other Writings of John Keats,* ed. H. Buxton Forman. 8 vols., New York, 1938-1939.

Kermode, Frank. *Romantic Image.* New York, 1957.

Lafourcade, Georges. *La Jeunesse de Swinburne (1837-1867).* 2 vols., Oxford and Paris, 1928.

_____. *Swinburne: A Literary Biography.* London, 1932.

_____. *Swinburne's Hyperion and Other Poems: with an Essay on Swinburne and Keats.* London, 1927.

Lang, Cecil Y. *The Swinburne Letters.* 6 vols., New Haven, 1959-1962.

———. ed. *A. C. Swinburne's* "The Chaotic School." To be published 1964.

Lee, Vernon [Violet Page]. *Baldwin: Being Dialogues on Views and Aspirations.* Boston, 1886.

McCarthy, Desmond. "Swinburne's Prose," *Empire Review,* XLIV (1926), 458-461.

Macaulay, Thomas Babington. *The Complete Writings of Lord Macaulay.* 20 vols., Boston and New York, 1900.

Madden, William A. "The Victorian Sensibility," *Victorian Studies,* VII (1963), 67-97.

Marks, Emerson. "Sainte-Beuve's Classicism," *The French Review,* XXXVII (1964), 411-418.

Musset, Alfred de. *Oeuvres Complètes de Alfred de Musset,* 9 vols., Paris, 1922-1940.

Nicolson, Harold. *Swinburne.* New York, 1926.

_____. *Tennyson: Aspects of His Life, Character, and Poetry.* New ed., New York, 1962.

North, Marianne. *Recollections of a Happy Life: Being the Autobiography of Marianne North,* ed. Mrs. John Addington Symonds. 2 vols., New York, 1892.

W. D. Paden, "Swinburne, The *Spectator* in 1862, and Walter Bagehot," in *Six Studies in Nineteenth-Century English Literature and Thought,* ed. Harold Orel and G. J. Worth (Lawrence, 1962).

Paintings and Drawings of the Pre-Raphaelites and their Circle. Cambridge, Mass., 1946.

Pater, Walter. *Works of Walter Pater.* 8 vols., London and New York, 1900-1901.

Patmore, Coventry. *Principle in Art.* London, 1898.

Pennell, Elizabeth and Joseph. *The Life of James McNeill Whistler.* 5th ed., Philadelphia and London, 1911.

Peters, Robert L. "Athens and Troy: Notes on John Addington Symonds' Aestheticism," *English Literature in Transition,* V No. 5, (1962), 14-26.

_____. "The Salome of Arthur Symons and Aubrey Beardsley," *Criticism,* II (1960), 150-163.

_____. "Some Illustrations of Carlyle's Symbolist Imagery," *Victorian Newsletter* (Fall, 1959), 31-34.

_____. "Toward an 'Un-Definition' of Decadent as Applied to British Literature of the Nineteenth Century," *Journal of Aesthetics and Art Criticism,* XVIII (1959), 258-264.

Praz, Mario. *The Romantic Agony.* New York, 1933.

Read, Herbert. *The Philosophy of Modern Art.* Cleveland, 1954.

Reul, Paul de. *L'Oeuvre de Swinburne.* London and Paris, 1922.

Rosenblatt, Louise. *L'idée de l'art pour l'art dans la littérature anglaise pendant la période victorienne.* Paris, 1931.

Rossetti, William Michael. *The Poetical Works of Percy Bysshe Shelley: Including Various Additional Pieces from MS. and Other Sources.* 2 vols., London, 1870.

Ruskin, John. *The Works of John Ruskin,* ed. E. T. Cook and A. Wedderburn. 39 vols., London, 1903-1912.

Russell, Charles E. "Swinburne and Music," *North American Review,* CLXXXVI (1907), 427-441.

Rutland, William. *Swinburne: A Nineteenth Century Hellene.* Oxford, 1931.

Saintsbury, George. *A Short History of French Literature.* Oxford, 1889.

Schueller, Herbert M. "John Addington Symonds: as a Theoretical and as a Practical Critic." Ph.D. Diss., Univ. of Michigan, 1941.

Scudder, Vida D. *The Life of the Spirit in the Modern English Poets.* Cambridge, Mass., 1895.

Shairp, J. C. *Aspects of Poetry.* Oxford, 1881.

—————. *On Poetic Interpretation of Nature.* Edinburgh, 1877.

Sharp, William. *Life of Robert Browning.* London, 1890.

Shelley, Percy Bysshe. *A Defense of Poetry,* ed. Albert S. Cook. Boston and New York, 1890.

—————. *Shelley's Poetical Works,* ed. H. Buxton Forman. 5 vols., London, 1892.

Sidney, Sir Philip. *The Prose Works of Sir Philip Sidney.* ed. A. Feuillerat. 4 vols., Cambridge, Eng., 1912-1926.

Starkie, Enid. *Charles Baudelaire: Flowers of Evil.* Norfolk, Conn., 1946.

Stedman, E. C. *Victorian Poets.* Boston, 1876.

Strachey, Sir Edward. *Talk at a Country House.* Boston and New York, 1894.

Sutton, Denys. *Apollo: The Magazine of the Arts,* LXXVI, No. 10 (1962).

Swinburne, Algernon Charles. "Changes of Aspect." MS. Huntington Library.

—————. "The Chaotic School." MS. ed. Cecil Y. Lang.

—————. *The Complete Works.* Bonchurch ed., ed. E. Gosse and T. J. Wise. 20 vols., London, 1925-1927.

—————. "Short Notes." MS. Huntington Library.

—————. *The Swinburne Letters,* ed. Cecil Y. Lang. 6 vols., New Haven, 1959-1962.

—————. *Undergraduate Papers.* London, 1858.

—————. Unpublished letter to John Addington Symonds. Bristol University, Bristol, England.

—————. *William Blake,* London, 1867.

—————. and William Michael Rossetti. *Notes on the Royal Academy Exhibition,* 1868. London, 1868.

Symonds, John Addington. *Essays Speculative and Suggestive.* 3d. ed., London, 1907.

Symons, Arthur. "The Lesson of Millais," *The Savoy,* III (1896), 57-58.

—————. *Symbolist Movement in Literature.* New ed., New York, 1958.

[Tennyson, Hallam]. *Alfred Lord Tennyson: A Memoir by his Son.* 2 vols., London, 1897.

Tennyson, Alfred Lord. *Works of Alfred, Lord Tennyson,* ed. W. J. Rolfe. 12 vols., Boston, 1895-1898.

Thomas, Edward, *Algernon Charles Swinburne: A Critical Study.* New York, 1912.

Vaughan, C. E. *English Literary Criticism.* London, 1896.

Watts-Dunton, Theodore. *Charles Dickens by Algernon Charles Swinburne: with a Preface and Illustrative Notes by the Editor.* London, 1913.

Welby, T. E. *A Study of Swinburne.* New York, 1926.

Wellek, René. "Walter Pater's Literary Theory and Criticism," *Victorian Studies,* I (1957), 29-46.

Bibliography

Wilde, Oscar. *The Complete Works of Oscar Wilde.* 12 vols., New York, 1923-1927.

Wise, Thomas J. *A Bibliography of the Writings in Prose and Verse of Algernon Charles Swinburne,* Vol. XX of Bonchurch ed. of *Complete Works.* London, 1927.

Worsfold, W. Basil. *The Principles of Criticism: An Introduction to the Study of Literature.* London, 1897.

Wright, Thomas. *The Life of Walter Pater.* 2 vols., London, 1907.

INDEX

Index

Index

Jacobeans: 111

Japan: art of, 84

Jerusalem: 27

Johnson, Samuel: 86

Jonson, Ben: on bourgeois reader, 26; style, 26; proper text for, 46; edition of works by Cunningham and Gifford, 47-48; shortcomings as lyricist, 100; excessive *tact*, 117; on style, 117, 134; on own obscurity, 173; *The Alchemist*, 39; *Every Man in his Humour*, 184; *Every Man out of his Humour*, 134-135; *The Silent Woman*, 134; *Volpone*, 39; *Discoveries*, 21, 184; 25, 32, 38, 39, 56, 75, 142, 184

Joubert, Joseph: 167

Jowett, Benjamin: 39, 169

Judgment: appropriate moment for making, 29

Justice: aesthetic tone, 108

Kant, Emmanuel: 85

Keats, John: Tennyson and, 33; strength of character, 33; "Johnny Keats stage of criticism," 33; and Shelley, 36-37; *empathy* and, 86; Fantin-Latour and, 92; use of detail, 92; diction, 96-97; beauty and truth, 97; Matthew Arnold on, 112; and Maurice de Guérin, 112; instinct for beauty, 112; sparrow and minnow, 114; on effects of poetry, 119; style, 50, 120-121; and "object," 159; failures as poet, 179; "To Autumn," 92; "On First Looking into Chapman's Homer," 104; *Hyperion*, 92, 143; "La Belle Dame Sans Merci," 92, 130; "Lamia," 92, 130; "Ode on a Grecian Urn," 112; "Ode to a Nightingale," 97; 25, 33, 88, 92, 105, 106, 111, 113, 114, 143, 144, 145, 157, 164, 177

"Keeldar, Shirley": 83

Kelmscott press: 77

Krakatoa: 78

Laforgue, Jules: 183

Lafourcade, Georges: 11

Lamb, Charles: as drama critic, 162; 51, 167, 169, 187

Landor, Walter Savage: as critic-praiser, 35; and Swinburne, 170; 24, 31, 78, 94

Lang, Andrew: 23

Lang, Cecil Y.: 11, 22, 168

Lanier, Sidney: system of notation, 180

Law in art: the impulse toward, 73

"Leading idea": 135

Lee, Vernon (Violet Paget): 148

Legros, Alphonse: *The Refectory*, 106

Leighton, Frederic: 103

Leonardo da Vinci: 143

Lesbian music: *vs.* Spartan understanding, 72

Leucothea: 157

Lewes, George Henry: 185

Leyland, F. R.: 10

Leys, M.: 60

Linnaeus, Carolus: 88

Literalism: and total impact of art, 84; uniqueness of Victorian literalism, 85. *See also* Detail, Nature, Objects, Science

Little Nell (*Old Curiosity Shop*), 171

Loire, chateaus of: 107

Longfellow, Henry Wadsworth: *Evangeline*, 39; 22

Longinus: 161

Lucretius: 46

Lust's Dominion: probem of authorship of, 48

Luxembourg Palace: 140

Lynceus: 135

Lyre: symbol of traditional poetry, 94; Aeolian, 151

Lyric power: variety of, 152

Macaulay, Thomas Babington: critical of Byron and Wordsworth as dramatists, 175; on eighteenth century poets, 178; 39

MacColl, Norman: 39

Macpherson, James: 30

Maginn, William: 31

"Maitland, Thomas." *See* Robert Buchanan

Mallarmé, Stéphane: 178, 183

Malory, Sir Thomas: *Le Morte d'Arthur* and Tennyson's *Idylls of the King*, 68

Man: piebald nature of, 66

Mangan, James Clarence: 30

Index

Manliness and poetry: 33-34

Marlowe, Christopher: and Aeschylus, 38; sublime effects, 162; *The Tragedy of Doctor Faustus*, 41, 117; *Edward II*, 41; *Hero and Leander*, 103; *The Jew of Malta*, 41; *Lust's Dominion*, 48; *Tamburlaine the Great*, 41, 155; 24, 52, 71, 99, 102, 141-142, 153, 162

Marston, John: rambunctiousness of, 155; 162

Marsyas: 94

Marx, Karl: 177

Massinger, Philip: deficient feeling, 117; *Sir John van Olden Barnavelt*, 44-45; *A Very Woman*, 163; 38

Medieval romance: 72

Medwin, Thomas: 46

Meredith, George: "Margaret's Bridal-Eve," 125; *Modern Love*, defended, 36; *Vittoria*, 83; 77

Mérimée, Prosper: 39

Meter: technicalities of, and color in painting, 95-96; anapests, 128-129; iambs, 129; spondees, 129

Method and material: relationship between, 30

Michelangelo: incompleteness of, 147; 46, 103, 143, 186

Middle class: morality, 59; 26, 132, 149

Middleton, Thomas: *The Witch*, 45; 38, 45-46

Mill, John Stuart: 155

Millais, Sir John Everett: loss of integrity, 60, 67; obituary, by Arthur Symons, 61; advice from Tennyson, 178; *Autumn Leaves*, 60; *The Blind Girl*, 60, 82; *Bubbles*, 60; *Pilgrims to St. Paul's*, 60-61, 82; *Sisters*, 60-61, 82; 81, 83, 85, 102

Millet, Jean François: 101

Milnes, Richard Mockton, 1st Baron Houghton: 168

Milton, John: virtue, 156; *Paradise Lost*, 21, 130, 170; *Paradise Regained*, 21, 130; sonnets, 37; 31, 34, 44, 51, 56, 79, 102, 117, 118, 137, 156

Mind, creative: 118-119, 146, 184

Molesworth, Mary Louisa: 171

Molière: 91

Moods of art: 52

Moore, Albert: *Azaleas*, 102

Moore, George: 52

Moore, Henry: 140

Moore, Thomas: 30

Moral ardour in Milton and Pindar: 51

Morgan, Evelyn de: 178-179

Morley, John: 25, 93

Morris, Lewis: 177

Morris, William: echoes of theories in Swinburne, 63; on culture, 63; formal growth in poetry, 133; tellingly even style, 133; *The Defence of Guenevere*, 124; "King Arthur's Tomb," 133; *The Life and Death of Jason*, 124-125, 133; 54, 77, 128, 132, 177

Moxon, Edward, and Co.: 56-57

Murray, John: 134

Muscular Christianity: 173

Muses, the: 119

Music: "visible" music in Solomon's pictures, 106; symbolic, 107; Pater's principle of, 107; art and "the condition of," 107; music of poetry, external, 150-156; music of poetry, internal, 156-164; poetry and, 186. *See also* Harmony, Onomatopoeia, Shelley, Whistler

Musset, Alfred de: *Namouna*, 115; 39

Nakedness: form in Rossetti's poetry, 93

Nash, Thomas: 38

Naturalism: Herbert Read on, 177; 70-73

Nature: actualities of, in Victorian art, 76-94 *passim;* an "animated body" (Coleridge), 85; sounds of, rendered in poetry, 154-156; poetry free of concrete nature, 156; in Keats, Coleridge, Wordsworth, Byron, and Shelley, 157; tangible and intangible worlds, 158; "living affinity" of, 161

Neo-classicism: in Swinburne, 26, 75; neo-classical form, 118; neo-classical aims, 132

Neo-Hellenism: aesthetic virtues of, 26

Neptune: 43

Nerval, Gérard de: 183

Nerves, in art: 52, 125, 126, 183

Index

Index

Index

"Changes of Aspect," 11, 22, 33; "The Chaotic School," 128-129, 168; "Emily Brontë," 21; *Essays and Studies*, 35-36, 83; *George Chapman: A Critical Essay*, 49, 118; "John Ford," 59; "Keats," 92; *Lesbia Brandon*, 21; *Love's Cross-Currents (A Year's Letters)*, 21; "Matthew Arnold's *New Poems*," 51; "Notes on Designs of the Old Masters at Florence," 101, 148; "Note on the Historical Play of *King Edward III*," 40; *Notes on Poems and Reviews*, 11, 57, 59, 173, 185; *Notes on the Royal Academy Exhibition, 1868*, 11, 60-61; "Notes on the Text of Shelley," 46; "The Poems of Dante Gabriel Rossetti," 119; "Short Notes," 11; *A Study of Shakespeare*, 129; "Tennyson and Musset," 39; "Thomas Middleton," 45-46; *Undergraduate Papers*, 11, 22, 52, 71; *Under the Miscroscope*, 25, 40, 71; *William Blake*, 10n., 13, 22, 35, 52-53, 63, 65, 101; "Wordsworth and Byron," 182

Note: Since this book was written, Cecil Lang's *New Writings by Swinburne: or Miscellanea Nova et Curiosa: Being a Medley of Poems, Critical Essays, Hoaxes and Burlesques* (Syracuse, 1964) has been published. The collection contains "The Early English Dramatists," "The Chaotic School," "Changes of Aspect," and "Short Notes."

Symbolism and Symbolists: "apprehension" of symbols, 41; Carlyle on symbols, 86; in Rossetti's *Sibylla Palmifera*, 113; French Symbolists, 52, 125, 178, 183; Rossetti's fanciful treatment of, 136-137; symbolist movement, 98, 178

Symonds, John Addington: unpublished letter from Swinburne to, 168-169; as critic, 171-172; 51, 52, 90

Symons, Arthur: "quality of nerves," 52; obituary notice of J. E. Millais, 61; on lyric poetry, 172; 101, 140, 144

Sympathies of perceiver: expanded through *gusto*, 159

Synaesthesia: as critical tool, 53; in Shelley,

100; method, not end, 108; 94, 95-108 *passim. See also* Baudelaire, Blake, Keats, Shelley, and Swinburne

Tact: defined and described, 111, 117; and harmony, 123-124; as "sense of right," 162; 109-126 *passim*

Taine, Hippolyte: 27, 39, 169

Talleyrand-Périgord, Charles Maurice de: 27

Tannhäuser: 79

Tate, Nahum: 104

Taylor, John: 92, 97

Taylor, Tom: 56

Tellus: 43

Temperament: of artists and works, 52; romantic, 126. *See also Virtue*

Tennyson, Alfred, 1st Baron: as moralist, 33; coward before critics, 33-34; "feminine art," 40; idylls as minor forms, 67-68; and Malory, 68; on passage on daisies (*Maud*), 78; sea imagery, 79; "eye and hand" are always to be trusted, 79; T. S. Eliot on, 81; writhing stylistic patterns, 80-81; verse techniques, 128; Swinburne's estimate of, 182-183; on art for art's sake (excoriated by Swinburne), 170; advice to J. E. Millais, 178; "Enoch Arden," 79-80; *Idylls of the King*, 68, 80, 175; *In Memoriam*, 87, 131, 175, 183; "The Lady of Shalott," 77; "Lancelot and Elaine," 79, 80-81, 176; "The Lotos-Eaters," 77; *Maud*, 78-79, 131, 183; "Northern Farmer," 80; "Rizpah," 130, 162; "The Talking Oak," 80; "The Two Voices," 183; "Will Waterproof's Lyrical Monologue," 80; 23, 32, 38, 39, 40, 54, 56, 71, 78, 79, 87, 142, 177, 178

Tennysonians: 94

Texts: dating of, 44; accuracy of, 26, 45-48; defilers of, lambasted by Swinburne, 45-46

Thackeray, William Makepeace: *Pendennis*, 41; *Vanity Fair*, 41

Thomas, Edward: 101

Thompson, Francis: "Corymbus for Autumn," 77; 79

207

The manuscript was edited by Alexander Brede. The book was designed by S. R. Tennenbaum. The book title was hand lettered by Andrew Molnar. The typeface for both text and display matter is Mergenthaler Linotype's Granjon, designed under the supervision of George W. Jones in 1928 and based on a face originally designed by Claude Garamond in the sixteenth century.

The book is printed on S. D. Warren's Olde Style Antique, white wove paper and bound in Bancroft's Kennett cloth over boards. Manufactured in the United States of America.